Praise for *Bla...*

A *New York Times* Edi...
A *Kirkus Reviews* Best No...

"Collins-Dexter compellingly ties her engaging assessments of the Black skinheads' artistic output to a broader political critique, often drawing on the history of media and labor movements and social justice.... Each essay reflects deep research, passion, and respect for her subject."

—*The New York Times*

"Brandi Collins-Dexter—a scholar, activist, and overall poignant voice on race and accountability (as well as a South Sider)—writes in *Black Skinhead* that she found in Kanye West a vessel for thinking about Black voters and rising disillusionment with Democrat politics. From there she spins a vibrant history of Black voters and assumptions."

—*Chicago Tribune*

"Seamlessly balancing the personal, political, and cultural, and enlivened with a sharp sense of wit, these standout pieces strike an essential note of warning for Democrats." —*Publishers Weekly* (starred review)

"How can the most reliable Democratic voters be the most dissatisfied with the Democratic Party? Why does the political class obsess over the shifting loyalties of white voters but ignore Black voters who are experiencing the same doubts? To explain why—and what to do about it—Brandi Collins-Dexter seamlessly weaves political analysis with cultural criticism, historical perspectives with deeply personal stories. She not only shows us what Black voters are yearning for, she tells us what will happen if we do not pay attention."

—Heather McGhee, *New York Times* bestselling author of *The Sum of Us*

"Brandi Collins-Dexter has written the book I wanted to read about Black politics in America, not just in the wake of Donald Trump's presidency but after the elections of Barack Obama and Joe Biden failed to deliver material results for Black people. With nuance, pathos, and an unflinching honesty, Collins-Dexter carefully explores the 'unsatis-fied' and 'unsettled' relationship between the Democratic Party and the Black voters (and would-be voters) they take for granted. She seamlessly and deftly weaves between what she's learned from thinking partners as different as Kanye West and his mother, Donda West, historian Leah Wright Rigueur, activist Kwame Ture, Black Trump supporters, radio host Charlamagne tha God, the Brotherhood of Sleeping Car Porters and—most personally—her late, basketball-dribbling father. The essays of *Black Skinhead* will haunt you, inspire you, and make you consider contemporary Black politics in America in profoundly new ways."

—Steven W. Thrasher, PhD, author of *The Viral Underclass*

"An influential media commentator on racial justice explores politics and Black voters in this sharp blend of memoir and cultural criticism. . . . Featuring a vivid mix of hard data, anecdotal details, and scholarly re-search, this book is a must-read for anyone interested in politics and Black lives in America. A remarkable work that leaves us feeling hopeful for change." —*Kirkus Reviews* (starred review)

"Tracing potentially tectonic shifts in American political behavior, Dexter-Collins here demonstrates impressive range and insight. The title she chose for her debut book references Black people who strongly reject a status quo that doesn't serve them, including the taken-for-granted alignment with Democratic Party politics. To illuminate the underlying roots of this alienation, Collins-Dexter blends ideological and cultural analysis with intimate personal narrative." —*Oprah Daily*

"Political activist Collins-Dexter's essay collection is timely as well as pointed. In it she argues that Democrats have taken Black voters for granted and that the consequences of this mistake have already begun—and will accelerate."

—*The New York Times*, "15 Works of Nonfiction to Read This Fall"

"*Black Skinhead* is the story we need, right now, of how Black civil society is disintegrating—and how we ignore it at our peril. Sharp, witty, poi-gnant, and honest, it is a tale of our generation and points to what we might do to stop ourselves from careening off a cliff of nihilism. In this political age, there is no more important task."

—Alicia Garza, principal of Black Futures Lab, cocreator of #BlackLivesMatter, and author of *The Purpose of Power*

"*Black Skinhead* masterfully weaves together a compelling personal story about coming of age as an activist disenchanted with the complacent attitude of politicians toward the needs of Black Americans. Brandi Collins-Dexter guides the reader to see the world as she sees it: lyrical, political, and cynical, at times. She does not take democracy in America as inevitable but rather as an ideal to be fought for, where all political parties must continue to earn the votes of Black Americans. If you're disheartened by party posturing, *Black Skinhead* is the political education you've been waiting for."

—Dr. Joan Donovan, research director at Harvard University's Shorenstein Center and author of *Meme Wars*

"Brandi Collins-Dexter knows how important it is to understand who Black people really are. Her eye-opening research, analysis, and storytelling reveal important undercurrents in Black culture, anticipating the major political waves they will soon become. *Black Skinhead* challenges every assumption and shows us how to see past the fiction of who politicians and pundits want us to be. This book cannot be ignored."

—Rashad Robinson, president of Color Of Change

"With *Black Skinhead*, readers will know what her fellow organizers have long known—that Brandi Collins-Dexter's indispensable leadership is propelled by rigorous research, expertise, and great clarity of voice."

—dream hampton, Emmy-nominated filmmaker, producer, and writer

"In her powerful essays, Collins-Dexter—an influential media commentator and former senior campaign director for Color Of Change—explores the fragile alliance between the Democratic Party and Black voters, in a mix of memoir, research, and analysis. Recommended for everyone interested in the US political landscape, Black lives, and identity in America."

—*Booklist*

"*Black Skinhead* should be a wake-up call to politicians and voters alike. Brandi Collins-Dexter challenges us to journey into the worlds of Black voters and people across the political spectrum. There were times where it felt uncomfortable, but the implications unearthed throughout the book must not be ignored."

—Michael Tubbs, former mayor (Stockton, CA) and author of *The Deeper the Roots*

BLACK
SKINHEAD

BLACK
SKINHEAD

**Reflections on Blackness
and Our Political Future**

BRANDI COLLINS-DEXTER

CELADON BOOKS  NEW YORK

www.celadonbooks.com

The Library of Congress has cataloged the hardcover edition as follows:

Names: Collins-Dexter, Brandi, author.
Title: Black skinhead : reflections on Blackness and our political future /
    Brandi Collins-Dexter.
Description: First Edition. | New York : Celadon Books, [2022] | Includes
    bibliographical references and index.
Identifiers: LCCN 2022016683 | ISBN 9781250824073 (hardcover) |
    ISBN 9781250824110 (ebook)
Subjects: LCSH: African Americans—Political activity—United States—History—
    20th century. | Group identity—Political aspects—United States. | African Americans—
    Politics and government. | Social change—United States. | Voting research—
    United States.
Classification: LCC JK2356 .C637 2022 | DDC 324.2734089/96073—dc23/eng/20220729
LC record available at https://lccn.loc.gov/2022016683

ISBN 978-1-250-82412-7 (trade paperback)

Our books may be purchased in bulk for promotional, educational, or business use. Please contact your local bookseller or the Macmillan Corporate and Premium Sales Department at 1-800-221-7945, extension 5442, or by email at MacmillanSpecialMarkets@macmillan.com.

First Celadon Books Paperback Edition: 2024

10 9 8 7 6 5 4 3 2 1

For Dad

CONTENTS

Prologue: The Stories We Die With
Reflecting on the Will to Keep Going, Even When Shit Gets Hard

I still haven't gotten my driver's license. I've tried. I've even gotten pretty close once. Then, I took the entire bumper off of my husband's Pontiac Sunfire. But I'm an excellent passenger, and I love a good road trip. Directions? I got you. Music and entertainment? I got you. Drink uncapped; snack unpacked and placed directly in your hand? I got you.

I have so many memories of being in the car with my dad. We would take all sorts of road trips. He hated planes, which was funny since my mom was a flight attendant. But he loved to travel, and he always preferred a car. My mom said that as soon as he could, he put me in the back of his car, and we drove.

He would play one of the mixtapes we used to make together for our fantasy radio station, W-JAMES-AM. There was no W-BRANDI-AM, which meant there was no Madonna, and most of the music was at least a decade old. But it was great music. We would sing along to the eclectic mix of old songs. My mom said I could sing before I could talk. Just strap me into the back of a car, and I would start making up gibberish in tune with whatever was playing on the radio.

Our road trip playlist included America, Creedence Clearwater Revival, and Three Dog Night—the perfect companions for highway driving. A lot of those songs we played were about the freedoms of being out on the open road, heading to some named or unnamed destination.

My favorite road trip was one we took from Chicago to Syracuse to see my grandmother. We were with my uncle William—or Uncle GI Joe, as we used to call him. He had been in the military as part of the medical staff that served in Vietnam. So he wasn't a GI, but the nickname stuck. He always traveled around with all of his things, moving around like a soldier with no safe place to call home. My family attributed his quirks to the things he saw and experienced over there. I wouldn't know. He came back before I was born, so I don't have a pre-'Nam frame of reference. But he has a fun sense of humor. Or maybe a dark sense of humor would be more apropos.

For a while, Uncle GI Joe even drove a camouflage car. But by the time we took our road trip in the summer of 1992, he had upgraded to a big, clunky white car. In my head, it was an '80s-era Oldsmobile Cutlass. It looked like that anyways, so now it's canon.

We took off on I-90, heading east. He had a cassette player in the car. But he only had tapes of the Soul Stirrers, the gospel group Sam Cooke performed with before he went solo. I sat in the car with my feet up, windows down, listening to the dulcet melodies.

My dad and uncle spent the trip harmonizing to their favorite songs and talking about old memories. Like one of the many times my uncle got married. He would talk about what a crazy bitch wife number X was. As we glided, or clunked, down the concrete highways and asphalt roads, I sat stretched out in the back with a book. I don't remember which one, but likely it was something from the *Sweet Valley High* series. Or *The Vampire Diaries*.

We kept the windows down to let the air circulate freely. I'm not sure Uncle's car had an air conditioner anyways. Every so often, the old white car would start smoking when it overheated, so we would pull over at a rest stop, and he would fill up a gallon jug he kept in the back with water. Then he'd pour the water into the radiator. While we waited for the car to cool down, I looked through the key chains or various tchotchkes in the shop. If I saw one I liked, Dad would buy it. Then we'd get back in the car and continue heading east. In hindsight, it's a good thing we didn't blow up. Thank God for roadside rest stops. And water.

We made a bunch of pit stops on the way to Syracuse. First was Niagara Falls, because I had never been. We stayed overnight at a motel that couldn't have been more than $25 a night, and we ate at the greasy hole-in-the-wall diner next door. You know the kind of place, where the waitresses are in their fifties and call everyone "hon," and don't bother to write down your order because they have it memorized. You can't have a good road trip unless you stay at a sketchy motel, get called "hon" by a waitress, and end up with a key chain or cheesy piece of memorabilia. These are the rules; I didn't make them up. I still make my husband abide by them to this day.

That was the year *A League of Their Own* came out. The movie is a fictionalized account of the All-American Girls Professional Baseball League. It was, and still is, one of my favorite movies. I saw it three times in the movie theater, and I dragged my dad with me at least one of those times. The movie ends in Cooperstown, New York, at the National Baseball Hall of Fame and Museum. I wanted to see it in person, so I begged my dad to add a stop on the way. It wasn't really along the way. It added a few hours and an overnight motel stay, but he and Uncle GI Joe were game. When we got to Cooperstown, it was like walking into heaven. Until I saw the women's baseball exhibit. It. Sucked. There was, like, one original baseball uniform and a bunch of pictures.

My dad wanted to make a short stop at the International Boxing Hall of Fame in Canastota, so we stopped there, too. A lot of our road trip stops tended to be sports related.

Sports are his life, and so, by proxy, our life, too.

Impossible Dream

> *To fight for the right, without question or pause. To be willing to march into hell, for a heavenly cause.*
> ROY HAMILTON, "THE IMPOSSIBLE DREAM (THE QUEST)"

In April 2020, my dad was supposed to be inducted into the New Mexico Sports Hall of Fame. We were all excited to support and cheer him on. In 1970, as a standout shooting guard and team captain, he led the New Mexico State University men's basketball team to its first and—as of this writing—only NCAA Final Four appearance. By 2020, he had already been inducted into the US Bank/New Mexico State Athletics Hall of Fame, the Corcoran High School Alumni Hall of Fame (Syracuse), and the Greater Syracuse Sports Hall of Fame as a player. And as a coach, he had been inducted into the University of Illinois Chicago Athletics Hall of Fame.

So one would think that by this point, he would have been jaded about this stuff. But ever since receiving the invitation, he had been excited. He'd had his speech written and music planned out months in advance, and we were excited to be together as a family. Even my husband David's parents were driving in from California. As the realities of COVID-19 began to set in, it was looking less and less likely he would be able to get to the Hall of Fame ceremony. But up until the last minute, he kept his plane ticket, hoping the United States would get a handle on the pandemic. Finally, we got word in March—there was no way the ceremony could go forward. *Don't worry, we're set for April 2021*, the facilitators of the ceremony promised.

Tell Me It's Just a Dream . . .

In early summer of 2020, my dad went in for what everyone had said was a standard procedure to address the early stages of prostate cancer. We were told when caught that early, the five-year survival rate for most men with local or regional prostate cancer is nearly 100 percent. COVID-19 was in full swing by this point, but we weren't too worried about what was an in-and-out procedure. He didn't even stay overnight.

Up until the day of that summer procedure, he had been walking four miles on the nearby nature trail, come sun or snow. While lifting weights. Even in his seventies, he still looked like he could drive to the basket and dunk the basketball like he did back in the day. I don't think he could still get up that high, though I wasn't willing to put money on it. But by the time early fall hit, it was clear my dad wasn't healing as he should.

For years, he ate a healthy diet. After the initial procedure he could barely get anything down. Soon, one meal a day became half a meal, became one or two bites, became barely a cup of water. One problem mounted after the next. Every time we went to the hospital, they found something else—a bacterial infection, blockage in his throat, ulcers on his stomach. He even had to have open-heart surgery. He continued declining. We thought he was being treated for his ulcers since that was what had prompted a visit in the fall, but then we learned he was being released without any of the medicines he needed to treat the ulcers. They had gotten so big, they covered his stomach. That was why he couldn't eat. Every time he'd left the hospital, he was worse than when he'd gone in.

The day after his seventy-fourth birthday, on November 24, 2020, we went to the doctor's office. My sister was allowed to go in with him, since he could barely walk and looked like death warmed over. My mom and I had to stay in the car. My husband, David, was on standby at the house. Dad didn't want to go. He didn't think he'd survive another trip to the hospital. But this wasn't supposed to be a hospital stay. He was just getting the long tube that pumped antibiotics through his arm to his heart removed. It wasn't supposed to take more than fifteen minutes. But he barely made it down the stairs and out to the car. His body was weak from the lack of food and nutrients. We all thought that once the tube was out and he was off the antibiotics, he'd be able to get some food down. But what we didn't know was that the untreated ulcers had also moved into his throat and would permanently block his road to recovery.

As I look back now, I think he knew even if the rest of us didn't.

He sat by the door, slightly hunched over. I handed him his cream-colored basketball cap and camel-colored coat to go with the cream sweater he wore. He looked up at me, smiling. "You finally learned how to put together an outfit, Ditto." "Ditto" was his weird little nickname for me, a gradual whittling down of "Branditto." He put the hat on his head. Once perfectly fitted, it now looked two sizes too big.

"Not that it matters now," he finished.

My husband, David, loaded him into the back of the car. My dad gave him a dap, said he loved him. Then he started singing "I'll Be Home for Christmas." David chuckled a bit as he closed the car's rear door. My mom pulled off. A couple of days earlier, Dad had randomly mentioned he knew I always worried he didn't like David because he was (in his words) "a white boy with slightly bad manners." Then he said, "But I love that boy; he takes care of you, Ditto. That's the only thing that's important . . . even if he is a little weird and mumbles sometimes."

Dad went in for a fifteen-minute procedure that turned into an overnight stay. He wouldn't be home for Thanksgiving two days later. And the Saturday after Thanksgiving, he flatlined. He lost oxygen to his brain for fifteen minutes, falling into a coma.

We called in every favor possible to get in to see him. COVID-19 had shut everything down, and the hospital was restricting patients, but they let us in when we told them who my father was. It was the ultimate flex, and a card we had always been hesitant to play as a family. But in the moment, I didn't care about any of that. I just wanted to see my dad. I wanted to see my dad walk out of the hospital.

It was bittersweet on multiple levels. The difference I witnessed in the medical and interpersonal treatment of James Collins, anonymous Black man, versus Coach Jimmy Collins, Illinois legend and Hall of Famer, was so wildly different. It was a reminder that while celebrity and class mobility may blunt the force of some racial bias, it never really goes away. All of my father's medical troubles were treatable and should not have gotten to this point. I don't believe that they would have were it not for a profit-driven health care system pushed to the max by COVID-19.

We got word we could get a couple of hours with him. The guilt of being granted a privilege so many people hadn't gotten was not enough for me to turn away the precious chance to tell him I loved him. I couldn't remember what I had last said to him before he went in. I wanted to make sure I could tell him that, even if he couldn't hear me.

Teenage Dreams

I turned to look at my mom in the back seat as my husband drove us to the hospital to visit my father. She was perfectly dressed in her St. John's blazer and starched white button-down blouse with her initials on the sleeves. She wore a pair of her South Sea cultured pearl earrings, an artfully wrapped scarf, and soft brown leather riding boots that had been handmade in Spain.

"Girls, we have to look good for Dad," she had told my sisters and me.

I looked critically at my uneven nails before brushing down my hair and putting on my plastic face shield.

I had taken to only listening to music that my dad liked. I had been doing little things like that—wearing his clothes, sitting in his chair, anything to keep him closer. Elvis Presley's "Can't Help Falling in Love" came on my playlist, and my mom smiled for a second.

"Every time I hear Elvis Presley, I think of Roy Hamilton. He's one of your father's favorite singers. He was going to walk out to one of his songs at the Hall of Fame ceremony."

"Oh yeah," I replied absently. "I don't know Roy Hamilton, which song?"

"'Impossible Dream,'" she responded after fumbling around a bit on her cell phone.

"The Impossible Dream." It was a fitting song on multiple levels.

My dad had lived what many would consider a remarkable life. He embodied the bootstraps rendition of the "American Dream." His story starts in Minter City, Mississippi, an unincorporated community in Leflore County. Between 1877 and 1950, Leflore County had the highest number of *documented* lynchings of Black people in the state of Mississippi. A lot more went undocumented. My paternal grandmother, Lorraine, had grown up hard. She married young to an undertaker named Earl Collins, who was nearly twenty years her senior. When Earl decided it was time to upgrade, he took his two oldest kids to live with his new wife, leaving Lorraine with a baby who was still breast feeding.

My dad's life is a testament to the sheer grit she drew from. Lorraine decided to get on a Greyhound bus to Syracuse, New York, by herself. Back then, it would've taken four days, virtually nonstop, to get there. It was like Black girl *Survivor*. But, clearly, she was already built for it. She was a teen mother with barely a fourth-grade education, taking a chance up North. Things could have easily gone wrong. But it would have been worse if she'd stayed. By the time a fourteen-year-old Chicago boy by the name of Emmett Till was lynched just five miles away from Minter City in Money, Mississippi, my grandmother had made it to Syracuse. A couple of her close girlfriends—Boo and Vivian—were already there. She secured a job as a cook, first at the Memorial Hospital and later on at the local Veterans Administration Hospital. They built a community of matriarchs raising their children together in an urban jungle.

Dad would wake up in the middle of the night and find his mother standing over him, praying out loud. Praying he would be OK and grow up strong. Praying he would survive the trials and tribulations before him. If there was one thing one could find in the 15th Ward, it was trials and tribulations.

But my dad also had male role models. There was Mr. Harrison, who ran what we would compare to a Big Brother program today out of a community center. And there was Uncle Joe, my grandfather's brother, who drove a motorcycle and towered over everyone. To Dad, that made him the epitome of cool. Years later, when my dad moved to Chicago in 1970, Uncle Joe—along with his tiny and pretty wife, Aunt Minnie—looked out for him. Still, out of my dad's circle of Syracuse friends, seven were incarcerated by age thirty. At *least* seven never made it to thirty. Others would die later in life from drug or alcohol overdoses or homicide, and some just died young—buried under the sheer weight of a hard life and the ailments that hard life attracted. Others, like Gus, Hicks, and Protein, remained fixtures in my dad's life (and ours) for years to come.

For Dad, prosperity and deliverance came in the form of sports. Though he preferred football, he found his body type and skill set were more aligned with the game of basketball.

So basketball was what he did. All. The. Time.

When he wasn't asleep, he had a basketball. Dribbling by himself while he read a book for class. Using the brick walls of the housing projects for passing and catching drills. Driving around with his friends to every street pickup game from Syracuse to New York City to Philadelphia, and even down the coast to Baltimore. He had one friend with a car. The group would scrape together the money to fill the tank with gas and hit the road. They hoped to win enough money to fill the car back up to get home.

It was never about the money for Dad, though. It was about the right to call himself the *best*.

He went looking for every single player on the East Coast he heard had game. And while he didn't always win, he always won the respect of anyone he took the court with. But playing sports wasn't the only survival skill he developed. He also had charisma for days. He was that popular star athlete who made you feel seen. The one who could make you feel ten feet tall with just a high five or head nod.

One look at all the handwritten notes in his high school yearbook could verify that. He was voted Most Athletic Male. In the accompanying photo, he's smiling playfully while pretending to be too weak to pick up a barbell. The girl voted Most Athletic Female proudly held a barbell of the same weight over her head.

As he began to make a name for himself, college scouts came calling. But those from Syracuse University did not. The rumor was they had an unspoken policy against recruiting Black athletes from within the city limits.

When considering things like income, education, homeownership, poverty, incarceration, and mortality—Syracuse ranks as one of the ten worst cities for Black Americans to live in. Before COVID-19, nearly 40 percent of Black residents lived below the poverty line compared to 11 percent of white residents.

My dad grew up in the notorious and oft-studied 15th Ward in Syracuse. The small community has been the focus of several national think pieces, including one in the *Atlantic* aptly titled "How to Decimate a City." There are few places in the country where quality-of-life disparities because of racial and economic segregation are quite so visible.

But it hadn't always been that way. In 1950, by the time my grandmother had moved there, eight out of nine Black people in Syracuse lived in that community. Once called a "refuge from discrimination," forged through Black-owned and operated institutions and community camaraderie, the neighborhood was ripped apart by Syracuse's urban renewal plan, which displaced 75 percent of the community and drove out whatever existed of the middle class. When I was a child, summer vacations in Syracuse often involved riding from my grandmother's comfortable suburban house in DeWitt, where Dad had bought her a home, back into the 15th Ward to visit relatives and some of my dad's old friends.

Every time we pulled up, people came out to welcome home a local celebrity. We sat out on the steps—often with my aunt Boo, aunt V, and cousin Ida. Random people from all over the neighborhood came out to say hi to James and "Little James," a nickname I hated. He would greet them all like family, reminiscing about some distant memory they shared. I think in addition to seeing loved ones, it was also about reminding himself and showing me where we came from. Moreover, it was about the importance of never severing our roots.

All-American Dream

While Syracuse University never came calling, other schools did. These schools included the University of Wisconsin, which, in Dad's words, had "too many weed heads back then," and St. John's University, which at the time had a bad reputation. But he had also gotten on the radar of Ed Murphy, a tall, husky Irishman from Syracuse. The son of a cop.

Murphy had played college basketball for the first integrated basketball team at Hardin-Simmons, a small Baptist institution down in Abilene, Texas. His college coach, Louis Ray Henson, was an Oklahoman with a slow drawl and the son of a sharecropper, who grew up during the Depression era with no electricity or running water. When Coach Henson moved on to New Mexico State University, one of his first assistant coach hires was Murphy.

By all accounts, Coach Henson liked to win. And when you want to win that bad, it doesn't take you long to figure out racism doesn't pay—at least not in the highest moneymaking sports. To be clear, I'm not saying Coach Henson's early integration of his teams was strictly transactional, or that he didn't care about racial injustices. Having known him since I was a child, I can say I saw him as a kind and genuine man. But he was also a smart man who liked to win. He even named his autobiography *Lou: Winning at Illinois.*

Coach Murphy's dad, the street beat cop, used to watch the kids playing pickup games while he was patrolling the neighborhood. If he saw a kid with potential, he would tell his son and Coach Henson, "Hey, come check this kid out."

To be clear, the relationship between the beat cop and the civilian in a Black neighborhood has never been as chummy as *The Andy Griffith Show.* Policing as an institution has always existed in opposition to Black people and our freedom. One of the origins of policing in the US was patrols charged with hunting down people attempting to escape slavery. From then until now, the link between law enforcement and white nationalism has not waned.

But while relationships between police and communities have been rigged from the beginning, the close physical proximity between where officers lived and the neighborhoods they patrolled made for different relationships. By all accounts, Officer Murphy had a rapport with the kids that showed a vested interest in maintaining safety, not just in being part of an occupying army.

If nothing else, Officer Murphy's situation was unique because most community cops didn't come equipped with college scholarships. He had been scoping out this one particular kid he kept seeing at every pickup game. His son was also familiar, having gone up against him in the summer leagues, and was also impressed with his grit. He was a six-foot-two forward, a skinny but scrappy kid who averaged twenty points per game. "You've got to have this guy," the Murphys relayed back to Henson. "He can really play." That was an understatement. As a high school basketball player, my dad was a three-time All-City selection. More than fifty years later, in 2018, he was voted the best high school player ever in Central New York.

Sight unseen, Henson gave Coach Murphy the sign-off to offer the kid a scholarship. And that was how an Irish son of a cop ended up in the 15th Ward eating neck bones and black-eyed peas, taking up space at my grandmother's tiny kitchen table while putting the full-court press on her and her son. He treated my grandmother with the highest respect, because he knew when he was recruiting my dad, he had to recruit Grandma, too. He had to be authentic. Later, my mom would recount that he was always a warm and booming presence every time they met up "and I never met a white man who could throw down on chitterlings like that," she laughingly added. He was someone that a protective mother could trust *just enough* with her teenage son's future.

But before my dad could get out of Syracuse, something happened that almost dramatically altered the trajectory of his life. One day, a police captain showed up at his school looking for him. Another kid in his neighborhood had snatched a white woman's pocketbook. In the scuffle, she had fallen, hit her head on the curb, and died. The police were out for blood, and they didn't care who bled.

The police were going around asking who did it and giving a description of the kid—a kid whose generic description almost verbatim matched my dad. So without evidence, people pointed the police in his direction. The police took him out of school, without a warrant and without reading him his Miranda rights—which hadn't yet come into effect. They didn't contact my grandmother. He was held at the police station for what my dad thought must've been about six or seven hours. They beat him with a phone book, trying to do whatever they could to make him confess to a crime he knew he hadn't committed.

He wanted to confess just to get it over with and stop the beating. But he also knew if he confessed, it would *all* be over. He had a future ahead of him that he had envisioned. That he had fought for. He knew everything he dreamed of would be truly impossible if he gave in. So no matter how much it hurt, no matter how long they kept him, he didn't give in. He also knew he couldn't show extreme anger or indignation at the situation. He had to stay calm and steady. In his head, he tried to put himself in the mindset of being in a high-stakes basketball game—keep his head, maintain focus, don't lose sight or awareness of the basket.

Eventually, the police got the word that my dad had been at a pickup game, with several witnesses around, at the time of the incident. There was no possible way he could've been involved. So, unceremoniously, they let him go in the middle of the night. Barely able to stand, he made the five-mile walk back home. He told his mother he had gotten into a fight at school.

When I think about this story, I find myself wondering if Officer Murphy had a hand in helping my dad get exonerated. Moreover, if my dad weren't a star player, would they have even bothered to investigate, or would they have called it "case closed" and thrown him in jail like so many others?

Innocent Black people are twelve times more likely than white people to be falsely convicted of crimes, and they also have to wait disproportionately longer for their names to be cleared, often years. Compared to that, eight hours is nothing. But from a psychological perspective, it can also change everything, especially for a scared teenager who doesn't know when they'll see home again. For Dad, it just reinforced the need to get the fuck out of Syracuse; he promised himself he would never move back.

In 1966, he graduated from Corcoran High School. I used to always flip through his yearbook and make fun of the photos. Now, in 2020, as I struggled to make peace with the reality that he would soon take his last breath, I stormed through my parents' house looking for it. I opened every closet and dresser drawer, combing through my dad's piles of paper. He had *a lot* of fucking papers. He wasn't necessarily a hoarder, but he kept everything that meant something to him. Now, I gathered them all up in my arms, trying to claim those pieces of him for myself.

There, under the table next to his spot on the couch, I found it, the Thomas J. Corcoran High School Class of 1966 yearbook. I opened it and stared at his senior photo. One time, I had posted one of his yearbook photos on Instagram, and more than one of my thirsty friends said he looked like Mahershala Ali, which, lowkey, he kinda did.

Next to his photo it said:

Collins, James . . . Colt 45 (nickname)
Crazy about sports . . . personality-plus
School spirited
Football 2: Basketball 3, 4: Track 2, 3
Goals: College, Travel
Top Five:

Pet Peeve: People who talk behind my back

Usually Found: Brewing in the West End
Suppressed Desire: To play basketball in college
Fondest Memory: Championship game in Oneonta
Theme Song: "Midnight Hour" [sic]

Last Will and Testament: I, James Collins, leave
Willee Wagner all my swinging teachers.

After graduation, he packed up what little he had. He couldn't afford a cross-country flight. Plus, no one in his family had ever been on a plane, and he wasn't sure he was ready to be the first one to try it. So, like my grandmother had years before, he sat cramped in a Greyhound bus for four days, but instead of going to Syracuse, he was making the trek to Las Cruces, New Mexico.

When he got off the bus, people called him "Jim," like the *Huckleberry Finn* character. "I hated that," my dad said, laughing. "Up until then, everybody called me James, sometimes Jimmy . . . but never Jim. Strange how people will just change your name like that unprompted." He thought to himself that he should turn around and get back on the bus, but he had no money. He'd spent everything he had just to get there.

Staying wasn't just the only economic option, it was the right choice. My dad would always light up when talking about his experiences in New Mexico. It was there that he flourished and expanded his worldview. His time as a school radio DJ diversified his musical tastes—something he passed down to me—and he wrote for the school newspaper. His teammates, a diverse group of kids from different walks of life, bonded with their love of the game. Because most friend groups tend to be segregated based on both class and race, it's rare to have some of your closest friends come from such different experiences, but he got that. In his words:

> I had never been treated with such open arms, especially by people who weren't Black. And Syracuse was diverse, kind of like New Mexico—there were Hispanic kids, and ethnic whites, not nearly as many Native Americans, but some. And, though we may have been integrated in certain public spaces, it really was segregated in most other aspects of life. But that wasn't my experience in New Mexico.

He went to New Mexico State University during a time of major cultural and political shifts in the United States. Throughout his high school years, Medgar Evers, President John Kennedy, and Malcolm X had all been assassinated. In college, Robert "Bobby" Kennedy and Martin Luther King, Jr., were assassinated. A year later, populist leader Fred Hampton would also be assassinated.

At the time, my dad stayed mainly apolitical. His focus was on basketball, and he was aware he couldn't be everybody's friend if he revealed how all these things were really affecting him. Life had shown him that he could get further by tamping down the pain, silencing the sounds of protest from within. His chances of survival would increase if he stayed on the right side of controversy.

But in 1968, when everyone was pulled into some form of political consciousness, standing on the sidelines stopped being a worthwhile option. The Olympic Games, held that year in Mexico, became the site of another political moment when millions around the world watched as US track gold and bronze medalists, Tommie C. Smith and John Carlos, respectively, stood on the Olympic podium while the US national anthem played—their black-gloved fists raised in the air, with black socks and no shoes to represent Black poverty in the United States. The moment resonated with athletes like my dad and his New Mexico State teammates who decided they wanted to follow suit.

When they did player introductions at the next game, the entire team ran out with their fists up.

> It was all of us, too—white guys, Black guys, Chicanos—we all ran out like that. You know I don't know if Coach Henson loved that, to be honest. But to tell you what kind of man he was, when the press asked him about it afterward and if he was going to discipline us, he said in that slow Southern drawl, "well you know, the boys were just doing 'Aggie power'; it's just a New Mexico State thing." And then he did it too. . . . It meant something that he stood with the team. That moment was one of the reasons why I was always loyal to him, because he was loyal to us. Whether he personally agreed or not, I don't know, but he never tried to stop us from being who we were. . . . As long as we were disciplined when playing the game.

At New Mexico State, my dad came into his own.

He became a consensus Second-Team All-American nationally after averaging 24.3 points, 4.6 rebounds, and 2.9 assists in a season. He was also on the NCAA All-District Team. As of 2020, he is the only player in school program history to earn multiple All-American honors, and he holds two single-season records: scoring (754 points) and field goals made (322). Mind you, all this happened before the three-point line existed, and as shooting guard, most of his shots were from what would today be in the three-point range. Oh, and he also made the cover of *Sports Illustrated* in 1970.

There's more, but you get it. He was lethal on the court.

For years, I never had the chance to see footage of my dad playing in his prime. Then, a few years ago, during the NCAA men's basketball tournament, footage was posted on YouTube from his Final Four game against UCLA. Watching my dad light up UCLA is a sight to see. He finished that game with twenty-eight points after a slow first half.

Pre. Three. Point. Line. You can hear UCLA-famed head coach John Wooden on the sidelines yelling, "Can somebody please go get him!"

Unfortunately, his effort wasn't enough, and they lost 93–77. Their dream run ended, as some sports dreams do, with a trip to the White House—the Nixon White House. After he died, we found video footage of him going up to the White House with his team, giddy and happy to be there. Honestly, how could he not be? A kid from the 15th Ward was invited to the White House??? That had to have been a special moment, no matter who was president.

Coach Henson and the Murphys changed the lives of so many men and boys, my father included. But my father also had to be exceptional to make it. He had to be ten times better than everyone else. He was constantly up against the odds and having to rise above adversity in ways that most of us—me included—simply aren't built for.

He knew that, and he never forgot it. He didn't want to forget it because then he would have had no reason to work to make things better for those who were still in Syracuse back in the 15th Ward. I think that was why he always went back home. That was why he showed me his home and made sure I understood it to be more than some scary nightmare from a news story or research study. He wanted to instill that memory in me, stuffed away like a rock in my backpack of Black middle-class privilege.

Sitting in his chair at my parents' house, sifting through his papers, I found an old copy of *Focus on Youth* magazine from 1968. It was a magazine about Black youth empowerment, and one section was earmarked:

> To accept a black person here and there is not enough. The whole black community must be accepted and allowed to change, as people within the group are able. Our prejudices will not disappear merely by having Negroes become clean and educated. We will still reject them; we have for a long, long time. We will not break down prejudice by having group discussions, by conducting surveys, or appointing committees. They are tired, tired of talk.

I thought about that passage for a long time and what it must have meant to him. I imagined him sitting there in that chair, thinking about all the things he had been given in life. Earned in life. Lost in life. Fought for in life.

He was a basketball coach for something like twenty-five years. Over the years, many of those players stayed in touch—those Dad loved, and those Dad didn't love but came to understand, as they sought to understand him. Players who had gone through tough times; some who were still going through tough times. But they never stopped calling, and he never stopped picking up the phone to answer. Many of them reached out and were there in his final days and hours. They had been there for my mom; some of them even called her "Mom." What a community he had helped raise.

James Earl Collins was born in 1946 in Minter City, Mississippi, to a young mother named Lorraine and her rolling-stone undertaker husband, Earl. He was raised in the 15th Ward in Syracuse, New York. He wasn't supposed to make it. He was born in a county with the highest rate of children's poverty in the United States. He was raised in a county with one of the worst racial income gaps in the country. And he turned a basketball into his one-way ticket to the American Dream. The impossible dream. This is why the Roy Hamilton song would have been such a fitting song to play while he walked across the stage at the New Mexico State Hall of Fame. It's why I have the lyrics tattooed on my arm today: to help me remember how easy it is for dreams to be deferred, and why we have to fight to remove the barriers deliberately put in the way.

I never got to go to Las Cruces with my dad. I would've loved to have been able to see it through his eyes. But I have been there with my mom, and while there, I saw a larger-than-life picture of him hanging up in the New Mexico State arena. He's wearing number 22, dribbling forward, and looks almost like he's skating on one foot while he smiles into the camera. When we went to the New Mexico Sports Hall of Fame in 2021 to accept the honor on his behalf, we heard so many beautiful stories from people in the community on whom he left an impression, even fifty years later.

The photo in the arena is also framed at the bottom of the stairs in my parents' basement, where I wrote most of this prologue. It's my dad's "man cave." As I write this, I can hear my mom pacing above me. I don't really know when she last slept. She cleans things, and she retells the story over and over again of the things that led to my father's demise. I don't think she can really stand to sleep in their bed alone right now. Above their bed, stenciled on the wall, are the words *Two people in love always kiss goodnight.* She wonders out loud if she should just paint over it.

On one of these last days, she hugged me tightly, whispering in my ear, "I know it's hard, but don't let this make you bitter. Your dad would never want you to be bitter."

"I'll try not to be bitter, Mommy," I whispered back. I never call her Mommy. I feel like I'm regressing.

It's hard not to be angry and disillusioned when there are so many lingering questions about the medical treatment he received and the life-and-death decisions that were made by the medical staff charged with his care. But I try not to focus on that, instead looking at his trophy cases full of awards commending him for sports and acts of community service. There is his ring from the New Mexico State Final Four, his trophies, his original Bulls uniform and original New Mexico State jersey. And all around, pictures of so many of the different kids he coached who grew up to be men able to create a better life for their families.

Sweet Dreams . . .

"Get up, honey, it's time to go home. The doctors in here are trying to kill you. You gotta tell them you want to go home."

We're in the hospital, in the ICU, hoping for some kind of miracle. My mom turns to the doctor with a slight smirk, even as tears fill her eyes. She says almost apologetically, but also defiantly, "I know I'm not supposed to say that in front of you." She rubs my dad's hands and feet as she continues to cajole him to wake up.

"Get up, baby, we gotta go home. You gotta survive this. You gotta fight for this."

Then she lovingly applies lip balm to his dry lips. She wipes the dried blood from his teeth and out from under his nails. She hangs a chain with all the championship rings he has accumulated over time around his neck. She says they're there so he remembers who he is, and also so *they* know who he is, too. She gives him a little basketball with his and his

Bulls' teammate Bob Love's signatures on it, softly encouraging him to grab the ball and get in the game, just like he always did.

My mom knew the right words to say to my dad. He was notoriously competitive—so much so that he never let me win at board games, never pretended to lose a game of H-O-R-S-E. If anyone could beat the odds and grab hold of the impossible dream, it was him.

I watch my mom tend to my dad with so much love and fierce devotion as I sit there fighting to keep my voice equally upbeat for him, trying not to show my heart breaking.

I keep reading this chapter to him as I rush to finish his story, hoping that somehow, he can hear me. That maybe he will wake up to fact check me.

Even though they say he can't hear me, I feel like he can hear me. I hope he can hear me. I hope I did his story some small amount of justice.

When he was gone, I didn't think I had any story left in me. Or, rather, I didn't know how to get it out of me. What was there left to say? What do you say when you watch someone fade away in front of you, knowing his story should have ended differently. Knowing how many people needed him. Still need him.

His death was like a chain breaking. Two weeks later, his sister Earlene died, and her son, my cousin Kevin, died shortly after that. A month earlier, his other sister Pam had died, as well as his niece (my cousin) Tina. A few months later, his brother Early died. I kept telling my aunt Linda that I was going to wrap her up in cellophane because we didn't want to lose her, too. Everyone was devastated.

It had already been a shitty year. My cousin Cola, who was closest to me in age, had died over the summer. I had two cousins fall into comas while my dad was sick. Thank God they both lived. My mom was heartbroken. Months later, she's still sending old family photos at three o'clock in the morning. My oldest sister sits in his car listening to his burned CDs, some of which I made for him.

But the world just kept going.

One day I was sitting in my dad's chair, staring out the window and hoping my computer had evolved enough to just write this book for me. I looked down at one of his stacks of papers. I picked them up. It was pages and pages of stuff he had written. He majored in journalism, but I didn't know he had continued to write.

There were little notes about all of us kids. There were basketball plays that he still drew up even though he had been retired for years. A speech he had written to read at the funeral of his best friend's son. There were random thoughts and observations. Reading them was like getting to take one last peek into his soul.

My mom told me that up until the end, he kept telling anyone who would listen that his baby girl was writing a book. The checkout woman at their local grocery store cried when she found out he was dead. He was so proud of me. Of all of us. But it was like he couldn't fathom that he had created a being that was writing a book. Once upon a time, he had dreamed of being a journalist. And though life had other plans for him, he'd never stopped writing.

I always promised my dad I would help him write his autobiography. Though we never got the chance, his story has become woven into this book's writing because although this is a political book, it's also a personal one and a cultural one. The three are inextricably linked. And for me, my dad's life is the origin of so much. Every time I got stuck on where to go next or got writer's block, I would stare at his photo or listen to some of those W-JAMES-AM songs. So I'm writing this for him. And in my mind, I imagine everyone my family lost is at a hole-in-the-wall bar in heaven, drinking shots of cognac and listening to Roy Hamilton . . . or Bobby Womack. Maybe they're there, too. And everyone is feeling free. And everyone is safe. But they're also waiting on me to tell this story. Our stories: the ones that kill us, and the ones that help us fight to live.

I've tried my best to do that.

BLACK
SKINHEAD

Introduction
Where Are We Going?

In the late summer of 2016, I was in Philadelphia for the Democratic National Convention. The convention was muggy and miserable. The weather, on the other hand, was pretty nice. Getting into the convention center was a shit show, and with Michelle Obama and Senator Bernie Sanders being two of the closers on the first night, anticipation was sky high. The theme that night was "United Together." Me, being the misanthrope I am, took a two-hour trip through the packed crowds back to my hotel so I could fully absorb their words in peace.

> That is the story of this country, the story that has brought
> me to this stage tonight, the story of generations of people
> who felt the lash of bondage, the shame of servitude, the
> sting of segregation, but who kept on striving and hoping
> and doing what needed to be done so that today I wake up
> every morning in a house that was built by slaves.
> —FIRST LADY MICHELLE OBAMA, JULY 25, 2016

I felt the first lady's speech in my soul. She talked about going high when others go low—and people have gone low against her, saying ugly things about her body, her private relationships, and even dissecting her facial expressions and features. She is the embodiment of the type of grace, intelligence, and strength I see in my mother. The climax of her speech rocked the house, and you could feel the electricity of the convention center through the TV:

> And I watch my daughters, two beautiful, intelligent, Black
> young women playing with their dogs on the White House
> lawn. And because of Hillary Clinton, my daughters and all
> our sons and daughters now take for granted that a woman can
> be president of the United States.

By the time she told the story of the American Dream fulfilled—her daughters playing out on the front lawn of the White House—I was in full-out ugly cry. I wanted to believe brighter days were ahead. But deep down I didn't think that would happen regardless of the outcome of the election. Though I did think one option was light years better than the other.

> So, look, so don't let anyone ever tell you that this country
> isn't great, that somehow we need to make it great again.
> Because this right now is the greatest country on earth!

For eight years, the Obamas had painted a striking picture of the Black American Dream—an idyllic representation of Black success combined with political and cultural power. They had presented a fairy-tale boot-straps narrative and leaned into the belief that we can all make it if we try. The Obamas' message was that the American Dream is for all of us; we just need the audacity, grit, and intellect to reach for it. And, in some ways, this was true. New doors were open for Black people, and anyone who had been implicitly and explicitly told that they could not make it to the White House because they didn't look the part.

The Obamas' message was also that if we work within the system together, pushing through lingering challenges, we can make it truly work for us. That you get what you earn. That those who previously held power can't keep us all out, and those of us who are able to break through will come back for the rest of us. That the public and private systems that shape our everyday lives aren't broken. That the real problem is those who control the systems and the people who don't show up to vote. Here's where they start to lose me a bit.

As aspirational as that moment of seeing Michelle Obama onstage was, symbolizing passing the baton from the matriarch of the first Black First Family to the presumed first woman president, her story wasn't a reality for many Black families. The success she had achieved by working within the system was still out of reach for a lot of Black Americans.

Going into November of 2016, we had been told that everything was fine, that America was working for everyone, and that the American Dream was attainable for all. But, in reality, everything was not fine, and nothing showed this quite as starkly as the election of Donald Trump as Barack Obama's successor. Shock and dismay reverberated through the media. How had this happened? Who had voted for Trump? How had such a seemingly seismic shift occurred overnight?

But for those who had been paying attention, there had been warning signs that the Obamas' version of the American Dream wasn't working for everyone. That it hadn't been working for many white Americans was immediately and loudly discussed, but the truth—and what I set out to write this book about—was that it hadn't been working for many Black Americans either. For many, President Obama's vision had been more illusion than reality all along.

As I set out on a journey to get to the heart of Black political identity, a process that involved extensive interviews with Black people from all across the ideological spectrum, the voices of Black Trump supporters loomed larger than most. They haunted my dreams, telling a different tale about Black politics and Black America, one that countered white America's long-held assumption that Black voters will always vote Democrat—and even that the Democratic Party is the best bet for Black Americans.

For me, the true canary in the coal mine was also perhaps the most unlikely: musician Kanye West, who had been trying to tell us for years. In Kanye's own journey, I found the perfect allegory to tell the story of how the once unshakable Black Democratic voting bloc has become increasingly fractured. In Kanye, I found a way to tell the story about a Black America that had become disillusioned with the failed promises of their country.

LOST IN THE WORLD . . .

The 2010 MTV Video Music Awards (VMAs) were MTV's highest rated in seven years. That year boasted a strong performance lineup—Rihanna, Eminem, Drake, Mary J. Blige, Bruno Mars, and Lady Gaga, among others. But for many, the most anticipated performance of the night was the closer: Kanye West. He was there to premiere his song "Runaway" off his upcoming album *My Beautiful Dark Twisted Fantasy.*

The album is still his most critically acclaimed work to date. It's a gorgeous album, from its musical composition to its lyricism. Its power is in its lush musical composition and seamless melding of music samples and sounds that in no way should go together. Sonically, it changed the direction music was heading in and even ideas of what music could be. And despite—or maybe because of—the ridiculous number of guest features and producers, it provided a soundtrack to emerging feelings of alienation and loneliness in an increasingly digitally connected world.

The album, and the feature film he released with it, was a deep dive into the pitfalls of excess, celebrity, consumer culture, race, sex, wealth, self-aggrandizement, and the death of the American Dream. But on a personal level, the album was also a voyeuristic and devastating look at the turn his life had taken since his mother, Donda—a massive influence in his life—had passed away unexpectedly in 2007, a day after undergoing several cosmetic surgery procedures. Her death and the manner in which she died would have a profound impact on his life and artistic trajectory.

In the years that followed, Kanye felt like he'd lost everything, especially after he famously interrupted Taylor Swift at the 2009 VMAs. In the backlash to what became colloquially known as Taylorgate, public perception turned against him. A scheduled coheadlining tour with Lady Gaga—Fame Kills—was immediately canceled, and Kanye felt the financial fallout. He received death threats. Even Joe Jackson—father of Kanye's idol, Michael Jackson—said publicly that Kanye should be blackballed out of the industry. He broke up with his longtime girlfriend, and then quickly experienced the crash and burn of a high-profile relationship with model Amber Rose.

The final blow seemed to be the hot mic moment when President Barack Obama referred to West as a "jackass" in a room full of laughing media people.

The country's first Black president had built his career in Kanye's hometown of Chicago. Excited by his candidacy, Kanye had produced celebratory songs that name-checked Obama, including rapper Common's 2007 track "The People," which had helped elevate the then-underdog presidential candidate to a pop-cultural icon with lyrics like *My raps ignite the people like Obama.* The instant summer anthem had not only been produced by Kanye but was released on the record label Kanye founded (G.O.O.D. Music) as well. The accompanying music video was on repeat on MTV back when MTV still played music videos, giving free round-the-clock promotion for the campaign going into the 2008 election. Though not the only one, Kanye had essentially used his own celebrity to help elevate the then-senator's profile in youth and pop culture. Now, that same person was telling the world that he didn't hold Kanye in the same regard.

In response, Kanye retreated into self-imposed exile in Hawaii in 2009. He called out to his community—the people he trusted, the people who held him down—and brought them together in Honolulu to record what would become *My Beautiful Dark Twisted Fantasy.* These were people from across genres of music, across genres of art. He brought together artists who hadn't broken into the public consciousness yet and people who were already well known. He, and they, created something as beautiful, dark, and twisted as advertised. I don't love how he publicly dogged Amber Rose—the misogynoir is hard to ignore—but the music is undeniable.

That night at the 2010 VMAs, one year after Taylorgate, over 11.4 million people tuned in to see an introspective, if chaotic, Kanye perform. Dressed in an extremely bright-red suit, he stood by himself on a minimalist black-and-white stage, playing the intro on what looked like a really high-end Casio keyboard. As the bass dropped, ballerinas surrounded him, and eventually rap artist Pusha T, all dressed in muted pink. Kanye performed with a focused intensity—aware of the audience that surrounded him on all sides but also clearly in his own world.

Kanye's lyrics fluctuated between apologetic and unrepentant—like the kind of begrudging apology people give when they say, "I'm sorry if you were offended." But the lyrics also showed self-awareness.

In "Runaway," he welcomes douchebags, scumbags, and jerkoffs instead of rejecting them. He didn't throw in jackasses, but he didn't have to because the message was clear. And in case it wasn't, in his song "Power," he raps the lyrics, *they say I was an abomination of Obama's nation, well that's a pretty bad way to start the conversation*. In that same song, he grapples with his desire to be childlike in his creativity and honesty while also falling deeper into the power trip that comes with success and wealth. He then flips it, calling out the broken education and criminal justice systems that have left people with nothing left to lose.

The album's final full song, "Lost in the World," a lyrical reflection of Kanye's suicidal thoughts, revealed that even in a moment when he was surrounded by people, he still felt alone. He felt misunderstood by voyeurs to his hard times, misrepresented by the media, and ultimately alone. He had become disillusioned.

It was a personal album, but Kanye had also laid bare the deep traumas of Black America, unafraid to lean into the darker and more complex side of the human experience. At times, he seemed to serve as a warning sign for the reckless desperation that can emerge when something or someone goes ignored for too long.

If Kanye was beginning to explore these themes on *My Beautiful Dark Twisted Fantasy*, on his 2013 follow-up, *Yeezus*, he was in full swing. In the years between the two albums, on the outside, it seemed like Kanye's life had become a fairy tale. *My Beautiful Dark Twisted Fantasy* had been a resounding success, spending more than two years on the Billboard charts. He got bigger; he dropped music collaborations that were hits. He released the Nike Yeezy sneaker—which broke sales records—and he married his dream girl Kim Kardashian.

But all was not well. Kanye, as an artist, wanted to break into the fashion industry. He'd worked as a low-paid intern at Fendi, putting hours and hours into learning the craft, but in corporate fashion houses, he was still seen as a joke. He was the biggest star in the world, and he had the biggest shoe at Nike, but even Nike wouldn't give him a long-term contract.

Kanye was incensed, voicing his frustrations with the company. The outburst seemed crazy to some people, childish even, but Kanye wasn't just talking about fashion. He was talking about the frustration of fighting to make it. The frustration of being willing to put in the work and still being denied access. Of being humble and spending entire nights in the Nike offices learning and perfecting the craft and still not being able to break through in corporate boardrooms that didn't see him as good enough. He had gone millions of dollars into debt ($53 million by 2016) to pursue his dream and the dreams of others, and he felt undercompensated in relation to how much money pursuing those dreams made for others. He was experiencing the broader exasperation of what it meant to be told all you have to do is work hard, pull yourself up by your bootstraps, do the right things, and say the right things, only to be told it is not enough. He was experiencing what it means to realize the American Dream is a lie. I'm not working with a multimillion-dollar budget, but that aspect of his diatribe was something I could relate to; perhaps it's a relatable feeling to many of us.

He went back into the studio and brought all that energy and frustration to his music—ultimately releasing *Yeezus*. The album was messy, chaotic, and dark. It mixed classic soul and the sounds of the '60s and '70s Black Power movement with techno and distorted rock sounds. He rapped lyrics like, *I am a God / So hurry up with my damn massage.* He premiered music from *Yeezus* by using guerrilla marketing, working with Black, cutting-edge, streetwear designers and beaming the first music video on a wall right outside of the Manhattan Prada store, like a fuck-you.

Yeezus took the themes of his previous album—excess, celebrity, consumer culture, race, sex, wealth, self-aggrandizement, and the death of the American Dream—and made that shit even darker. It sounded damn-near unhinged. To me, it's his Blackest album to date on multiple levels. Maybe that's why it's the one I still listen to the most.

The vision Kanye painted of himself and of America on both *My Beautiful Dark Twisted Fantasy* and *Yeezus* sat in direct contrast to the Obamas' Black American Dream. Through his music, Kanye was telling a different story of what it means to be Black in America. He told the story of striving, yes, of putting in the work, doing all the things you are supposed to do, being great at what you do—perhaps even being the best at what you do—and still not gaining access into the halls of power. A story about having all the supposed cultural and social power that one could garner and still being told you don't belong in that White House, that you will never truly belong in that White House. That you could never earn that right, no matter how much you fought for it.

Kanye argued it was a lie to think we could get ahead by merely doing better and working harder within systems not built for us. The problem,

Kanye said, was all the government and corporate institutions that maintain carefully groomed racial and class inequities. The realization he was having, we would later learn, was leading him increasingly toward economic libertarianism and a type of social conservatism that was further away from the Democratic Party he had once supported. He no longer needed Nike— Adidas was more than willing to place a higher premium on his products. He didn't need the government, either, and fuck them for trying to take taxes out of his hard-earned money.

To me, it was on these albums that Kanye became that canary in the coal mine. And it's also when he became what I have come to identify as a Black skinhead.

WHAT IS AND WHAT COULD NEVER BE . . .

In 2016, in the aftermath of that hopeful Democratic Convention and the radically different election outcome that would soon follow, I began to think more about disillusionment in Black America. If the Obamas' American Dream was an illusion, then what was the reality, and how were Black people reacting to it?

From the beginning, before I knew what twists and turns this book would take and before I knew I had a full book to write, I knew I wanted to call whatever I was doing the *Black Skinhead* project. It's a direct reference to a song from *Yeezus*. But also, the pairing of Black with skinhead—while seemingly counterintuitive—made sense as a way to describe how Black culture and nationalism have shapeshifted with the loss of community spaces. It made sense as a way to describe a declining faith in our individual or collective ability to move government.

"Skinhead" today is often associated with white nationalism. But the term was originally used in the 1960s to define an emergent post–World War II British multicultural working-class subculture rooted in Black—primarily Jamaican—music. The subculture presented a type of working-class counter to the whimsical, happy-go-lucky and high-end mod version of England (think the TV show *The Avengers*) being culturally exported around the world. Buzz cuts and a preference for Doc Martens reflected the rugged practicalities of youth who were working industrial jobs and manual labor.

Beyond aesthetic and musical taste, skinheads were united by a frustration with the status quo and a sense that the working class was being left behind. This resulted in a movement that, while cultural, was also inherently political. As economic conditions worsened and the rhetoric of scarcity ramped up, ethnonationalism increased, driven by a rising fear of being replaced by a new labor force—the Windrush generation and their children. This is how *skinhead* came to carry the connotations it has today. But at its core, the skinhead movement was about being a disillusioned outsider, and it is this definition of the term that I have found so useful in understanding the current state of Black political identity.

This disillusionment was the sinking feeling I felt watching Michelle Obama's speech at the 2016 Democratic National Convention. As much as I wanted to believe in her assertion of a Black American Dream, I knew that for so many it wasn't a reality. And it was this disillusionment with the status quo that I saw in Kanye West—perhaps the archetypal Black skinhead—over the course of *My Beautiful Dark Twisted Fantasy* and *Yeezus*.

In this book, I tell the story of the Black skinhead, to explore what this shift has meant for Black culture and politics. Through stories and anecdotes, I show how we've arrived at the present moment and what it means for our collective future.

For our purposes, I define Black skinhead in three ways:

Black skinhead (*noun*)
1. A disillusioned political outlier who is underrepresented in mainstream media discourse.
2. A Black voter who is only defined by their voting history and not their expressed ideology.
3. A Black person who rejects their societal value or cultural identity being defined by their willingness to vote for the Democratic Party during presidential elections.

As I see it, Black skinheads live in the cracks and uncertainties of the dominant American national culture. They live in our shifting understanding of what it means to be Black (especially politically). They live outside of the bounds of fetishized Black political identity. Though not yet a fully formed subculture or community, these people are finding their way into various microworlds or alternative political factions in response to a mainstream story of Blackness that they don't feel a part of.

While a Black skinhead mindset manifests itself strikingly in terms of political ideology—and we will spend a lot of time exploring that—at its root, it is about rejecting a status quo that does not serve Black people. This status quo permeates all aspects of society, from music to economic opportunities to sex work to media representation, and so we will spend time exploring these avenues as well.

This book is as much an attempt to understand Black skinheads as it is to answer the crucial questions they raise. When someone tells you everything is fine, but around you, you see evidence it's not, where will the quest to find answers lead you? Moreover, how are Black people being led away—not toward—each other, and what do we lose when we lose each other, when we lose Black spaces and Black community? When we feel lost in the world.

In 2016, months after the Democratic National Convention had projected the comfortable idea that everything was fine and we were all now "with her," Trump's election revealed things were definitely not fine, and that many people did not feel secure within the boundaries of political norms. Four years later (or eighty-four in Trump years), as we waited for the results of the 2020 presidential election battle between Donald Trump and Joe Biden, things were still not fine.

November 7, 2020, was an unseasonably warm Saturday in Baltimore. My husband, David, was enjoying the last traces of summer on our rooftop deck. I had slept in later than normal, drifting somewhere between dreaming and waking. It had been five days since we had done our civic duty and voted for a ticket topped by former vice president Joe Biden and former senator Kamala Harris. I hadn't been particularly happy about it. From the beginning, I hadn't been interested in Joe Biden as a presidential candidate. My vote was definitely an "anti-Trump vote," not a "pro-Biden" one. My gut said the election would be called for Biden, but I couldn't shake the 2016 PTSD.

By then, I had been working on this book for months, and sound bites from all the interviews I had conducted drifted through my mind. I couldn't shake the voices of Black Trump voters and their zealot-like fandom. The physical signs of white anxiety that littered the highway from Chicago back to Baltimore had sent cold shivers down my spine. I wondered if it would bear out that Trump, not Obama, was the manifestation of a "post-racial" president in a multicultural society. I wondered if my mind was playing tricks on me.

As news flooded in from across the country, county after county set new records for voter turnout. Absentee ballots poured in; youth turnout skyrocketed. Despite orders from the head of the United States Postal Service and ongoing budget cuts, the disproportionately Black fleet of postal workers around the country had worked extra shifts, fighting to make sure every ballot cast would be counted. The loser of the 2020 election would still pull more individual votes than President Obama had in 2008.

I lay in bed mulling over these things, half awake and half dreaming. I was feeling paranoid, the four walls closing in despite the mounting evidence Biden would win by a fairly wide margin. Suddenly, somewhere in the distance, I heard the pounding of a djembe, raucous honking, and yelps of relief. My husband popped his head in, having come down from the roof.

"They called it. Georgia."

Georgia. Huh. Who knew? I had been putting all my eggs in the Pennsylvania basket.

"Want to go for a walk?" David asked.

"Sure, let's get outside!"

We masked up and ventured out into the Baltimore sun. It was November, but you would've thought it was the Fourth of July the way people were celebrating. We walked through the park among the large group of people celebrating. It was a multiracial cornucopia of relief, elation, and unapologetic joy. There was BMORE LICKS ice cream on tap for everyone. "Fuck Donald Trump" by YG, featuring Nipsey Hussle, played on cell phones, drifted out of cars passing by, and floated out of the windows of the row houses that populated our neighborhood.

In a lot of ways, it mirrored the euphoria of election night in 2008, when the first Black president had been voted into office. Biden's victory seemed to say we weren't the monsters we thought we were. That democracy had been saved, and all was right with the world. I almost expected a cartoon bluebird to land on my shoulder and start chirping the words to "Fuck Donald Trump." But I couldn't stop the uneasy feeling that, much like 2008, the dream would not live up to the reality. Despite Donald Trump looking like a monster from the worst corporate shark-infested waters, he had still gotten more votes than any of the last nineteen presidents.

So even as I walked through our neighborhood, smiling with my eyes at all of the shiny, happy people and enjoying the sun tanning the upper half of my face, I still felt thoroughly unsatisfied, thoroughly unsettled. Despite the election of my "chosen" candidate, as a voter, I felt more alienated than ever. Those feelings of alienation would only increase as I watched Biden's victory speech later that night.

> I've long talked about the battle for the soul of America. We must restore the soul of America. Our nation is shaped by the constant battle between our better angels and our darkest impulses. It is time for our better angels to prevail.
> —PRESIDENT-ELECT JOSEPH BIDEN, NOVEMBER 7, 2020

I listened as the future forty-sixth president talked about uniting the country in the face of adversity. He spun a beautiful story of America— the America we could be and the America we always were. He talked about bipartisanship, the middle class, and the restoration of America's soul. It was a lovely vision, one that flowed as beautifully as a sermon from a Southern Black preacher.

But it bothered me that what he was saying sounded an awful lot like a more palatable version of Make America Great Again. He was presenting himself as a welcome alternative to Trump, but both men painted a picture of an idyllic time when America made sense. They both offered promises of delivering a political and moral time machine that would take us back there. But going back in time actually sounded like a complete nightmare to me. It made me wonder where that left people like me, people who thought America needed some serious home improvement and not just a return to the past.

As a country, we had won, or so everyone kept on telling me. Black people were the heroes whose votes had saved our country's soul, or so liberals kept on telling me. So why did it feel to me like we had lost? Why did I spend the rest of the night searching online for Black women psychiatrists who specialized in primal scream therapy while listening to *Yeezus* and my Tears for Fears playlist?

And why would a bunch of Trump-loving psychos storm the United States Capitol months later, chanting racist shit while wearing Yeezys? Why would one of their leaders, Nick Fuentes, fan the flames of racial animus, xenophobia, and damn near any phobia you could think of while blasting Kanye songs on his internet show?

I have a lot to say about that stuff, but this is (mostly) not a book about that. This is a book about Black people and our political future.

I hope to show readers that the instinct to dismiss 2016 as a fluke and embrace 2020 as an unmitigated success—particularly when it comes to Black voters—obscures the crisis at hand within the Democratic Party. I hope to show readers just how much the Democratic Party has taken Black voters for granted, and why that fragile alliance is beginning to fracture—and the ramifications this has for us all.

But while this book is about Black political identity and electoral politics, it is equally about Black culture, media, economics, and community building. In each of these spaces, I'll show you where hope ends and disillusionment sets in.

Because politics and culture are so intertwined, we will chart the rise of Black skinheads through both, understanding that to only look at one or the other misses the full picture. Politics is culture, and culture is politics. It is why we started with both the Obamas and Kanye.

One final note is that while this book is an outward look at Black America, it is also deeply personal. And so, as I interrogate the systems around us, I will keep returning to my own experiences, charting the course of my own disillusionment. Embarking on this journey awakened me to certain hidden and forgotten truths about our country and its institutions, challenging me to ask myself, *am I a Black skinhead, too?*

While this book will take us to many places, ultimately, it is a warning about the threats to Black culture and identity, the fracturing of communities on and off-line, and what losing our safe spaces will cost us as individuals, as a community, and as a society.

1

Black People Love Me, and Other Things You Should Not Assume About Black Voters

A Look at the Prevailing Myths About the Black Vote and Black Media

CHARLAMAGNE THA GOD: Listen, you got to come see us when you come to New York, VP Biden.

PRESIDENTIAL NOMINEE VICE PRESIDENT JOE BIDEN: I will.

CHARLAMAGNE: Because it's a long way until November. We got more questions.

BIDEN: You got more questions, but I tell ya, if you have a problem figuring out whether you're for me or Trump, then you ain't Black.

CHARLAMAGNE THA GOD: It don't have nothing to do with Trump. It has to do with the fact I want something for my community. I would love to see—

BIDEN: Take a look at my record, man. I extended the Voting Rights Act twenty-five years. I have a record that is second to none. The NAACP has endorsed me every time I've run. I mean, come on, take a look at the record.

BIDEN'S HANDLER (TO CHARLAMAGNE): All right. Thank you so much. I really appreciate it.

Ever have one of those moments when you feel like you're watching an agonizingly slow car wreck play out in front of you? And you just keep saying "oh no, oh no," while the driver sluggishly spins out of control? If you have, then you have a sense of how I felt watching this clip of former vice-president-turned-presidential-candidate Joe Biden's interview with Charlamagne tha God on *The Breakfast Club* morning show.

And it wasn't just me. In the last week of May 2020, this clip became instantly infamous as Biden's "You ain't Black" gaffe. The cringeworthy joke had been an attempt to deflect from serious questions about engaging younger Black voters who, unlike their grandparents, hadn't yet gone all in for Uncle Joe. And it revealed, with painful clarity, just how deeply Biden assumed support from Black voters was a done deal.

The stakes were high. *The Breakfast Club* is heard by eight million listeners each month. More than half of those listeners are Black, and many of them are in the 18–34 age group, a prime voting demographic. Their YouTube channel has around five million subscribers. But the number of ears and eyes their content reaches is harder to quantify, given the virality of the juicy sound bites they're adept at getting. Over the years, they have become the go-to place for politicians like then-senator Hillary Clinton, then-senator Kamala Harris, and Senator Elizabeth Warren to speak to young Black voters. It hasn't always gone well. In 2019, for example, Senator Bernie Sanders found himself in hot water when, during his interview, he declined to support reparations for descendants of enslaved Africans in America.

Biden's interview had been tense from the word *go*. Charlamagne jumped into a series of questions about Biden's disappearance from the public stage as other political leaders, like state governors, became more vocal about COVID-19. Biden didn't react well. He was defiant and immediately on the defensive, spouting his record with the NAACP and referencing polling data he said showed Black people were universally in favor of him. He used the predictable—and at this point, clichéd—"But I have Black friends" excuse when asked about the 1994 crime bill, which is now widely regarded as having had a devastating impact on the Black community. In lieu of acknowledging the bill's failures, he began to rattle off a list of the Black leaders who'd supported it back then.

Perhaps seeing their jobs flash before their eyes, Biden's handlers tried desperately to cut the interview short. But Biden was off and running, delivering sound bite after sound bite that all seemed to reaffirm how out of touch he was with younger Black voters and their concerns with the Democratic Party.

CHARLAMAGNE THA GOD: I don't know if you saw a couple of weeks ago . . . [Sean "Diddy" Combs] said what I believe a lot of Black voters, including myself, feel, and that's that Democrats take Black voters for granted. Votes are quid pro quo, right? It's not like I don't want to vote. I just want to know what candidates will do for us. . . . Do you feel like Black people are owed that from the Democratic Party?

JOE BIDEN: Absolutely. What would I say? Remember when they said Biden can't win the primaries.

CHARLAMAGNE THA GOD: Yes.

JOE BIDEN: I won overwhelming [*sic*]. I told you when I got to South Carolina, I won every single county. I won a larger share of the Black vote than anybody has, including Barack.

Responding to the question of *what will you do for the Black community?* with *Black people love me even more than Barack* . . . wasn't chill, to put it mildly. Beyond just alienating listeners, the interview raised serious questions about the Democratic Party as a whole. Was the Democratic Party taking Black votes for granted? Was it time to rethink what many considered unwavering loyalty to the party? And did anyone [Black] actually prep him for this interview?

In my mind, more than anything else, the interview revealed a set of assumptions about Black voters—assumptions that are widely held and perpetuated not only in white media but within Black social spaces. Namely, that being a Democrat is part of what it means to be Black. This raises the question: What are the implications when Black cultural identity is tethered to one political party?

Mainstream discourse and media narratives are often produced by a socially ingrained need to distill Blackness and Black people into standardized patterns and data points that can be read, interpreted, and ultimately controlled. Flattening Black political thought into one cohesive narrative is an effective way to do this while also stifling political expression that may pose a threat to institutions and industries that prop up clearly defined partisan politics. As long as Black votes are predictable, they don't really have to be negotiated.

From an electoral standpoint, we're not allowed the same political nuance as others. We have two jobs as Democrats: turn up, and vote for the party. Failure to do those two jobs well enough dooms us to a hell of having to read an onslaught of articles by white people talking to other white "experts," one Black politician from the South or New York City, and *maybe* one Black voter they found at a bus stop or the grocery store about why Black people didn't do their jobs. From a Republican party-line perspective, because Black voters are assumed to be Democrats, it's better to put energy into delegitimizing our votes than trying to convert our votes. Ultimately, it's tied to an inability by partisan institutions and their gatekeepers to really grapple with how racial and economic caste systems have required Black people to organize outside of individual ideologies.

But another major reason for the reductive narratives around Black political thought is more hidden and more insidious: the disappearance of Black-owned-and-controlled media spaces for diverse political discourse and organizing.

The World's Most Dangerous Morning Show

The tagline for *The Breakfast Club* is "The World's Most Dangerous Morning Show," and it's not called that ironically. It's because careers and reputations have been murdered on the show. They know it, and anyone who goes on the show knows it. It's called this for many reasons, but for Biden, the reason was not necessarily because of the character of the hosts or a "gotcha" mentality. For Biden (and Sanders, and other white politicians), it's dangerous precisely because of how the complex constellation of Black political identity interacts with the media—and how often politicians underestimate that.

The Breakfast Club is a syndicated radio show based in New York City and hosted by DJ Envy, Angela Yee, and Charlamagne tha God. It currently airs in over ninety radio markets across the United States and is also televised every morning. Charlamagne got his start as a radio hitman for Wendy Williams, who would go on to host her own television talk show.

They made their name by going after celebrities and took great pleasure in doing it. Charlamagne once made singer, author, and TV personality Kelly Rowland cry. Who does that? Who makes *any* member of Destiny's Child cry anything but tears of joy? To be fair, he has expressed deep regret for that, made amends, and even offered to "suck a fart out of her butthole," which is . . . charming.

In the last decade, Charlamagne has evolved into one of the biggest political interviewers in the game. While his interviews have shifted to become less about gotcha moments and more anchored in a Black political consciousness, he still pulls no punches.

This kind of radio personality is by no means unique, but what sets *The Breakfast Club* apart is its position as a prominent Black-controlled media outlet. In the book *News for All the People*, Joseph Torres and Juan González detail the history and ongoing fight for people of color to own and control emerging communications technology in America. It may be shocking for some people to hear this, but Black radio isn't just good for quiet storm, baby-making jams and suspect car loan commercials. Black-owned and controlled radio stations have long been crucial hubs for Black political organizing.

Dr. Martin Luther King, Jr., for instance, had an office in the same building as historic Black radio station WERD. Every time there was a boycott announcement, or Dr. King wanted to address Black communities, he would use a broom to tap on the ceiling and the DJ would announce breaking news. In the modern internet age, radio DJs with primarily Black audiences have continued this savvy tradition, intermixing politics and pop culture to draw listeners in while also informing them.

Beyond entertainment value, there's another reason (well, many reasons) why Black listeners often prefer receiving information from outlets like *The Breakfast Club*, rather than from places like the *New York Times* (whose readership is only 4 percent Black and two-thirds white): and that's the fundamental concern about whether mainstream media outlets can be trusted to accurately report Black news. They have consistently shown they cannot. Whitewashed newsrooms, blanket reporting on Black issues without layered context, and chronic underreporting of both Black trauma and success have left a major gap that's made even more clear in times of crisis.

This disconnect has historically led to the off- and online development of alternative public spaces that many Black people see as much safer forums to hear about and explore the diversity of Black politics. Black-owned and controlled media outlets, yes, even the ones that play the music your parents hate, have long been core to building consciousness and consensus across Black political ideologies and covering the stories wiped from the pages of dominant local and national media outlets. And those Black newsrooms and media spaces have long been seen as a threat to people in power.

Media 2070, a project started by the organization Free Press, is an ambitious effort to radically transform who has the capital to tell their own stories by the year 2070. They documented story after story of how mainstream media has been weaponized against Black communities and how Black people are consistently blocked from maintaining our own media. For all the bullshit claims about bias in the media against conservatives, the record shows conservatives' fear of Black power is the real story of what's creating media bias.

I was an advisor for Media 2070, and I have to say, even though I knew the game was rigged, I was flat-out stunned by much of what the project leads were able to dig up. For the sake of time, I'll share just one example.

In 1919, when white people were showing their asses and burning Black communities to the ground in at least twenty-five documented occurrences of white rage in cities across the country, guess what the United States Justice Department was doing? Well, let me start by saying what they weren't doing. They weren't investigating the destruction of Black Wall Streets in Tulsa, Oklahoma, Chicago's Bronzeville, or Elaine, Arkansas. Instead, they were investigating the Black press. The Justice Department released a report called *Radicalism and Sedition Among Negroes as Reflected in Their Publications*, and then lobbied to block free speech protections out of fear that Black people were getting too uppity.

The Justice Department was salty because the Black media had the *audacity* to say, *Um, hey, Government, y'all wanna do something about all the lynchings and inequities we gotta deal with? Will something happen to the people burning down our communities, or nah? And, oh, by the way, can you stop calling these massacres "riots" and making them seem like fair fights when they're basically just white people carrying out terrorist attacks on Black communities?* And the government was emphatically like *Nah, we good . . . but since you brought it up, we wish y'all would shut the fuck up and just be happy we're not formally enslaving you like we used to.*

To stop paraphrasing, here's a fun section from the Justice Department's actual report:

> Underlying these more salient viewpoints is the increasingly emphasized feeling of a race consciousness in many of these publications, always antagonistic to the white race, and openly, defiantly assertive of its own equality and even superiority.

In other words, Black people were getting too unified and that was scary for the government that had already walked back a number of promises made as part of the Reconstruction Era post–Civil War. People often say of voter suppression that if someone tries this hard to stop you from voting, that means your vote is powerful. I feel that way even more about media access and ownership. For decades, media consolidation has been the silent war waged on Black communities. When people try that hard to steal your voice, we all ought to be worried.

All of which is to say that spaces like *The Breakfast Club,* in all their pop-cultural and political glory, are vital for Black communities and power— especially since for decades, Black-owned, controlled, and created media has been dying. In a time when corporate juggernauts have devoured smaller, independently owned companies, Black people have been on the losing end, and Black information integrity has suffered.

Y'all, we don't even really have Black Entertainment Television (BET) anymore. One of the few national Black-owned television stations, it was sold to Viacom in 2001, and within the next few years, Black-centric news and public affairs shows on the station were canceled. The quality of content has declined ever since. Honestly, I'm *still* salty they canceled *Teen Summit* and all of their various nightly news programs. They don't even show football games from historically Black colleges anymore.

This slow crumbling has meant that spaces like *The Breakfast Club* are some of the last places where we can be heard in all of our complexity. Imagine if there had been no Ida B. Wells-Barnett to document lynchings in the South, or no *Pittsburgh Courier* calling for policy protections to address the racism veterans on the frontlines faced at work and home.

Or no *Black Enterprise* to report on how Black-owned businesses, despite being the fastest-growing businesses in this country, can't access capital and are further compromised by any move to eliminate the Minority Business Development Agency? Imagine if there were no counterpoint to the dangerous untruths told to us and about us. We're getting closer and closer to that.

It is within this context that social media emerged as an alternative avenue for political discourse, and Black radio shows like *The Breakfast Club* only increased in their already-important role in offering a range of Black political thought and debate.

Fighting to Find Space

In the late 1990s and early 2000s, Black people created their own digital safe spaces and technological innovations not just to fill the void left by traditional media, but also to build community resilience and speak to audiences directly—free from traditional gatekeepers. These blogs, message boards, and email lists offered the freedom to create and amplify important narratives about Black trauma and joy, fact-check inaccurate reporting, and provide authentic places to process conspiratorial framing. Even today, the ones that remain continue to deploy many adaptive content moderation standards and community practices to maintain the space's integrity.

Black technoculture—or the experience of Black social joy and inventive creativity through technology—is the result of decades of hobbyists, engineers, activists, and entrepreneurs throughout the African diaspora operating at the cutting edge of internet and computing technology. Frequently, these actors leveraged and created innovative technologies and communication vehicles in service of civil rights, starting as early as the 1960s and picking up steam in the 1970s and 1980s. Adam Clayton Powell, Jr., A. Philip Randolph, Martin Luther King, Jr., and Bayard Rustin openly discussed the negative implications of "cybernation" and automated technologies. But they also saw technology as both inevitable and a space for opportunity when in Black people's hands.

In the late 1990s, Barry Cooper—then a sportswriter at the *Orlando Sentinel*—knew connected computers would fundamentally change the news business. He also saw Black people were over-indexing in their use of AOL. Bringing these two ideas together, he launched Blackvoices .com, a Black message board and news website that would eventually gain over a million registered users. Shortly thereafter, in the early 2000s, Chris Rabb launched *Afro-Netizen,* one of the first successful internet news blogs. His circulation rate was so high, he became one of just forty blogs credentialed to cover the 2004 Democratic National Convention.

ColorOfChange.org (later Color Of Change), where I spent years as a senior campaign director, would launch in the aftermath of Hurricane Katrina, eventually building to a national circulation of millions. They sought to fill the void left by the decline of Black newspapers and the absence of Black voices at media outlets. By 2008, they would play a more significant role in political organizing and turnout for various elections, something they continue to do to this day.

As Dr. Charlton D. McIlwain notes in the book *Black Software,* Black movements built dense and diverse networks that stretched across affiliated activists, journalists, public officials, and even mass groups of anonymous strangers. This was used to "both hijack and resist media influence." Doing that consisted of producing and distributing at scale compelling, consumable, and usable content to inform, persuade, and organize large audiences. Earlier in the chapter, I talked about Dr. Martin Luther King, Jr., using a broom to knock on the floor at WERD radio. Decades later, Black folks found a digital version of that on the early internet.

Today, Black millennials and Gen Zers spend more time on social networking sites than any other ethnic group of those generations. Additionally, Black people of all ages over-index in membership on several social media platforms and in ownership of gaming devices, and they are also more likely than other ethnic groups to be considered tech trailblazers by their friends and colleagues. This isn't a new phenomenon. Historically, Black people have consistently been early adopters of new media sources such as newspapers, radio, and television.

Black radio and media spaces on- and offline have long allowed for the articulation and processing of divergent Black political thought. We have needed those spaces because predominantly white-owned media are neither able nor willing to platform more diverse Black political thought unless it serves their broader purpose or story.

We've lost a lot of Black media. And because of tech consolidation, we have lost a lot of Black-owned and controlled spaces online as well. What outlets are left, for better and for worse, are those that keep us anchored in a shared purpose and offer a loose outline of a Black political agenda. These are outlets that at least attempt to accommodate the unique constellation of Black political identity with all its points of division and union.

I don't think it's an accident that the ones centered on music and entertainment have had a better chance of survival than the ones only focused on news. If a lot of white people think the radio hosts are just talking about which political figure carries hot sauce in their bag, it enables those hosts to fly under the radar. Also Black music and its related aesthetics has been one of the most commodified elements of our culture.

But what can make these spaces delightfully dangerous—perhaps the real meaning of "The Most Dangerous Show on Earth"—is that they do offer a low-stakes way for Black people to become more politically engaged and activated. I'm not sure if I should be telling you this because next thing I know, those in power might be coming for those shows, too—and these spaces must be protected and expanded at all costs. But it's important for us to talk publicly about it and collectively understand why these sorts of fights for media ownership and tech accountability, which often take place at regulatory agencies like the Federal Communications Commission or the Federal Trade Commission, matter as much as other justice fights like criminal and economic justice. I would even go as far as to say that without *media justice*, there is no chance for criminal or economic justice.

Radio remains the most popular medium among Black listeners. It reaches 93 percent of all Black Americans weekly, and the number of people tuning in over the last decade has increased, especially as radio shows have become adept at adapting to an internet environment. Despite this, of the ten major radio conglomerates that target Black audiences, only two are Black owned, and of the eleven thousand commercial radio stations across the country, fewer than 250 are Black. This means someone else makes the final call on what content gets greenlit, taken off the air, given primetime slots, and many other decisions that impact who we get to hear from in the Black community, and who we don't.

Shows like *The Breakfast Club* feature Black thought leaders and figures who want to talk to Black people from all over the political spectrum—not just Democrats. And in doing so, they provide a space for more robust Black political dialogue. Throughout the years, there have been guests on the show who have been openly critical of the Democratic Party from the Right and the Left. Some, like Angela Stanton-King and Kanye West, have been open Trump supporters. Radio and media shows and personalities like *The Breakfast Club*, #RolandMartinUnfiltered (which, at its current peak, has an estimated 9.2 million views monthly), and Marc Lamont Hill have attempted at varying levels to hold the container for all the political ideologies white people assume don't even exist.

Their power and influence in Black spaces mean anyone who wants Black people to purchase their music, watch their movie, forgive them for a transgression, or vote for them should plan to make a stop through at least one. But one shouldn't expect these visits to be the breezy and laidback interviews you may find on a network television morning show. Even if you think you're politically aligned, one can't expect political allegiance to act as a shortcut to earning listeners' and viewers' support. These shows demand more than that.

They are a venue for political and quasi-political figures to demonstrate to Black audiences they will throw down for Black people, and they will support policies and agendas that uplift Black people. Don't get it twisted; just because your segment may run in between "ass up, face down" songs doesn't mean it's one to take lightly. The interviewers and the listeners can spot the fake from the real, and your card will get pulled.

It's not a place, for example, to blow it on the question of reparations as Bernie Sanders did. If you're going to come on and say you don't support reparations for Black people, you need to have an alternative economic plan you can offer to Black listeners that sounds like reparations. Otherwise, you're probably going to get clowned. To your face, not after you leave.

This is why, historically, these kinds of spaces have proven to be stronger than standard political ideologies like Left, Right, center. Especially as these spaces have dwindled in number, the few that remain—shows like *The Breakfast Club*—have become increasingly powerful and important.

This is why, coming full circle, Joe Biden's *Breakfast Club* interview was so disastrous—and so telling. Assuming that appearing on a Black radio show would inevitably mean a supportive audience for the Democratic candidate, Biden miscalculated what it would take to win over the full spectrum of Black voters. He miscalculated the purpose of a space like *The Breakfast Club,* and he miscalculated the nature of Black voters' collective consciousness.

Over the past few decades, the Democratic Party has benefited from that collective consciousness, but Black identity and culture are by no means tethered to the Democratic Party. And the uneasy alliance between Black voters and the Democratic Party can and will be broken, especially if Black voters become increasingly disillusioned with a party they feel is taking them for granted. Some people would say that this sounds impossible, but it's happened before. If you had told a Black person in 1922 that by the mid-1980s more than 90 percent of Black voters would support only Democratic Party candidates, they wouldn't have believed you. It was unthinkable to imagine so many Black people leaving the party of Lincoln. But there were people who were alive during the Civil War still walking the earth when the Black vote began to make significant shifts to the other side.

Right now, it's hard for me to imagine a scenario in which 90 percent of Black people are voting Republican by 2084. But the thing is, the Republican party doesn't need 90 percent of the Black vote to control everything. If they could climb up into the mid-20s percentage-wise then that alone would have a huge impact . . . which is a possibility that feels very much within reach.

2

Are You Being Served?
Do All Black Voters Think Alike?

In the lead-up to the 2020 presidential election, I was not in a good place. As a Bernie broad, I had *a lot* of questions about whether or not Biden was the best choice for the Democratic Party. In the last several decades, the Republican Party has established itself as the party of grievances, a fear-of-a-Black-planet type of party. Make America Great Again, a tagline that had been successfully deployed both by Donald Trump and Ronald Reagan, had obvious shades of white replacement and was rhetorically tied to the 1920s-era Ku Klux Klan. I wasn't about to place my allegiances there. But I didn't want to be held politically hostage by the Democratic Party either. And I knew many other Black voters felt that way as well.

If Biden's understanding of Black voters as a shoo-in for Democrats was so flawed, then the question is: What is a more full and complex view of Black political identity? In writing this book, I formally sat down with more than forty Black voters and non-voters between the ages of 18 and 108 in my quest for a more accurate picture. I can't even put a number on the informal interviews, but, suffice it to say, it's amazing what you can get your taxi driver, hairstylist, or COVID-19 testing person to talk to you about if you just ask. When all is said and done, I talked to self-identified Black people in about twenty states. When I first started doing interviews and was seeking guidance, someone told me to keep doing interviews until I start to hear the same things. But over the course of my interviews, that moment never happened. Everyone I talked to said very different things, which spoke volumes because, according to suburban legend, all Black people think alike. Clearly, this was not the case.

At the very least, it was immediately apparent that, contrary to Joe Biden's beliefs, there was no way I could lump the majority of Black voters I talked to into being a "capital D" Democrat. I couldn't even organize them into the two-party system. So, what was going on here? How could Black voters be all over the place ideologically, yet still be considered the most cohesive political voting bloc in the United States?

"Capital D" Democrats and Other Myths About Black Voters

Whenever someone tries to tell me Black people are simping for the Democratic Party, I have to question whether they actually know Black people at all. Like, seriously, I wonder if they've had a conversation with a Black person that wasn't about sports, music, or their discovery of cocoa butter, Jamaican castor oil, and/or lotion. Because Black Democratic support is complicated, and it only tells one part of the story of Black political engagement.

In 2001, after years of data collection, Dr. Michael Dawson, a political scientist at the University of Chicago, published *Black Visions,* the most important summation of Black political thought and its nuances to date. In it, he breaks down Black politics into six categories. For our purposes, we're going to examine his theory through a non-academic metaphor. Picture yourself in the Blackest school cafeteria in America. You have your tray, and you're deciding where to sit, which conversation you want to have. Here are your options.

At the center table, you have the racial egalitarians, the reformist-but-all-in Democrats. This is the largest table, the one where the Democratic Party cheerleaders and quarterbacks sit. The president of the Black student body might be posted up there, too. They're the ones who may have a keychain with a photo they took with President Obama at a convention once. They see white ignorance as a leading—but fixable—vehicle for racism, and one of their responses is to appeal broadly to Americans to live up to the country's stated values, ideals, and aspirations so the American Dream can be possible for all of us. They see liberation through complete integration, social safety net programs, and relentless

Black excellence. Their playlist might include Curtis Mayfield's "Move On Up," Sam Cooke's "A Change Is Gonna Come," or "Devastated" by Joey Bada$$.

Slightly off to the left, you've got the emo table of disillusioned liberals. These may be the theater or art kids, the reluctant but consistent democrats (lower case d) with a lot of side-eyes toward capitalism. But they will also be wearing the flyest fits because having a critique of capitalism doesn't have to involve wearing only one outfit for the rest of your life. They talk about investment in Black-owned businesses, infrastructure, and spaces. They are a proponent of luxurious socialism and see liberation through social safety net programs, socialized health care and education, and employment opportunities that can ensure a high standard of living. Their playlist might include "Who We Be" by DMX, "III. Life: The Biggest Troll [Andrew Auernheimer]" by Childish Gambino, or "Shove It" by Santigold featuring Spank Rock.

Off in the corner even farther left, you have the Black Marxists, who are side-eyeing the disillusioned liberals because they are not in any way here for hedging on capitalism. But they also reject the idea that a conversation around class struggle and policy-making can happen without looking at the relationship between race and class. They view any political power built through the economic control of labor, income, and ideas as a primary vehicle for systemic racism. They see liberation through self-determination, land ownership (through community-owned cooperatives), and a united worker-led movement centering colonized communities and people of color globally. They may be those people you see with, like, twenty thousand patches, buttons, and badges (or flair) all over their jean jacket and backpack. Their playlist might include "This Land Is Your Land," preferably the Sharon Jones and the Dap-Kings version, "War" by Bob Marley and the Wailers, or "Whitewashed" by Minority Threat.

Going the other way, to the right of center you've got the Black conservatives, rolling their eyes because they are not in any way here for your bullshit communism, socialism, anarchism, or whatever the hell the Black Marxists and liberals are doing. But also, White Republicans who claim they don't see race (yet call you by the name of the other Black guy at the Future Business Leaders of America meeting who looks nothing like you) are super annoying, amirite? They see, as a leading vehicle for racism, perceptions of Black people as charity cases who receive undeserved benefits. They see liberation through a free-market economy, self-help, and financial independence. Their playlist possibly has "Git Up, Git Out" by Outkast (featuring Goodie Mob), "Power" by Kanye West, "All About the Benjamins" by Puff Daddy, or alternatively "Rasputin" by Boney M.

Then there are the table-hoppers, like Black nationalists. They may be more fluid or at times party ambivalent in terms of what they see as the best ideological vehicle for change, but they're clear that shit is not working, and Black people need independent capital and economic models. They support complete Black autonomy and various forms of cultural, social, economic, and political separation from AmeriKKKa. They don't see economic or political power as a leading vehicle for systemic racism. It's all about race and anti-Blackness. That's it. That's the tweet. On their playlist is probably "American Pharaoh" by Jase Harley or "Fight the Power" by Public Enemy—though if we're being honest, all the Black factions have probably rocked to "Fight the Power." I'll also throw in "DNA." by Kendrick Lamar.

Finally, there are the Black feminists, who may also do some table-hopping, but they may also be outside the cafeteria setting up for the after-lunch student council meeting because the president of the student council is too busy flexing at the racial egalitarian lunch table. They are done waiting for all the movements and movement leaders to recognize how much Black women have been holding it down out here. And not in a Black-women-are-magic-and-saving-people's-asses kind of way, but in a way that recognizes we have to take care of ourselves because no one else seems up for the task. Like, seriously, get y'all's shit together. They are often assumed to be hanging out at the left flank of lunch tables, but at any given table, the Black woman turn up can get real. They may have on the playlist "U.N.I.T.Y." by Queen Latifah, "Lost Ones" by Lauryn Hill, "Juice" by Lizzo, or "Brujas" by Princess Nokia, depending on the vibe.

These different identities have often disagreed throughout history, but there also have been moments when everyone has pushed their

tables together, forming a Black consensus based on four shared agreements:

- Racism exists,
- Racial justice is necessary,
- Self-determination and land ownership are fundamental
  goals, and
- A shared Black agenda is critical to achieving success.

Because everyone is complicated and three-dimensional, Black people
may carry more than one of these ideologies. I would probably place
myself somewhere in the disillusioned liberalism/Black Marxist/Black
feminist realm. It depends on the day and what someone has done to piss
me off. Hopefully, Dr. Dawson will eventually turn this into an online
quiz so I can know for certain. But people within these ideologies have
traditionally understood that at some point, you have to play together to
win together.

Historically, playing together did not mean sitting at the same ideological table. Dr. Leah Wright Rigueur, who studies twentieth-century
African American politics and history, notes Black Americans weren't
always so tied to the Democratic Party. In fact, in 1936, Black voters were
split 44 percent Democrat, 37 percent Republican, and 19 percent Independent. But in the second half of the twentieth century, there was a
growing belief that the Republican Party did not support racial egalitarianism or value Black conservatives. Instead, leaders of the party chose to
eschew the Black vote and stoke racial resentment to court white voters
as part of the Southern Strategy. This led to a migration of Black voters
to the Democratic Party.

Black people's voting behavior is often driven by a desire for efficacy
more than ideological alignment. Through this lens, voting is not intrinsically valuable; it only matters as much as it can be seen as effective for
the greater good. This is why in today's electoral climate, some perceive
voting third party or voting for a candidate deemed unviable as a waste
of time. But even during eras when Black voters were more split between
different political parties, how one used their vote was an extension of

race consciousness, not just indicative of who someone likes the most. In fact, race-conscious voting is so strong among Black voters that many do not consider the individual but the group when making the decision to vote and for whom. Dr. Dawson calls this linked fate. This instinct is so strong that Black communities will vote against what may be seen, to outside observers, as individual self-interest if they feel a different candidate will be better for the Black community as a whole.

One result of this is that social and religious conservatism among Black voters does not always (or even often) correlate with the decision to vote Republican. Black people who don't believe in abortion will often vote for the pro-choice party because, ultimately, they believe Black people as a constituency will be better served by the Democratic Party. Or they believe abortion laws will be weaponized against poor Black people and so the risks outweigh the value. Even class doesn't trump group identification. Because of this sense of linked fate, affluent Black people tend to be more likely than affluent white people to support liberal policies and tax codes that benefit the working class.

Linked fate is also essentially the reason why even Black people who fundamentally don't agree with President Obama's policies or perspectives are still instinctively protective of his legacy and family. The inability to understand the power of linked fate is why non-Black progressives and leftists who sympathize with what they consider "Black issues" express disdain and dismay at Black people who display public empathy toward the Obamas or don't always choose ideology or party over Black identity.

The result of this is that today, the Democratic Party has ended up an imperfect, one-size-fits-all—or perhaps none—home for Black voters. It's why even though Black voters have such diverse political thought, they often vote as a cohesive Democratic bloc, and why there is a unique pressure on the Democratic Party to encompass a wide spectrum of Black thought, including conservatism.

But this doesn't mean there's some magic negro funk dust keeping Black people tethered to the Democratic Party or primed to vote. On the flip side, for example, we also see Black voters sometimes choosing to opt out of elections. Contrary to what the finger waggers say, this is not merely because they are disinterested in the business of politics. Interest in voting drops at a higher level when Black people begin to believe elected officials either cannot or will not serve the community's needs. Hence, reinforcing that voting in and of itself is not the point. For the last several decades, many have chosen to disengage rather than switch their vote to a Republican Party that doesn't even pretend to cater to a Black political agenda. When connected to intentional strategies like targeted disinformation or voter intimidation, this is what Dr. Leah Wright Rigueur and others have called "voter depression." Voter depression is when a significant number of potential voters from a specific community (geographic, racial, cultural, etc.) decline to participate in electoral politics because they have become convinced the outcome of an election will have no impact—for better or for worse—on the material and social conditions of their lives, families, or broader communities. It's the moment when "yes, we can," becomes "we never will."

Black people rolling strong as a voting bloc has only ever been possible due to organizing and proximity, a byproduct of forced segregation. For decades, Black people, regardless of class, have lived in the same neighborhoods, and even when families relocated from urban to suburban areas, they continued to worship at the same religious institutions, shop at the same businesses, and socialize with one another. These everyday engagements and relationships allowed for Black people of different political ideologies to debate, develop, and align on strategies to build Black political power.

In an ideal scenario, we push our tables together and everyone, including the table-hoppers, has a seat. We figure out together how everyone gets what we need to create a happy, harmonious cafeteria. The Black Marxists bring in their organic, farm-to-table food and herbs. The Black conservatives use their business acumen to figure out how to increase the resources to expand the supply to meet the demand. Instead of waiting for Shady Sadie to bring out her bland-ass vegetables, we decide what we want as a collective and use our power and the tools at our respective tables to make sure everyone gets fed nutrient-rich food and the nourishment can be sustained. And then we put on our Black visions ideological mixtape, and we enjoy our lunch. Sometimes we yell across the tables to each other, and sometimes we're just happy to be posted up at our table. But we are clear we're still working toward a shared Black agenda with an integrated menu.

In our modern era of political engagement, increasingly the focus has not been on pushing the lunch tables together and figuring things out but occupying the same center to progressive ideological tables. The failure to account for—and make room for—Black radical or divergent politics to the left and right of center has meant people do not see themselves within the current party framework. And the erosion of Black political organizing and public spheres—ranging from media to religious to business institutions in communities—has left a whole heap of people dissatisfied. A study released in 2019 by Gen Forward, a University of Chicago–based polling initiative, found that 1 in 3 Black voters between the ages of 18 and 36 said that they believed the Democratic Party does not care about them. A survey of more than 30,000 self-identified Black Americans, conducted by Black Futures Lab, found that 1 in 5 respondents viewed the Democratic Party unfavorably, and 52 percent of respondents said that "politicians do not care about Black people or their interests." That's a lot of disgruntled potential voters the Democratic Party has to rely on to keep showing up.

Take me, for example. I can't even tell you the mental gymnastics I have to do to vote for some Democratic candidates. During the primaries, I vote with my heart, but in the general election—once a candidate is chosen—I tend to vote for survival. Not always, but probably about 90 percent of the time these days, the survival candidate has a D by their name. Sometimes I've stared at my ballot and thought, *fuck it, I'm just going to write in Fannie Lou Hamer.* But my conscience won't let me risk the chance that my vote could be the *one* thing standing in the way of the election of an alleged Klansman's son. But, damn, I'm thirsty for something different. At what point is "good enough, I guess," actually not nearly enough?

3

Who Will Survive in America?

A Look at the Reemergence of the Black Political Outliers Moving Away from the Democratic Party to the Left and Right

G od, it must be so hard for you. Stay strong, sweetie."

"What?"

I looked up at the waitress, confused by her sympathetic whisper. She looked down pointedly at the book I had lying facedown on my table: *The Loneliness of the Black Republican* by Dr. Leah Wright Rigueur.

I was in some off-the-beaten-path town in a Boston suburb, in the area to spend a week at Harvard University doing a deep dive on Black political thought. I was cheap and late about booking my hotel and had ended up in this strange place. Starving, I looked at the different restaurants in the area and settled on going to a generically named Mexican spot. Yes, I deserve to be clowned for that; I own it. I posted up at my table for one, diving into my book about the history of Black conservatives. Clearly, my white waitress had now mistaken me for one of those lonely Republicans.

"You know," she continued in a hushed whisper as she filled my water glass. "I totally understand how you feel; there aren't many open Trump supporters around here."

Wait—what?

"You're MAGA ... er ... too?" I lowered my voice to a conspiratorial tone, throwing in the "too" at the end just to see where this was going. She looked around. I did, too. Nothing but white people.

Damn.

I should've gone to IHOP.

"You know, I'm not racist. . . ." *Oh God, people really say that?* "I know some Mexican people, really good, hardworking ones. They came here the right way." I glanced back toward the kitchen, hoping to catch a glimpse of the chef preparing my Mexican meal for the evening.

"But we have to make sure that our country is safe, you know?" she continued on, oblivious to my discomfort.

"Totally, there's [*sic*] some really terrible people out here," I responded, nodding slowly.

"Oh, absolutely, sweetie. We have to protect our communities. You know how it is." I glanced around again. "We have to keep fighting the good fight. Some people don't get it, but you have to do your research on these things."

"For sure."

"See, you seem smart. We just have to make sure that we get out there and vote next November. The DemocRATS are already trying to make sure we can't. We need all the real people out there making sure our voice is heard."

"I have been saying we have to make our voices heard. People need to get enlightened."

"Good for you, girl!" The white waitress nodded proudly. "Did you have your order ready? The street tacos here are amazing."

"For now, can I just get a margarita on the rocks, extra shot of tequila on the side?"

"I got you." She winked at me before walking away.

Damn, I *really* should've gone to IHOP.

As we've established, I'm not a Black Republican. But I know they're out there. There are some in my family. One even went to the January 6 rally before the Capitol Hill insurrection. I know they're more common than many white people think they are.

The question, of course, is why; what does it really mean to be a Black Republican? In fact, what does it mean to be a Black person outside of the Democratic Party—on the Right or Left? What does it mean about these people's political ideologies, and what does it mean about the Black political community as a whole? We saw the inklings of this in the fallout from Biden's comments and the work of Dr. Dawson, but I wanted to understand these splinter groups further and get to know some of these voters across the spectrum.

I decided to start with the Right.

Team MAGA

> **BRANDI:** Ooh! Did you have any Pullman porters in your family?
>
> **LISA:** I did not have any Pullman porters in my family.
>
> **BRANDI:** Do you get asked that a lot?
>
> **LISA:** You know, not as much as you might think.

In 2020, I went searching for Black MAGA people and, thanks to my friend Katara, I found one: Lisa. Lisa grew up on the South Side of Chicago in the storied Pullman community, which I immediately found almost as fascinating as the fact she's a Black MAGA supporter. Here's why:

Pullman is one of the oldest model company towns in the United States and was founded by George Pullman in the 1880s. It has lovely little brick row homes and treelined streets. They were all designed by Solon Spencer Beman, a nineteenth-century architect with a Queen Anne vibe. Everyone who once lived there—in some way, shape, or form—was affiliated with the Pullman railroad company. When you go there today, you get a really clear picture of where the executives once lived and where the working-class employees lived. Pullman workers of all races played a crucial role in labor and working-class struggle in the late nineteenth century and for a significant portion of the twentieth century.

You should look that up later. But this is a book about Black people, so I'm gonna talk about the Black people.

After the Civil War, the Pullman Company became one of the largest employers of Black people in the country. Many were from former slave states in the South and were considered the perfect servants by George himself. About a fourth of them ended up in Chicago with others living in different hubs across the country, like Pittsburgh. Pullman believed the Black male porters and female caretakers would be docile and more invisible to his white passengers, increasing their comfort. He was so committed to their invisibility that porters were called "George" or "boy"—they weren't even allowed the dignity of having their own distinct identities or names.

George misplayed his hand on that one. Pullman workers were a force to be reckoned with, eventually forming the first Black labor union in the United States—the Brotherhood of Sleeping Car Porters. The movement to unionize was co-anchored by noted Black conservative figure and labor organizer Milton P. Webster and noted socialist figure and labor organizer A. Phillip Randolph. Their organizing skills, movement strategy, and bipartisan leadership not only laid the groundwork for the mid-twentieth century civil rights movement, but also created its playbook, with Pullman leaders having a fingerprint in everything from the Montgomery bus boycott to the historic March on Washington for Jobs and Freedom.

But the legacy of the Pullman workers isn't just their labor organizing and economic power, which was crucial to building the Black middle class. They were well-traveled and engaged with white elites, making them conduits for those in power. They collected and shared information, recommendations, and experiences with Black people. They knew where to go, where not to go, and didn't hoard information—instead sharing it for the greater good and benefit of the culture. They helped expand their community's collective consciousness and were able to open more doors for their children to seek higher education or explore other careers and opportunities not previously available to them.

In this way, you could say the Black Pullman workers were the social media and micro-influencers of their day. Maybe with fewer thirst trap photos. But I don't really know because I wasn't there. Regardless, the porters' social impact is undeniable. Supreme Court Justice Thurgood Marshall and former San Francisco mayor Willie Brown were descendants of Pullman porters. Malcolm X and the photojournalist Gordon Parks were porters themselves. That's just to name a few.

Porters, in preparation for their route, would go to newspaper headquarters and pick up as many copies of the *Defender,* the *Pittsburgh Cou-*

rier, and other local Black papers as they could discreetly get in their bags, and toss or pass them out in Black communities along their route. This was a risk for the Pullman workers, as their routes often took them through sundown towns. In places like Oklahoma, the porters were forbidden from coming into town even to eat, and they often relied on the kindness of Black locals. But this also meant they were building power and influence without relying on white resources and institutions.

Which brings us back to my new friend, Lisa. Her family moved into the Pullman community during the 1960s and 1970s and bought a house from a white person. This was during a time of white flight, when people were running to the suburbs, and Black lower- and upper-middle-class families were seizing homeownership opportunities. For Lisa, this was an ideal environment that she remains nostalgic for—a place where neighbors were close to each other and looked out for each other. She particularly appreciated "the ability to see Black success" when she looked around. But in the 1980s and 1990s, the Pullman community had fallen more and more into economic decline and middle-class families had moved out. Many of the houses that had once been impeccably kept were now falling apart.

So when she heard Donald Trump talk about Making America Great Again, it evoked a longing for a specific place and time when Black communities of mixed-class status lived together, worked together, built together, and believed in each other. This is remarkably similar to things I've heard in my own family from the South Side of Chicago.

Lisa owns a staffing agency, and her priority is to see more Black-owned businesses be retained in communities like Pullman. Lisa says as she's grown up, she's seen more and more that businesses invested in the community's wellness and safety have moved out, and the current businesses are just in it to make a quick buck, and then will leave. The Black dollar is not circulated within the neighborhood borders at the same level it once was, nor is it "safe or appealing for people who are successful to stay here." And, in her eyes, the local (Democratic) alderpersons have failed Black communities, reinforcing the need for more limited government.

> So, I'm all for someone being able to give me the resources that
> I need in order to create a better lifestyle for myself. That's what

I need. That resonates with me versus the government having their hands in your personal information and dictating how you can live your life and use your money. What I want from our government is manufacturing jobs, tighter trade agreements. Fix the streets; help people feel safe in their own homes. I want aldermen who do their job and fight to maintain successful, thriving businesses in the community. That, to me, is the role of the government. Tools and opportunities for self-sufficiency. That's what we need.

This, Lisa says, is why she became a Trump supporter after a lifetime of voting for candidates from the Democratic Party. She believes Trump's public stance on trade, manufacturing jobs, and nation-centered economics offers a better pathway for Black people than the 1990s style of accelerated globalization championed by economist Alan Greenspan. The "public stance" is doing a lot of work in that sentence.

Though Lisa voted for President Obama in 2008, she was unhappy with the way he had responded to the 2008 recession. And in 2012, she didn't vote. It was only through Trump's emergence that she found herself energized as a voter.

In Trump, she saw someone she felt was passionate about the country in a way that could help her community. While Lisa did not vote for Trump in 2016, in 2020, in addition to planning to cast a vote for him, she spent her time organizing Black MAGA voters and creating a community space for them to discuss how to take ownership of the Republican Party. Trump does not represent the things to me that he represents to her, but what I hear in her words is that it's as much about building a Black economic base in this country as it is about a disconnect from the Democratic Party. Talking to her certainly challenged my ideas about Trump supporters as extensions of white nationalism.

For Lisa, Black survival means prioritizing saving Black businesses and building independent wealth. It means using Black wealth to sustain communities through trickle-down economics. And, apparently, it means supporting Trump. Her love for her community and for Black people is what sent her to the Republican Party, directly contradicting the public narrative that Black Republicans are isolated from Black communities.

But what about the other side? What does survival mean for a Black voter whose progressivism has pushed them to the left of the Democratic Party?

One result of Black voters' consolidation in the Democratic Party that we discussed in the previous chapter is that conservative Black voters have a choice. They can find a home in the centrist space of the Democratic Party and even have the potential to move back toward Republican politics, as Lisa has. But Black leftists don't have a lot of options within a de facto two-party system. Often, their only recourse is finding a third-party candidate with whom they align or settling for a party that shows open resentment toward its most-left politicians and voters.

As I was writing this book, I really wanted to see what signs of Black radical organizing were happening on the Left. I met someone who, like Lisa, is passionate about Black people, Black community, and our future. But while Lisa's passion has led her toward Trump, my left-wing Black skinhead's passion led her to organize a third-party write-in campaign in the 2020 election cycle, unable to support either of the major-party candidates. Oftentimes, we're told voting third party or for a write-in is as good as throwing your vote away. But I spoke to someone who disagrees with that.

Team Wild Card

> **BRANDI:** OK. My dad's family is from Minter City, which is in Leflore County. I've been through Clarksdale, which I think is kind of around—
>
> **QUERRIDA:** (*laughs*) That is funny to hear you say, MENTER City.
>
> **BRANDI:** Because I don't know how to pronounce it! (*laughs*) My grandma left, moved to Syracuse, and never went back. How is it pronounced?
>
> **QUERRIDA:** They don't say that. It's not that proper. It's Minner City.
>
> **BRANDI:** Minner City?
>
> **QUERRIDA:** Yeah. You gotta read it together, like one word.
>
> **BRANDI:** OK. That's good. I have to know this because I don't want to mess it up and sound like a carpetbagger.

In 2020, I went searching for Black, progressive, third-party candidate voters, and thanks again to my friend Katara (who introduced me to

Lisa; she's got a diverse group of friends), I found one: Querrida. She has a welcoming laugh and a twinkle in her eye but a sharp, no-bullshit presence about her. She grew up partly in Greenwood, Mississippi, in Leflore County, the same county as my dad's family. Minter City, to be exact. That was almost as fascinating as the fact she's a third-party voter. And like with Lisa, Querrida's connection to the place explains a lot about her politics.

In Leflore County in the late 1880s, the (white) Southern Farmers' Alliance, a populist movement organizing for labor and land rights, was one of the region's major agricultural organizations. Because Black people had been barred from membership, Black farmers organized the Colored Farmers National Alliance and Cooperative Union. White populist farmers and law enforcement in the area didn't like that uppity shit. In September 1889, major American newspapers claimed hundreds of Black people were fighting against white people in Minter City, and there was a potential race war brewing. Lawmakers and officials in the area rushed to say some troublesome Black people had to be arrested.

If you're side-eyeing that story right now, you definitely should be. Contemporary Black newspapers describe the incident as less of a race riot and more of an all-out massacre. When all was said and done, as many as one hundred Black people had been killed or disappeared. On the ground, stories emerged of home invasions and Black people ruthlessly shot down like dogs. One person told a story of watching a white man hold a Black couple at gunpoint and forcing them to watch as his sixteen-year-old brother beat the brains out of their baby daughter.

Several sources reported the terrorists targeted well-known leaders of the Colored Farmers' Alliance. Ultimately, everything was covered up, and the actual number and names of the people killed remain unknown. Needless to say, the message was heard loud and clear, and the Alliance was no more.

In the years that followed, Leflore fell into decline. Automation and mechanization of the agriculture industry, as well as the later relocation of plants overseas, reduced the job market in the area significantly. Also, as you can imagine, the racist massacre wasn't really an enticing reason for Black people to stick around. Ultimately, these shifts—combined with the absence of educational and vocational development opportunities—triggered an exodus of Black workers not only out of Leflore County, but out of Mississippi for good. To this day, Leflore County has the unfortunate distinction of having one of the highest levels of child poverty of any county in the United States. As an aside, a study by Citigroup (I know) found anti-Black discrimination cost the United States $16 trillion between 2010 and 2020. Cleopatra could still be alive, having spent a million dollars a day, and wouldn't even come close to spending a trillion dollars. I wonder how much racism has cost Mississippi.

This is more or less the community Querrida grew up in, going back and forth between Greenwood, Mississippi, and Detroit, Michigan. In both places, her family had been deeply involved in politics. Querrida told me that every Memorial Day weekend there's a homecoming celebration called "I'm so Greenwood." It's a time of celebration, joy, and remembrance of those forgotten in Leflore. But over the years, there had been something of an exodus out of Greenwood, and there is a reluctance to discuss the past. When I asked her why, she said:

> It's not a place for Black people, even though they could take over and run it. But the memories are not good for the older people. I had to leave Greenwood to find out about Greenwood . . . if that makes sense. You have to remember the guy that killed Medgar Evers ran away to Greenwood (Mississippi), and they didn't arrest him. You have all these people living side by side, the descendants of the murderers and the descendants of the murdered. And no one talks about it.

But then there's the other side of this. When I asked Querrida if her family had been deterred from engaging in radical Left politics, she said on the contrary—it made them organize louder. Her aunt, in fact, was a well-respected civil rights leader in the community.

There's a long history of this kind of Black outsider leftist organizing in the United States, which Dr. Dawson explores in *Blacks in and out of the Left*. Throughout its history, the Socialist Party in the United States has included the presence of Black radical leadership stretching back into at least the early part of the twentieth century. But the party's persistent unwillingness to combat racism within its ranks and within society has made it an unsustainable political home for many Black leftists.

The construction of race in the United States throughout the seventeenth and eighteenth centuries was clinically used to stamp out a growing number of multiethnic worker-led rebellions. Those in power intentionally created an economic caste system based on characteristics that presumably could be detected by the eye. It became a way to distinguish a worker class that could eventually work its way to liberation and social acceptance from those who had been enslaved for generations and were never meant to be free. So, for many Black people who inherited that story of multigenerational enslavement, race cannot be severed from class.

This clashes with the popular myths that race-neutral, class-based organizing can work, and that addressing class will automatically solve racism. Time and time again, building a successful and sustainable multiracial class struggle has proven easier said than done. Continued tensions have played a role in shaping not only white and Black views about race and racism today, but also how Black leftist radicalism has been defined in American politics.

In my ancestral homeland of Mississippi, the soil is soaked in the blood of Black working-class struggle. But there is also a beautiful and irrepressible line from the Colored Farmers' Alliance to civil rights icon Fannie Lou Hamer and the Mississippi Freedom Democratic Party to unapologetically radical Jackson mayors Chokwe Lumumba and Chokwe Antar Lumumba. It's built in the will of people like Querrida to organize out loud no matter how many people say they can't win, or that Black organizers should shut up and just toe the line. Making Black struggles and fights visible has proven throughout history to be the only effective strategy to bending the arc toward liberation. The only way to counter white nationalist guerilla warfare—which has often gained traction by operating in secrecy—is by forcing decision-makers to not only bear witness to anti-Black violence but also explain why they haven't done anything to stop it.

Talking with Querrida also made me think about my friends Malcolm and Chelsea. Malcolm grew up on a farm outside of Oxford, Mississippi. He was raised in the All-African People's Revolutionary Party, a Black socialist party with a Pan-African bent. The leader of the party when Malcolm was growing up was Kwame Ture (Stokely Carmichael), who stayed with Malcolm's family when he came to speak at their conference. For Malcolm, his party affiliation was not a stand-in for Democrats or Republicans. Voting in national elections had not always been his priority—it came second to doing the community work. But that did not mean being disconnected from the process of building political power.

Kwame Ture is a Black Power icon who worked tirelessly in places like Mississippi, calling for radical self-determination and political, economic, and cultural power for Black people. Malcolm said that growing up, his community always talked about the system as a whole:

> The system is going to be a system pretty much, regardless of the puppets that they have out there. My mindset has always been changing the way we as a people think about who we are, not necessarily backing people for crumbs off of the table.

Politics, Malcolm said, artificially divides people along party lines. To him, it's the United States of America that's the problem. Two-party politics, like law enforcement and standardized education, are all extensions of a system in place that functions to hold down Black people. They are all geared toward stifling the imagination and controlling public knowledge, limiting what's possible for Black people as a whole.

Within the Black community, there have always been disagreements about the best way to get liberated. There are always some people who say, *Work the shit out through reforming the system,* and some people who say, *Nah, burn this shit down,* and some people who are going to be, like, *Forget all this shit; why can't we all just get along?* The people who practice the first strategy tend to be chosen as public spokespeople and the second group gives rise to populist Black leaders who are chosen by the people when the "right way," stalls out.

Chelsea and Malcolm have a son named Stokely Baldwin (after James, of course). I asked Chelsea what she thought about President Bill Clinton, who at the time of the interview had recently come under fire for disparaging her son's namesake Stokely Carmichael (Kwame Ture's government name) at the memorial services for the late congressman and civil rights icon John Lewis. Somehow, Clinton thought paying homage to Congressman Lewis required him to positively compare Lewis's leadership to Carmichael, who—in Clinton's estimation—was dangerously close to taking the Black civil rights movement "too far" in the 1960s, whatever that means. As you can imagine, Chelsea wasn't impressed:

> I was stunned that he even thought that that was an appropriate thing to say, considering that Stokely Carmichael has provided so much, so many roots and so much knowledge for the Black community. He's given a really good backbone to the Black Power movement. OK, you can say that he was radical. Yes. But in order to get action, sometimes you gotta be radical.

This was something Congressman John Lewis also understood, making Clinton's comments that much more flabbergasting. This seemed to be what Querrida was also saying—the idea we could reform the Democratic Party and do things "the nice way" had gone out the door. It was time to get more radical in our thinking as Black voters. And if being radical from the outside helped move the Democratic Party in the right (or Left, as it were) direction, then maybe we could make even more necessary changes at scale.

Returning to Querrida, at the time of our interview, she and her family lived in a DC suburb. She is a former revenue agent for the IRS and gets really riled up about taxes. "People said they were upset that Donald Trump only paid $750 in taxes. I was shocked he paid that much; he needs a new lawyer. I bet you Jeff Bezos (Amazon founder and billionaire) didn't pay $750. People at that level pay nothing." (According to published reports in 2007 and again in 2011, Jeff Bezos paid nothing in federal income taxes).

One of Querrida's biggest goals is a rewrite of the tax codes, which are currently unfairly levied on the middle class and specifically, she informs me, Black people.

> You know what demographic pays the most money in taxes? Black people, especially women that [sic] have gone to school and gotten a graduate degree. Black women are the most educated

demographic in the country. A lot of Black women have middle management jobs and no kids. That puts them in a higher tax bracket right there. And then a lot of Black people are afraid to take the deductions they're owed because they don't want to deal with the IRS calling them or trying to put them in jail. See! That's the kind of stuff I'm talking about right there.

She says that people shouldn't blame Trump or billionaires for taking advantage of failed policies. In her mind, it was the Democratic Party that let down Black and working-class voters because when they had both the House and the Senate, they did not move to massively overhaul the tax codes. "How can I be mad at Trump?" she asks. "How can I be upset at the scammers and not be upset at the people who made the scam possible?"

When I met up with her, Querrida was organizing a write-in vote for former Bernie Sanders surrogate Nina Turner (who's Black, FYI) among like-minded Black leftists. In the presidential primary, Querrida voted for Bernie Sanders because he shared her agenda. But in the open presidential election, Querrida saw an opportunity to push not just someone who supported the same platform as she did, but also who she believed would best support and excite Black people as left-wing voters. She aligns with Turner's stance on Medicare for All, unions, and infrastructure. The major reason she couldn't bring herself to vote for Biden in the primary was his lack of support for Medicare for All as well as his continued defense of the crime bill and other policies that have negatively impacted Black families. "We should be out here demanding something and someone better," she proclaimed, her frustration evident.

Similar to Lisa, Querrida disagrees with the old adage that we should vote—or vote a certain way—because of what people in the past have done for access to the ballot box. Not when so little has changed over the last fifty years. She refused to go out with her aunt and uncle to march during Black Lives Matter protests in 2020, saying, "We shouldn't have to be marching. It should be changed by now." She continued:

They didn't march and die in the streets for us to have a racist person in office, for us to vote for people who want to deprive our children of a good, debt-free education, debt-free health care, stable jobs. Our people didn't die for us to vote for people who go to DC and pass laws to put us in prison.

For me, the fight for power for Black and working-class people at scale feels further away than it should at this point. Like Querrida, I feel disillusioned by the prospect of spending the rest of my life marching for basic rights to humanity.

In the days after BLM II over the summer of 2020, members of the Democratic Party wore kente cloth hats in solidarity with Black people. It looked beautiful—clearly, they had high-end kente cloth. Then, the national Democratic Party quickly silenced calls for legislation addressing police violence. President Biden rushed to say he would increase funding to police departments for sensitivity trainings without adding any stipulations attached to militarized equipment, or auditing unarmed killings, or really anything that has been proven to actually address the problem of police killings in Black communities.

Solutions like rerouting funding from police departments to other services, such as mental health and anti-homelessness programs, would provide substantive support not just for Black people, but all people— reforms people across the political spectrum agree are needed. But those options were immediately pulled from the table, and we were left with just the token feeling of seeing Nancy Pelosi and Chuck Schumer wear kente cloth for my community's benefit.

We have symbolic gestures of solidarity with Black struggle. We have Black representation in several places. But it's not enough. My old boss, Color Of Change president Rashad Robinson, puts it this way:

> Black people are deeply present in so many aspects of society. From food to fashion to music to culture, we drive so many things. America can love Black culture and hate Black people at the same time. And those things don't actually have to be in conflict; they can actually work quite well together. Though I say don't mistake presence for power, the presence in and of itself is not bad. Visibility is not bad. It's when we think it's enough, and we think that a Black president means that Black people have achieved equity, that the danger emerges.

Black people are visibly present at all levels of power in America. Although there should be more of us, we're there. But representation without material gain is not enough. Can never be enough.

No Church in the Wild

When I first opened up the chapter, we were in Massachusetts at a shitty Mexican restaurant outside of Cambridge. I didn't fully explain why I was there in the first place. It was 2019, and I had somehow talked my way into Harvard. I was there on sabbatical from Color Of Change, completely indulging in my nerdiness on the picturesque Harvard campus where I was studying the degradation of the online information ecosystem and its impact on Black communities. Specifically, I was looking at how disinformation funneled by Russia in 2015 and 2016 impacted Black voters in the US during the 2016 presidential election.

But the more I looked at how internet communities operated online, the more it became clear to me that buzzwords like *disinformation* and *misinformation* were only part of the story of what was happening online. Because of algorithmic segregation, people were being put into ideological echo chambers that offered limited ways to work across the internet aisle. Across the spectrum, this had left people more politically polarized than ever.

Much has been made about how the 2016 US elections, and living in Trump's America, have divided families. A 2016 survey conducted by ABC News found 37 percent of Americans reported experiencing increased tensions with relatives and friends because of the campaign. A long trail of tweets and social media posts recount family fights at the dinner table, at birthday parties, and at holiday celebrations.

Many of those stories are told through the lens of non-Black families, yet now I had talked to Black MAGA supporters who had issues with the Clinton-era neoliberal trade policies that had hit Black communities hard. I had talked to leftists who expressed disappointment with a Democratic Party that, to them, seemed complicit in Black economic disempowerment. These were people who, despite their commonalities, couldn't find space to organize around an economic agenda like the ideologically diverse Pullman workers of the past.

I knew what we were seeing online was a clear projection of broader political dynamics in the real world, and the deeper we all retreated into our online communities, the harder it would be to work through divisions in the Black community. The picture that was emerging was this: a once more-or-less unified Black nation and culture, connected through linked fate, was now becoming a fractured network of Black skinheads, reconfiguring into online micronations that are primed to be at odds. Even as, in our own minds, we were still fighting for each other.

The primary driver of this was a growing sense that a Black political agenda anchored in racial and economic justice had been pushed farther away, that we have too often settled for symbolic wins while the realities of closing the racial wealth gap and seeing other signs of Black political and economic empowerment have become more and more a losing battle—something that I, too, feel.

Talking with Lisa and Querrida, despite all their obvious differences, I was struck by their similarities. They're around the same age, both Gen X. They're both passionate about Black people and our well-being. They both believe deeply that Black economic autonomy should be a goal and feel the Democratic Party has failed them. They are two sides of the same coin of Black skinhead identity—disillusioned outsiders, moving away from the establishment.

After I concluded my interviews with Lisa and Querrida, I found myself wondering what they would say to each other if they were in a room together. I found them both to be strong, smart women who cared about their Black communities. Could they find common ground with each other? I'd like to think that they could, but in this increasingly fractured nation, I'm not certain.

Interlude: Feminism for Black Girls Who Have Stopped Caring About What You Think
Rediscovering Black Feminist Politics in the Modern Era

My senior year of college (#AgnesScottCollege, #Black RingMafia), I went to support one of my roommates in the school's production of Ntozake Shange's *For Colored Girls Who Have Considered Suicide/When the Rainbow Is Enuf.* It was a beautiful production. The seminal choreopoem, written in the 1970s, is a collection of flowing, poetic monologues woven together into a tapestry of experience of what it means to be a Black woman in a society that compulsively undervalues her. It's about loneliness, isolation, and the desire to be loved at any cost, even if the price is your heart and spirit. As if to underscore that point, each woman performing a monologue remains nameless, only identified by the color of the dress she wears and the city she is from. In my memory, my roommate played the orange lady from St. Louis, but this was a really long time ago.

At the end of the play, the women come together, their sorrow and tears fading as they find joy and love in each other and themselves. As it turns out, *we're* the ones we've been waiting for this whole time. We're enough. The women in their brightly colored dresses join together as a cohesive rainbow, chanting the words over and over again:

> *i found god in myself*
> *& i loved her/ i loved her fiercely*

It was incredible to watch, and it's still one of my favorite plays to revisit. The journey to get to the point where you can genuinely say that you are enough can feel like a never-ending road. The ability to embrace ourselves as Black women and say we are enough is priceless.

In *For Colored Girls,* every character has been mistreated in some way by the people in their lives and society at large. Today, we would say that they were navigating misogynoir, which has shaped both a certain construction of sex and sexuality in our society and ideas about how Black women are expected to move through the world. But back then I didn't have language like that to grapple with. The themes that surface in the play swirl around all the ways that Black women can be seen as both *too something* for others and *not enough something* for ourselves. We're both too masculine and too voluptuous. We're too uppity *and* too hood. We're expected to project soothing maternal energy even as we're not valued as mothers, and we're dismissed as angry when we speak up about others' transgressions. But, ultimately, for the women in the play, their autonomy and humanity are reasserted through finding one another, themselves, and finding God underneath the scars and trauma. It is a harsh but realistic look at what it means to be a woman, and, specifically, a Black woman in our society.

Today, Black women are more likely to experience sexual, psychological, and physical violence in their lifetime than women in most other ethnic groups. We are more likely to be disbelieved when trying to seek help and more likely to be arrested after calling the police to report violence from an intimate partner. The Georgetown Law Center reported that adults view Black girls as less innocent and more adultlike than their white peers. By the age of five, Black girls are perceived as needing less nurturing and protection and are perceived as more sexual.

This is the treacherous terrain Black girls must navigate in a world that does not care for them as it should. We deserve to love freely and be loved, to be protected from abuse, and to be taken seriously when we ask for help. We deserve recognition of the full scope of our humanity. The intersecting strikes of being Black, women, and majority working class can automatically render our truth inconsequential, our stories invisible, and our minds and bodies at risk.

There's much to be said about this. There's even more that needs to be done about this. There are so many systems that must be disrupted and challenged. Black women and girls are treated as second-class citizens when it comes to health care, employment, and treatment within legal systems, just to name a few. The fights can't be tangential to broader justice fights—we have to bring the unique challenges Black women and girls face sharply into focus.

When I think about what drew me to my form of Black feminist politique, it was the desire to see and talk about Black feminism as a matter of economic and sexual liberation and personal freedom. For all my love of *For Colored Girls,* I was drawn to a feminism that felt lighter and joyous, and not like a form of traumatic bonding.

After seeing *For Colored Girls,* I remember sitting on a swing on the porch outside my dorm room, smoking cloves and drinking Strawberry Boone's Farm wine out of a water bottle. On my burned CD, Meshell Ndegeocello switched seamlessly to OutKast. Le Tigre transitioned to Trina. My friends and I were talking about all the pretentious things one talks about when they're at a women's college during the height of third-wave feminism.

We discussed what it meant to be a hip-hop feminist, a term that had recently been coined by Joan Morgan. Morgan's work had been the first reading assigned in my feminist studies class that I actually felt. It was the first book I remember to identify the tension that existed for me as a middle-class Black girl who had a disdain for Black middle-class politique. I resented respectability politics, the idea that as Black people, our worthiness depends on behaving and existing in a way that satisfies the white gaze. I hated the respectability politics that came with proving that being Black and being American and being Human and being a Woman weren't nearly as disconnected as others seemed to think they were.

And I also resented the idea that I had to check a long list of criteria that qualified me to identify as a feminist. I didn't want to confine myself to a life of going to parties that only played "conscious rap." Some of it kinda sucks, to be honest. I didn't want to smell like sage either. No disrespect to those who do. At the time, feeling the pressure to adhere to a certain feminism or Blackness, we were unsure whether we could even call ourselves feminists. We sat outside the dorm, grappling with where we could find our own space.

"I don't know . . . do you consider yourself a feminist?"

"I mean, probably not, because I just got into a fight with homegirl in sociology class about 2Pac and C. Delores Tucker. He probably didn't have to call her a motherfucker, but I still feel like she *is* a hater."

"I mean, she's kinda right about the corporations and their control over rap music though . . ."

"Yeah, but 'How Do You Want It' is still my shit."

"True. Put that on."

Second-wave feminism had left a bad taste in many Black women's mouths. Women like my mom, who felt fights around the right to work, or the right to birth control, or the right to burn your bra, or whatever, were not the fights Black women were up against. Black women were already out in the workforce. We were already hypersexualized and hypermasculinized at the same time. For them, the challenge of being Black in America obviously came before the challenge of being a woman in America.

And to the extent that we looked to the previous generation for inspiration, it was to second-wave rebels like bell hooks, Grace Lee Boggs, Dolores Huerta, or The Combahee River Collective, which included one of my (still) favorite writers and scholars, Audre Lorde. It was the Collective who introduced the first use of "identity politics" and talked about Black feminism as something distinct from other liberatory movements, including mainstream feminism.

> Above all else, our politics initially sprang from the shared belief that Black women are inherently valuable, that our liberation is a necessity not as an adjunct to somebody else's but because of our need as human persons for autonomy . . . We realize that the only people who care enough about us to work consistently for our liberation are us. Our politics evolve from a healthy love for ourselves, our sisters and our community which allows us to continue our struggle and work.
>
> —*How We Get Free: Black Feminism and the Combahee River Collective*

Black women are the backbone of political thought, feminist wins, and labor organizing in this country. Full stop. This is often only acknowledged when Black women "march to the polls," to bail out the country or operate as public surrogates for party politics. But the work and labor done between election cycles are often taken for granted. My friend Chelsea says this in a way I appreciate:

> I feel like in this country, it is the responsibility of Black women to do the labor. Black women have no other choice but to do the labor. And that shows in our vote every time. That shows in our work, every time. But it never shows up in our paycheck. It never shows up in the result. And I think that is the ongoing evolution of how Black women are viewed in our society. From the beginning, in this country, Black women were expected to do the labor. We were also expected to give birth, then breastfeed our children, and then someone else's children, and continue to do everything else. And I just think that is literally where we are in this country, always and forever.

People want to "support" Black women, "listen" to Black women, and deify Black women. But only the right type of Black woman, and only when it's convenient for people to do so. They value only the Black women who are seen doing labor for party and ideological politics, and that's true in both the Democratic and Republican parties. That's true in the nonprofit industrial complex and in the broader political ecosystem. And it's also true when we're talking about myriad justice issues and fights.

People only want to listen to Black women when we are saying things they want us to say. This is what I mean when I talk about respectability politics. But when Black women go rogue, that "listen to Black women" shit goes out the door in a hurry. In the blink of an eye, Black women can be knocked off that pedestal as quickly as we were put on it. Take Congressperson Maxine Waters, who has served in Congress for decades, frequently working across the aisle to get legislation passed. She is quite respected on the Hill for her efficacy and savvy, which is not enabled by adherence to decorum.

Despite this, she has been shut down by members of her own party for "stepping out of bounds," she has offensively been referred to by Trump as having a low IQ (she most certainly doesn't). She has been a target of members of the media and other public discourse spaces to show her as anything but civilized. Terms like "wild" and "unhinged" are routinely thrown around. No matter how long she's been working in Congress to get things done, ultimately her civility is not seen. Instead, she's painted as a savage, or whatever term for savage people is being more comfortably used in public these days.

The true fuckery of respectability politics is there's no way to win. By pinning our worth not on our intrinsic value but on our ability to perform a set of white expectations, respectability politics makes it so Black women are never truly valued anywhere—not as sex workers, flight attendants, congresspeople, or as human beings walking this earth just like everyone else. And the social capital we've accrued through attempts to be "respectable" can be taken away in an instant.

So, for us riding the third wave of feminism, it was like, *If the game is rigged, then fuck it, let's enjoy being fucking savage.*

In that way, though we gave a head nod to these sister influencers, we also embraced the ruthless posturing of the hip-hop era. Newly emerging feminist icons in hip-hop broke all sorts of molds. Queen Latifah stood with a regal presence—calling for U.N.I.T.Y. even when a rude person had to get punched dead in his eye. Lady of Rage rocked rough and tough with her Afro puffs, meeting the lyrical relentlessness of her colleagues at Death Row Records, while Da Brat's rapid-fire cadence remained unmatched by her colleagues at So So Def. TLC channeled a tomboy aesthetic while literally wearing condoms as not just a fashion, but also a political statement. Lil' Kim and Foxy Brown muddied the waters of what it meant to be sexually liberated even while projecting an image that seemingly catered to the male gaze. Then Missy Elliott blew everyone out of the water and completely changed what a pop-cultural icon could be, introducing Afrofuturism through a hip-hop lens. In some ways, you could say many of these women leveraged proximity to masculinity via their record labels and hip-hop cliques in order to achieve success. In some ways, their success at the time was not as transgressive or iconoclastic as we've come to expect in today's world. But their presence and power created a new range of possibilities that didn't feel as possible before. We found inspiration and qualities that were—and continue to be—worth deifying in all of them.

We weren't just trying to find the god in us; we wanted you to see us. All of us. Not just a nameless woman in a vibrant dress. In the Y2K era, we still felt we were left in the void between the respectability politics of being Black and the respectability politics of being feminist.

The third wave was about the right to own your own image. We needed to be able to exist and live out loud in whatever way we damn well pleased. That could mean aesthetically. That could mean sexually. That could mean subculturally. That could mean your whole identity and rejecting the way the outside world wanted to label you. No purity tests.

"What about you? You a feminist?"

"I don't know, after what I did freshman year at FreakNik, I may not be allowed."

"I doubt anyone kept photos of that."

"Well, they should have, cuz I looked good . . ."

All of us, in one way or another, were looking to break the bonds of normalcy, and that included destroying the idea that feminism was a specific fight or struggle, or there was one way to be a feminist.

I came out as a feminist to my family around 2002-ish. It was a minor spectacle. My oldest sister kept telling everyone I was a feminist, but the whispered emphasis she put on the word made it seem like she was saying devil worshipper. My other, openly sexually fluid sister was like, "Huh . . . why?" I don't think my dad had any inkling of what that could mean so he just shrugged his shoulders and kept it moving. My mom was fine, but she did wince a bit.

The reaction was odd to me, as it seemed obvious that everyone in my family was a feminist. How could they not be? I came from a family of strong, take-no-shit, do-for-yourself-and-love-your-community Black women. My dad always encouraged me and my sisters to be our own people and always be inquisitive. He wanted us to be smart, capable women conquering the world. How could that not be feminist?

What I realized later was that calling myself feminist implied to my family that I was dropping the "Black" in my personal identifier. For my mom in particular, her experiences in the second-wave feminism movement of the '60s and '70s were that white women were quick to call on Black women to support whatever they were fighting for at the moment, but as soon as they got their win—be it increases in wages or more opportunities to be in executive positions—Black women were left behind. "We were never seen as equal partners," she added, "even when we were right there marching with flags, taking the risks, and even taking the hits. They wanted us for numbers, not because it was important to see *all* women win."

But to me, it meant really taking on the fights Black women are up against across all spaces. It meant taking my mother's activism to the next level. It wasn't just about approaching broader justice fights with a Black feminist lens, it was about taking up fights that were for, about, and centered Black women. Our labor is primarily valued when it benefits others; our joy and pleasure are only valued when they're comfortable for the white gaze. And for us, we had gotten to the point where we were saying fuck that game and were trying to figure out (to varying degrees of success) how to play our own.

As a broader Black culture, that is what has served us historically—the ability to cultivate our own systems, processes, community engagement, and sustainability efforts that operate outside of the ones that, from the day they were built, have been formed to work against us. In the Y2K era, we embraced being unapologetically iconoclastic. It wasn't about breaking glass ceilings; it was about tearing down the room and using the pieces to reconstruct a home of our own. It was about forcing everyone else to bear witness to that reconstructed life—something that felt both intensely personal and oddly performative at the same time. And with the newest technology at our fingertips, it became easier than ever to move those iconoclastic ideas from the margins to the center.

4

Obama for America
Learning from How Obama Won America

Election night in November 2008 in Chicago was the happiest I had seen Black people as a collective. People were dancing in the streets, and Stevie Wonder and Curtis Mayfield played from boomboxes on the sidewalk. Even my normally moody bus driver was upbeat. In Hyde Park, the South Side neighborhood where I lived at the time, stores had signs in the windows that read, "Obama ate/shopped/got his hair cut here."

And this was before we had even seen the election results. People were just that happy to have cast a vote for what could be our first known Black president. You should have seen how happy Black people were when we found out we had *actually* won. In the moment, it did feel like WE had won.

When I started writing this book, I found myself thinking about that day a lot. I reminisced about it with my best friend, Jay. Though we weren't together that night, we both remember how electrifying it had been in Chicago. To be a Chicagoan. To be a Black Chicagoan. It was an unforgettable night, watching the Obama family in Grant Park. It had been a long time coming, but change had finally come. That was what it had looked like. That was what it had felt like.

> JAY: And it was something I've never, ever experienced before. Ever, ever, ever. I'm not sure that I will ever experience that type of joy. You could see it in people's expressions and in their eyes. It felt like a

whole bunch of dead people, soulless people had come to life. It felt like before, people were zombies and now, (*exhaled breath*) it was like someone put life into them. We could be free, we could be us. We were whole now. It didn't last, but that's what it felt like that night.

When thinking back on that November night and everything that came after it, what stands out to me is President Obama's symbolic legacy of flipping every single thing about this country over on its back. Not because of his nebulous message about hope, which ultimately meant too many things to too many people to be sustainable, but by being perceived as part of an unapologetically Black family that was "for the culture." It was like having the Huxtables in the White House . . . minus Bill Cosby.

Being Black in America has always been seen as inherently destabilizing to the idea of America. There's a constant war between the official version of who we are and the underground version we are forced to keep hidden. For many Black people, we constantly feel implicit and explicit pressure to hide the part of ourselves that is perceived as monstrous to the outside world. What the Obamas did with little things like their fist bumps, or by bringing hip-hop artists to the White House, was to humanize certain facets of Black culture and integrate them into the idea of what it means to be as American as the Fourth of July. And Black Americans could, at least for that moment, feel like their whole selves.

Seeing the Obamas as this perfect picture of a successful Black family—a real one, not one on a television show—does reaffirm that Black people can win. It did make me walk taller and feel prouder of who we are as an extended community. They felt not just unapologetically Black, but authentically Black. Many of us projected onto them all our hopes for an equitable society.

Hit Me with Your Best Shot

Just so we're on the same page, Black voters were the difference in both of Obama's presidential elections. Black voters got in formation and marched in steady streams to the polls, with 95 percent voting for him in 2008 and 93 percent in 2012. Comparatively, only 43 percent and 39 percent of white voters in those respective years could say the same. That fifty-plus-point spread was the widest since the 1984 presidential election. In that year, President Ronald Reagan beat the Democratic nominee, Vice President Walter Mondale, in a landslide. People hadn't even finished their election day dinners before the race was called. The difference-maker between 1984 and 2008 was turnout—Black and youth turnout hit record levels in 2008. They would not be denied the promise of change they were so longing for.

But the stories of joy around Obama's victory and what he and his family meant (and still mean) to Black people can make it easy to forget that it wasn't always this way. In fact, some readers may be surprised to know (or may have forgotten) that it took a hell of a lot of work to get Black voters to jump ship on Hillary Clinton in 2008. Going into the primaries, Clinton had the upper hand.

To the extent you can make a sweeping judgment about Black voters and what drives high turnout, it often comes down to three basic factors that contribute to a belief in our collective ability to hold a candidate at least somewhat accountable to a Black agenda: trust, authenticity, and viability. It's easy to forget that at the start, Clinton checked more of those boxes than Obama did.

I spoke about this with Marlon Marshall, who joined Hillary Clinton's 2008 presidential campaign as field director in Nevada, Ohio, and Indiana, but after the primaries, became the election director in Missouri for Obama for America. Marlon is Black. He said in 2008's Democratic Party he could see there were two movements building, both offering something he wanted to be a part of, both offering something that had previously felt out of reach.

Marlon had friends in both the Obama and Clinton campaigns, and he was excited to be a part of a wave of energy that was not just about a candidate, but also about investing in people, empowering them to achieve the change they wanted to see. He felt conflicted on which campaign to join, but after eight years of George W. Bush, his leading value was "We need experience to go right in and get it done." And Hillary felt like the best person to jump in on day one and just get it done.

Clinton had perceived viability and trust, and that mattered to Marlon both as someone who worked on campaigns and someone who wanted to see the country move in a different direction. Obama just didn't have that reputation, or any reputation yet, at the national level.

But what Obama *did* have was perceived authenticity, which was what spoke to Kwesi Chappin, who organized for Obama for America in South Carolina in 2007 before becoming deputy director at Get Out the Vote for President Obama's 2012 re-election campaign in Ohio. Kwesi's interest in politics first began with "The greatest mayor of Washington, DC, mayor for life, Marion Barry." Growing up just outside of DC and having friends that lived in the city, Kwesi saw the mayor several times in social settings. "He was just being human. This really set the tone for what a politician can be for the people." Kwesi recalled seeing old clips of the mayor when he still had an Afro and was wearing dashikis.

> He cared about maintaining afterschool programs and education initiatives. He fought for that despite not having any federal or outside resources . . . because DC isn't a state, right? Taxation without representation and all that. He just had a Chocolate City left out there with no supports, and he still fought to get tangible benefits for the community.

Kwesi grew up watching Barry around town and at events ranging from street basketball tournaments to strip clubs. Always be politicking. What Barry was doing so effectively was retail politics. Retail politics means meeting with voters directly and building personal connections. This is the kind of "kiss the babies" (or tip the dancers) stuff that gets spoofed when people talk about politicians. But it gives voters a sense that they have access to the politician. It humanizes the politician, and it helps people feel heard. It might up the cringe factor from time to time—like Tom Steyer backing that thang up in South Carolina—but it works.

Retail politics goes a long way toward creating a sense of authenticity for all voters, but it particularly matters for Black people, who often feel unheard in between election cycles. Many Black working-class communities rarely see state and federal politicians unless they visit, accompanied by security teams, to cut a *say nope to dope* PSA.

That's why Barry became so iconic not just in Washington, DC, but also in Black culture more broadly. Kwesi noted that even when crime was going up in the city, people still trusted him. Where did that trust come from? Because they believed he knew a path forward, yes, but moreover, because he never ran from challenges to hide away in an office or ivory tower. Retail politics is crucial because, at its best, it can build loyalty that allows people to back you up when you're out on a limb fighting for policies and money that will help the community. And for better or worse, it can help people overlook a candidate's fatal flaws.

Like Marion Barry, then-senator Obama is really good at retail politics. And Kwesi noticed that. He watched clips of Obama listening to people about why they were mad. But more than that, Obama was bringing on volunteers—people Kwesi knew and trusted—and he could see they were true believers and not just part of the political hustle.

"And Michelle. I was rocking with Michelle; she was a real one," Kwesi added.

It's been criminally understated, in my opinion, how much Michelle Obama brought the president into critical Black spaces. Even my sister (a staunch Hillary supporter in '08) likes to tell the story of running into Michelle Obama at Medici's bakery in Chicago's Hyde Park and telling her that she was only supporting her husband—then running for senator—because of her. "Hey, as long as you vote" was allegedly her response.

Beyond that, Barack and Michelle's interactions with each other and their daughters cultivated a type of Black nostalgia and familiarity that made people fall in love with the idea of them as a First Family. If there was one unquestionable thing in 2008, it was then-senator Obama's love for his family and the ties they had to the Black community in Chicago. I remember all of that, and it definitely left an impact on Kwesi:

> For me and for a lot of people, when we saw him on *Oprah* with Michelle Obama, it felt safer. She felt real. They felt like a real Black family. Obama reminded me of my dad. He was cool and chill, and I felt his patience. It reminded me of how my dad dealt with my brother, who has special needs. Same energy. There was a sense of authenticity that came through those series of interviews. I wasn't the only one who felt like that; I heard that from a lot of folks.

So Marlon saw Hillary Clinton had viability and trust. He didn't say she lacked authenticity. On the contrary, it was that many voters didn't value her brand of authenticity for a variety of reasons (misogyny, anti-elitism, conspiracism, hatred of pantsuits, take your pick). Some deeply resented it. On the other hand, Kwesi saw in Barack Obama and the Obama family an authenticity that couldn't be duplicated by other candidates. Also, being much newer to national politics meant he didn't really have a voting record or decades of quips that he had to go back and explain. He also saw Obama had the trust of a rapidly growing volunteer team that would eventually encompass an email and outreach list of 2.2 million, an unprecedented amount at the time. But Obama didn't have viability ... yet. That made the South Carolina primary particularly important. It was the first time during primary season that Black voters could have a major impact. And it was up for grabs.

Carolina on My Mind

Despite Obama logging a surprise victory in the Iowa caucus, Clinton was the favorite going into South Carolina. Most people assumed Clinton would torpedo Obama's momentum with a decisive victory in South Carolina. And that might have happened were it not for one person. In South Carolina, the Obama campaign knew they needed young voters and Black voters to turn up. With Hillary Clinton holding more name recognition and trust with many who would vote in the primary, Obama needed to pull an ace card. And he found his ace in *the* person who (especially in '08) could break the meter on trust and authenticity in a way no one else could.

Oprah. I'm talking about Oprah.

At least that's what the streets say. And by the streets, I mean my friend Kwesi.

The Oprah effect already did its thing in Iowa; her events with then-senator Obama throughout the state were widely credited in the media as helping to influence the state caucuses. When Oprah arrived in South Carolina, there was a big announcement in Columbia at Williams-Brice Stadium. Damn near twenty thousand people pulled up to see her. And, Kwesi noted, the audience was mostly women ... Black women. It's no secret that Black women are the key to any Democratic Party win. Kwesi said that was especially true for the primary in South Carolina. Obama had already built a lot of energy with younger voters, especially because of his anti-war (particularly the Iraq War) and climate change stances. But when Black women of all ages started becoming believers and began to trust, that was the pivot.

In that moment, Obama finally gained that third factor—the viability— that he had been missing. This was ultimately what led Marlon Marshall to join the Obama campaign after Obama became the Democratic Party's nominee. This was despite numerous public reports about how contentious things had gotten between Obama and Clinton and their respective camps. "Everyone could tell it was about something bigger," Marlon said.

Loves Jesus, and America, Too

Obama's traction only snowballed from there, and it did because of his and his team's commitment to community engagement—the same kind of engagement that had gained him authenticity in the first place. The Black women who went to see Oprah and got hyped about the Obama campaign became local evangelists, organizing house parties and other events that helped build a community of people excited about the political process.

The matriarchs that hosted parties for Obama across the country were the same people who ran the neighborhoods. And they ran their churches, too. Here's a pro-tip: People think if they get a photo op with a pastor of a mega or prominent Black church, then they've done their job. They think that if they sit in the front row people will say, "Oh, this politician must care about us."

Wrong.

The pastor is always going to get that photo op, but if you want that to translate to votes or donations, you have to go to the deacon, the first lady (the wife of a senior pastor), or one of the elder women who runs the choir, Sunday school, or church fundraising. That was something that Kwesi learned, and he used it to build out his network of volunteers on the ground.

> That for me was a lesson in who really has power and influence. Especially the first lady or the ladies in the front to third pews. They're the ones who will literally take carloads of people to the voting booth on election day. They're the ones who people listen

to and trust. They're also the ones who don't trust easily, so you have to put in genuine work. I have to get Miss Nettie one-on-one. That's the big hurdle you have to clear. But it's not just her. Once I build up that trust, I ask her, "Who else do I need to talk to? Can you introduce me? Can I get you to host an event?"

Kwesi was one of many young Black organizers who helped run the South Carolina Obama for America '08 barber and beauty shop program and house parties that, if you know about them, are the stuff of legends. Here's a secret about Black people in the United States that you would only know if you've ever watched a movie made by, with, and for Black people. Family house parties, barbershops, and beauty salons are where shit really goes down. Barber and beauty shops are where people discuss not just what color to dye their hair or the specifics of a legit fade, but they're also where a lot of Black political and pop-culture discourse takes place. When you're stuck in a salon chair—or at a shop waiting for a chair—for hours at a time, you can rotate through a lot of different topics.

Catherine Knight Steele discusses this dynamic in her research about Black online communities, which she refers to as the "virtual barbershop." Steele explains that both "the barber and beauty shop symbolize a space of retreat." Steele states Black communities have long relied on nonpolitical spaces for political discourse, in part because of the systemic exclusion of Black people from public debate and political power.

Historically, Black people have often had to find alternative spaces to build resistance and engage in political discourse free from surveillance. For example, getting caught talking about abolition in the pre–Civil War era, regardless of whether you were in the North or the South, could lead to you, your friends, and your family being killed or targeted. After the Civil War, working against Jim Crow racial segregation laws was also not a thing you could do out in the open. Over time, Black folks got adept at turning spaces that seemed nonthreatening—Black-owned barber/beauty shops, restaurants, and even local music radio stations—into places to build private and public revolutionary agendas. The only reason I'm sharing this is that the FBI is already aware, so I'm not breaking confidence here.

The same pressures applied not only to the spaces but also to the conversations themselves. Being able to talk in coded language allowed people the freedom to have discussions that may have appeared apolitical to the unaware ear, involving relationships, popular culture, and work.

Black organizers in places like South Carolina knew knocking on doors and asking voters to throw their weight behind a young, upstart candidate with an unusual name, in lieu of going with the more familiar Clinton name, would be an uphill battle. Oprah could only get you so far. Breaking down barriers couldn't happen in more overtly political settings where Black people would have their guards up.

If you could get people in their comfort zone, and you could deploy organizers (like Kwesi) who could cultivate an authentic representation of an Obama agenda and who could shoot the shit with the best of them at the barbershop, maybe you could move people. If you were willing to talk with not just your head, but also your heart and your gut, you could build trust. You could get Black voters to break patterns of voting more conservatively for a candidate they considered more of a sure thing. The barbershop program was not in the original Obama campaign plan—it was a modification by Black folks who knew their people and knew where and how to talk to them.

For Kwesi, building genuine relationships is what it's about. He compared it to his time working at Best Buy. I laughed, dubious at the comparison. But for him, any place where he can see new people every day, interact with them, and be genuine is his jam. As an introvert, that scares the hell out of me, but to each their own. Working the Obama campaign, he said, was like selling computers without commission. You have nothing to lose or gain by saying this is a shitty-ass computer or that is a good one.

> I told people, "Hey, here's a candidate. He's running for president, but you're gonna have to hold him accountable to get what you want. Yes, he's really that fucking cool; yes, he speaks very well. But this is not going to work without you holding him accountable."

As Kwesi talked about his work in South Carolina, you could tell he was really embedded into the community. The Obama for America model is often lauded in part because they used a neighborhood team model, gave their volunteers autonomy, and hired organizers who were overwhelmingly from the community. In other words, it was Community

Organizing 101. But there were also people like Kwesi, who was going to make himself at home no matter where he was. He wasn't from South Carolina, but he could reach people in ways that can't be taught at an organizing boot camp. That made him highly effective as an Obama surrogate. While certain journalists and politicians were starting to push the fantasy that America was post-racial, he and other Obama for America field organizers understood that for Black people, you can't back away from talking about race. Moreover, they knew that Black identity remains a source of pride and safety for many, especially in a world that tells us Black culture, families, and people are corrupt and powerless. By confronting and upending that myth over and over again—in churches, house parties, and barber shops across South Carolina and then the rest of the country—it solidified a feeling of linked fate between Black voters and Obama that became a call to action. He was able to build trust and authenticity with people in a way that didn't feel transactional.

I tell you all of this as a reminder that the story of DIY cooperative economics and organizing in Black communities is one with a long history that is detached from campaign strategies. The ability of both digital and ground organizers in the Obama '08 campaign to tap into that is part of what made it possible for Obama to become a more viable candidate. Instead of just casting harm-reduction votes and making the safe choice (Clinton), Black voters were moved to vote for a Black future, even if it were one they would never experience for themselves. This was the power of Obama for America.

The Way It Is

So, what happened? Did Obama for America live up to its full potential, or did it leave too much unfinished business? Well, it depends on who you ask.

When I asked Kwesi whether OFA was a missed opportunity, he didn't hesitate.

> They made poor moves strategically. It was so hard for me to understand. You've got all these Obama folks who are fired up, who want to run for office, who want to volunteer in their community. We told them to hope, we told them they could do real work to hold elected officials accountable. In South Carolina, we told

them that universal health care was possible because that's what we believed. So now that the election is over, what does it mean to live what we preach?

After the election, the Obama campaign found itself with a list of 2.2 million people who were activated, excited, and ready to go. But no one really knew what to do with the list. It was still low-key surprising to some that Obama had even won. People wanted to figure out how to keep volunteers engaged, but how engaged and to what end was a point of contention.

At some point, the decision was made to formally change the name from "Obama for America" to "Organizing for America." It was also decided that the organization would be housed within the Democratic National Committee. When that decision was actually made is another point of contention. For example, Shireen Mitchell, who was part of the digital infrastructure as a blogger and social media creator, told me it had always been planned for Obama for America to get rolled into the DNC. As she tells it, everyone has to sign a contract in order to run for president as a Democrat, and in the contract there are elements that include an agreement on fundraising, contact list sharing, and all the stuff in between. This is a standard practice across political parties, and it's in part why you can't seem to get off various political email lists no matter how hard you try.

The problem, Shireen said, is that the goal was to use OFA as a strategy to reform the DNC, not just let the program fall apart. But once it was moved over, it didn't have the same level of resourcing, access, or support to galvanize the energy of '08. Because of the lack of resourcing, some people who were core to the success of the tech model lost their jobs or went to work in Silicon Valley.

According to Kwesi and others I spoke to, a December 2008 meeting in Chicago was held with various leaders of Obama for America, including field organizers and DC strategists. Debates quickly spiraled and lines were drawn between ground organizers, digital organizers, and Beltway strategists. Whether a byproduct of the predictive demographics of those various roles, or other factors, lines seemed to be drawn along race, age, and class divisions. When the smoke cleared, the DC political machine was left standing.

So even though the whole concept of OFA stayed, it was a shell. And while it worked for Obama again in 2012, it didn't do as well. People wanted to neatly standardize, package, and sell the Obama '08 magic in a box, but this entirely missed what had been so effective about the model in the first place.

The infrastructure had worked because it was adaptive and responsive. Volunteers had the power to shape it and instill a sense of responsibility in people, even ownership, over the election and their community. They had the freedom to incorporate cultural and hypergeographic aspects into canvassing to persuade people to move away from their typical voting patterns. And that kind of power redistribution and loss of control over what happens on the ground wasn't something many campaigns were willing to do. Certainly, it wasn't something the DNC was ready to do.

By the time Hillary Clinton's campaign picked up what little was left of OFA in 2016, not only was the core infrastructure lacking, the entire landscape of the internet and how people were interacting with each other on- and offline had begun to shift. According to published reports, the Clinton campaign took a more top-down approach to the structure. Organizers were sent to places where they had no knowledge of the community and no connections or personal stakes.

So where are we now, post–Obama for America?

For Marlon, who after the 2008 election went on to work in the Obama administration, the question of did OFA live up to its full potential is a hard one. They had built a campaign that, in many ways, was unlike anything that came before it, and it was all around a finite goal of getting one man elected. Obama for America had brought together a lot of strange bedfellows who otherwise may not have been aligned. So, in that way, it made sense to Marlon that when it came time to decide what to do next, not everyone agreed. But because of that, maybe it was always meant to be temporary. Maybe we should just appreciate it for what it was and what they were able to accomplish. Marlon was philosophical about it all: "The rigamarole of policy-making and organizing support is a different animal from campaign organizing and certainly from movement organizing."

For Arisha Hatch, a former OFA volunteer who later went on to oversee campaigns at Color Of Change, Obama for America was a gift, one that would manifest into building out an organizing program at Color

Of Change that would galvanize millions of Black voters in future elections. Not just in presidential elections, but local and state races as well. "Yes, the president is important," she said, "but every day, your district attorney makes hundreds of decisions that directly affect you and your community. The ability to make sure we have people who value Black lives occupying that office—that's the type of change you can immediately see and feel."

Color Of Change's community organizing program started by connecting with local leaders and inviting Black women in cities like Detroit, Miami, Philadelphia, New Orleans, and other places to brunch. It's a space to laugh together, dance together, eat together, and plot for the future. At its heart was a definitive framework for creating a public narrative—something OFA volunteers had learned through the Obama campaign—the power in telling your personal story and welcoming people into a positive vision for the thing we were being asked to collectively do together. Not just "get X elected," but change the material conditions around us, change the neighborhood, the state, the country, even the world. And make change that is driven and led by those who have been directly impacted by the failures of decision-makers.

Arisha would remember the joy and empowering experience of being a part of the '08 campaign—the house parties and community-based strategies and how different it felt from social justice and political organizing that stems from community trauma.

But for me, it was hard to grapple with how this movement—and Obama for America was a movement as much as it was a campaign—could have just been collapsed and handed over to the Democratic Party. Even if that's just how politics often goes, is that how politics should go? How did that ultimately serve Black people? Or working-class people? Or most people?

It remains frustrating that there are so many unanswered questions about how the power of that moment in '08 and the Obama for America infrastructure could have been harnessed. I can't help but feel like OFA was neglected and left to die, whether intentional or not. We still sit with the ripple effects of what it meant to have hoped things could be different, only for many to wake up eight years later with little change to their material conditions. For many, things were worse.

In the case of Black people in particular, estimates for how much wealth Black people lost from 2005 to 2009 range from 53 percent to 61 percent. Our collective net worth plummeted 43 percent from 2007 to 2013 as a result of the financial crisis. Our material gains didn't come back. We as a people didn't come back from that either.

I honestly don't know how much of that to blame on the Obama administration because we had gone through nearly three decades of corruption, rapid deregulation, erosion of labor rights, overreliance on computers, and faulty automated decision-making before Obama even set foot in office. He immediately walked into a recession not of his making. But it also feels like things could've been a lot better eight years later than they were. Certainly the failure to address concentrated economic power—or use enforcement mechanisms geared toward curbing the predatory behavior of corporate actors like those in the banking, housing, and tech industries—has direct ties to the rapidly widening economic, racial, and social inequities that are the hallmarks of a new Gilded Age. Regardless, the Trump '16 campaign benefited from the collective hopelessness that had fallen over the nation. In the years since Obama for America, we saw the rise of Tea Party politics, #Occupy, and Black Lives Matter. That was layered on top of the losses suffered during the recession. We were not the same as we were in 2008.

In 2016, 4.4 million voters who cast a ballot in 2012 stayed home, and at least 1.7 million cast a ballot without voting in the presidential election. However you want to slice that, at the end of the day, there were millions of people who either didn't think their vote mattered or hadn't found a presidential candidate they believed in.

Fruits of My Labor

The question of whether or not Obama '08 results could ever be achieved again by just bringing in Black people and giving them the autonomy and resources to organize is a tough one. The combination of the 2008 recession and the COVID-19 economic shock in 2020 wiped out a lot of the Black-owned business and cultural spaces that had been so core to building community. Many of the restaurants and barbershops volunteers went to are no longer there. Some people no longer own the homes or spaces where they once hosted parties.

Instead, we've built more and more of our community in the online realm. The virtual barbershop and beauty shop aren't quite like the one down the street where you go in and see people week after week who know you and your kids. Online, you don't necessarily know who it is that you're building community with, what their motivations are, or what they want. And, moreover, because of the siloed ways in which the internet works, we're getting pushed further into echo chambers, which means that often, we don't get the opportunity to have conversations with people who may not see things as we do. Instead, we're all hyping each other up in our respective corners and getting more and more agitated about all the shit that's not working. And there's a lot that's not working.

At this point, we can only deal with the fact that we are increasingly moving toward polarized thinking without any sort of authentic check on what we feel. And we've been trained as people to seek out more and more spaces where we find people like us instead of people who can challenge us and move us. Under the current conditions, I'm not at all certain the Obama campaign would have been able to win South Carolina in 2016, let alone today.

That's what worries me. Not the question of whether Obama himself as a candidate could (or should) win today, but the idea that more and more, we're moving away from the ability to even embrace a candidate who doesn't immediately feel politically safe or viable. That we're losing the ability to vote for a candidate who may have authenticity but is lacking trust and viability. That we're becoming so disillusioned that the thought of voting for a Black future is usurped by the immediate need to just survive, even if barely.

Meanwhile, for all the jokes and sarcastic remarks Republican leaders made in 2008 about Obama's experience as a community organizer, the book *Groundbreakers: How Obama's 2.2 Million Volunteers Transformed Campaigning in America* became required reading for the party's staffers in 2016 and 2020. The book documents the Obama for America ground and digital game, creating a playbook that the Republican Party has been able to draw from. Instead of offering hope for a better future for all of us, the core messaging panders to fears of white replacement, individualism, right-wing nationalism, and fears of losing power. Though it didn't get Trump over the finish line in 2020, it's been a critical model for electing a new, younger pipeline of lawless leaders. People who have shown a willingness to take over a country they've proclaimed theirs by *whatever means necessary*. Whether it's through blocking access to the ballot box or giving tours through the halls of Congress to insurrectionists plotting armed violence (allegedly).

Everything about where we go from here scares the fuck out of me.

5

Kanye Was Right-ish
Maybe We Don't Need Instant Replay on Black Trauma

ME: WHEN IT'S ALL SAID AND DONE, REMEMBER THE FEARLESS, RE-MEMBER THE DREAMERS, REMEMBER THOSE WHO REPRESENT THE GHETTO . . . THE FAIRY TALE OF NOTHING TO SOMETHING. . . . I CAN HEAR YOU SCREAMING 'COLOR INSIDE THE LINES!!!' WELL FUCK YOUR COLORING BOOK, COLOR BY NUMBERS [*sic*] APPROACH TO LIFE. AT THE END OF THE DAY WHO ARE WE HURTING??? OH "THE NEW BLACK"??? SINCE BARACK IS PRESIDENT BLACKS DON'T LIKE FUR COATS, RED LEATHER, AND FRIED CHICKEN ANY MORE [*sic*]?! WHEN YOU TRULY UNDERSTAND CULTURAL SETTINGS, BOUNDAR-IES, AND OUR MODERN DAY [*sic*] CASTE SYSTEMS, THEN YOU CAN FEEL THE GLORY AND PAIN FROM THE DAYS OF KINGS IN AFRICA TO THE NEW KINGS OF THE MEDIA. LET THE BALL PLAYERS [*sic*] DANCE AFTER THEY SCORE! IT'S LIFE MY NIGGAS, IT'S LIFE! REMEM-BER CLOTHING IS A CHOICE. WE WERE BORN NAKED!!! FRESH IS AN OPINION, LOVE IS OBJECTIVE, TASTE IS SELECTIVE, AND EXPRESSION IS MY FAVORITE ELECTIVE. NO MORE POLITICS OR APOLOGIES!!!

DAVID: Are you sending me Kanye blogs again???

Between 2009 and 2010-ish, my now-husband David and I were work colleagues at Safer Foundation. Realizing we lived around the corner from each other, we took the bus together after work, talking from Union Station in downtown Chicago all the way back to our Hyde Park neighborhood on the South Side. Often, our conversations revolved around current events, news, music, and pop culture. I introduced him to Funkadelic's *Maggot Brain*. He introduced me to The National and their *Alligator* album. We found musical common ground around A Tribe Called Quest and Gang of Four. We later shared our dismay when Gang of Four's "Natural's Not in It" turned up in an Xbox commercial. Eventually, our after-work conversations drifted onto our work Google Chats and nighttime texts.

As I was writing this book, I cracked open my archive of those chats. A ridiculous amount of that time was spent debating and analyzing the various shenanigans and exploits of Kanye West. You could even say that arguing about Kanye played a pivotal role in sparking our relationship. In lieu of doing stuff like . . . ya know . . . working, we went back and forth analyzing his big moments, like the "I'mma let you finish" run-in with Taylor Swift at the 2009 MTV Video Music Awards, and smaller moments, like his super-random stream of consciousness, fully capitalized blogs like the one I opened the chapter with. Like others, we could never really agree on if we were bearing witness to a public breakdown or breakthrough.

For decades, Kanye has provided eager viewers countless jaw-dropping moments to analyze. It's no small feat that Kanye has somehow managed to keep the public's attention for decades without even having to drop a sex tape. Well actually, he does have a forty-minute sex tape in circulation, but that doesn't even crack his top ten most tweeted about moments.

Kanye West is both unpalatable to the mainstream and irresistible to the masses. That's because he has a persona that is perfect for the age of internet celebrity. He blurs the barrier between what people think should be private versus public. He does it in a way that feels camp and at times grotesque. And through it all, Kanye gives an authentic, if imperfect, voice to trauma and a disaffected generation. But there can be a cost to breaking decorum.

All Falls Down

Ever have one of those moments when you feel like you're watching an agonizingly slow car wreck play out in front of you, and you just keep saying "oh no, oh no" while the driver sluggishly spins out of control? If you have, then you have a sense of how I felt watching the infamous clip of Kanye West on *TMZ Live* in May 2018.

It was a weird setup to begin with. In the clip, Kanye is at the TMZ studios with Candace Owens—a YouTuber-turned-political-pundit who simultaneously demonizes "identity politics" for white conservative audiences while using her own identity as a Black woman to launder Far Right ideology. So, Kanye is there with her, but she's off camera at this point. He's seated next to *TMZ* host Charles Latibeaudiere (Black), while founder Harvey Levin (white) is standing next to them. Harvey is probing Kanye about why he's a Trump supporter. Kanye says Trump's his boy, that Trump is one of rap's favorite people, and that he routinely appeared in hip-hop videos before people decided it wasn't cool to like him.

And that's when it goes down. Kanye gives the sound bite that would briefly break the internet:

> When you hear about slavery for four hundred years. For four hundred years? That sounds like a choice. You were there for four hundred years, and it is all of y'all? It is like we are mentally in prison.

In the clip, the shot of him calmly talking to the two men is edited so that it then cuts to him standing up, waving his hands wildly and addressing the rest of the TMZ staffers as he exits the studio. He challenges them, asking if they thought he was "being free and thinking free" by speaking his mind. Popular *TMZ* personality Van Lathan, Jr. (Black), who was not a part of the original conversation, responds, "I actually don't think you're thinking anything." He continues:

> Kanye, you're entitled to your opinion, you're entitled to believe whatever you want, but there is fact and real-world, real-life consequence behind everything you just said . . . And while you are making music and being an artist and living the life that you've earned by being a genius, the rest of us in society have to deal with these threats to our lives . . . We have to deal with the marginalization that's come from the four hundred years of slavery

that you said for our people was a choice. Every day we have to walk into that truth while you choose to say things that, to be honest with you, dog, are nonsensical . . .

It was a raw moment between two Black men who felt strongly about the sides of the line that they were on and so unlike anything one would expect to see on *TMZ*. Van Lathan's words were poignant, and you could feel the earnestness behind them. When he said he was disappointed, appalled, and unbelievably hurt to see whom Kanye had morphed into, I felt all of that flowing through him.

"You gotta be responsible, bro," Lathan kept saying, now standing.

"Bro, I'm sorry I hurt you," Kanye kept saying as he walked toward him.

The clip ends before you see how the conversation concludes.

As the edited moment circulated online, Lathan became something of an internet folk hero for daring to call out Kanye for his bullshit, for telling him to his face that celebrity had gotten the better of him. The implication of Lathan's words was that Kanye was not the same man he had once been. And, specifically, that he was not the same man who had spoken up for Black people during Hurricane Katrina over a decade earlier.

At first glance, I agreed. It felt like a shift from the 2005 Kanye who had resonated with me. In August of that year, I remember looking at photos and videos of Black people on their roofs in Louisiana, begging for help, for food, for any sign that someone cared. I read about them being treated like animals and gunned down in their most vulnerable moments while the police chief blatantly lied about the threat they presented.

And during a live telethon raising money for those communities washed away by Hurricane Katrina, I saw my favorite musician vocalize what I had long felt.

"I hate the way they portray us in the media," Kanye West said.

If you see a Black family, it says, 'They're looting.' You see a white family, it says, 'They're looking for food.' And you know that it's been five days because most of the people are Black. And even for

me to complain about it, I would be a hypocrite—because I've
tried to turn away from the TV because it's too hard to watch . . .
and they've given them permission to go down and shoot us.

His copresenter scrambled to salvage the script, but Kanye wasn't finished. He concluded with the words: "George Bush doesn't care about
Black people."

The day before the benefit concert and telethon, New Orleans police
officers had shot six unarmed residents, killing two of them. That same
day, Roland J. Bourgeois, Jr., had gunned down three Black men attempting to seek refuge after the hurricane. Bourgeois had used racial epithets
before the attack, telling one neighbor, "Anything coming up this street
darker than a brown paper bag is getting shot."

These were stories that for the most part would go un- or underreported in the immediate days after Katrina made landfall. But even
without those stories, Black people knew every bit of what Kanye was
saying was true, even if some of them wished he hadn't said it in mixed
company. It's the type of traumatic processing we like to do in private.

But when Kanye West said those words, "George Bush doesn't care about
Black people," it was like finally, someone was willing to cut through the
bullshit pretense of civility. Kanye in 2005 was someone who spoke to me
and for me. He spoke to many other people.

But 2018 Kanye on *TMZ* saying slavery was a choice? Nah, he could
keep that one. What had happened in the intervening years? What had
changed?

People interpreted Kanye's slavery comments in many different ways.
For some, "Slavery was a choice" translated to a statement on the inherent
dumbness of Black people in America. The implication is we were willing
participants in our own physical enslavement. For others, it showed the
inherent dumbness of Kanye and his eagerness to be a tool of the Trump
show. But in hindsight, both of these conclusions are flawed.

Look, I can admit it's a weird fucking sound bite and definitely
the wrong venue and audience for that conversation. It's one of those
things you say when you're the controversial cousin at the family Easter
dinner and everyone wants to debate hot takes in private. It's not really
the thing one says during a performative spectacle at the offices of a

company that specializes in trashy gossip and painting people in the worst possible light.

But there's nuance to what he's saying, especially when taken in the context of his tweets the next day explaining that by "choice," he was referring more to mental than physical enslavement.

> Of course, I know that slaves did not get shackled and put on a boat by free will. My point is for us to have stayed in that position even though the numbers were on our side means that we were mentally enslaved. The reason why I brought up the four hundred years point is we can't be mentally imprisoned for another four hundred years. We need free thought now. Even the statement was an example of free thought. It was just an idea. We are programmed to always talk and fight race issues. We need to update our conversation.

There's a lot in this that's true, in particular, the fact that mental terror was inflicted upon Black communities to keep those enslaved subservient. Psychological warfare was deployed, including public murder, rape, and beatings, not just of people who tried to escape but also anyone they loved. Slave owners and their enablers also spread vengeful ghost stories and conspiracies that tapped into the idea that supernatural forces were watching, even while the slave master slept. So in that way, Kanye was right about mental enslavement being able to do a lot of work that physical enslavement alone could not do. He was right about the impact of psychological abuse.

Where I and so many others took issue with his comments is that it's a dangerous and false idea to suggest if you cannot break the binds of psychological terrorism, it's because you're a mentally weak person. That is just another way to pathologize Black people and blame us for slavery's evilness. So I'm not feeling the comments for that reason. But how people responded to the comments both at the moment by *TMZ* employees and later on the internet—as if there was no nuance to what Kanye said—was a very narrow interpretation of what he was actually trying to articulate.

Days later, Kanye further clarified his statements by visiting whom else but Black radio and media personality Charlamagne tha God.

Charlamagne got straight to it, asking Kanye what he was thinking and pushing him to provide more context (edited for clarity):

> **KANYE:** We definitely are dealing with racism. But I want to push future concepts . . . It's like . . . all the slave movies . . . why you gotta keep reminding us about slavery? Why don't you . . . put Michael Jordan on a twenty-dollar bill [instead of Harriet Tubman]?
>
> **CHARLAMAGNE:** But Harriet Tubman was a slave who rebelled, though. Like, her and Nat Turner had a different frequency . . . They were like you were; you said you didn't feel like being controlled.
>
> **KANYE:** Man . . . I know this is gonna cause an uproar, but [pauses] certain icons is [*sic*] just too far in the past and not relatable. And [that's] what makes them safe. Like, they'll let you go on the Grammys and talk about slavery and all that, and racism, because it's not talking about buying stock; it's not talking about buying property.

As a Kanye-whisperer, I feel relatively confident that what he's saying here is the constant showcasing of Black trauma as the main story about Black people is another form of psychological warfare. And I do agree with him about this. For example, research suggests Black people—and people of color in general—experience long-term mental health effects from frequent exposure to the graphic videos of police killings circulated online. The experience of watching those videos, combined with the lived experience of racism, can create severe psychological problems: heightened fear, anxiety, and distrust of the people around you—symptoms that are very similar to the post-traumatic stress we see in veterans.

Research also shows repeated exposure to violent videos in general and Black death specifically makes people numb to the pain and suffering of others. During George Floyd's murder trial, one thing that stood out was how the defense attorney kept playing the footage of the last moments of Floyd's life over and over again. There are several reasons why he claimed to have done this, but one purpose it served was to bombard the jury with a constant onslaught of images that would desensitize them to Floyd's death. Desensitize and dehumanize, leading them to forget they were seeing the unnatural snuffing out of someone's life. For me, it's chilling to process that.

I recognize white people often perpetuate the constant media loop of Black trauma in the name of acknowledging Black pain. But whatever the motivation, the impact is disempowerment. It reinforces a narrative that Blackness is something undesirable, unsafe, and subhuman.

There are many implications in that for white people. One is an implicit superiority from, and comfort in, inhabiting whiteness. Here's some of what it means for Black people. If Blackness is assumed inherently traumatic, built solely on the memory of enslavement and murder, then there is no room for Black nostalgia and the resulting comfort and pride. There is no room to embrace the complexity, nuance, and joy of present-day Black existence. Nor is there room to work toward a Black future free of trauma because it's hard to even begin to imagine what that could look like. It becomes easier to imagine Black extinction than it does Black liberation. Easier to imagine Black pain than Black joy.

Now this desire to encompass joy and nuance by no means erases the pain Black people have faced throughout this country's history. Indeed, it is the acknowledgment of this pain that can render "Make America Great Again" a threatening statement for Black people. When people talk about making America great again, they are not talking about making it great *for* Black people. So when Kanye, who has often supported Trump, says the phrase, it is typically only seen as hostile or impervious to Black struggle, which then informs our interpretation of everything that he says and feeds into the same simplistic interpretation of his slavery comments. But in Kanye's statements to Charlamagne, we can see his embrace of MAGA as an attempt to reclaim, for Black people, a positive view of the past. And as important, it invites us to imagine a possibility for things to be great for Black people.

I often fear that in our collective memory and story, we have stripped all of the beauty of how Blackness came to mean something other than a census box, such that a reminder of our history becomes synonymous with pain. In front of the white gaze and through the white gaze, to be Black is to be brutalized. And because there are so few Black media outlets left to tell and celebrate our stories in our own voices, the dominant narrative persists that to be Black is to be disempowered; that to be Black is to be lynched. I think it says a lot that it took a Black media outlet—in this case, *The Breakfast Club*—to draw that deeper contemplation and nuance out of Kanye.

When we strip all of that away, when we make Blackness something we have to rise above, Blackness becomes a traumatic bonding experience that is temporal, hard, and eventually hateful. And in some ways, this is what Kanye was voicing in his *TMZ* interview—the all-too-real ways that a narrative of trauma can be harmful. We need a different version of Black history, built from the stories that don't make the front pages of the *New York Times* or TMZ's website.

Follow Kanye

In 2019, Kanye released the gospel album *Jesus Is King,* an album that tackles themes of imperfection, liberation, salvation, and new birth. The lead single for the album was called "Follow God." Its accompanying music video is fairly sparse, especially when compared to some of the more lavish videos he's offered in the past. The video starts with Kanye walking in front of his father, Ray, through the snow on the artist's expansive Wyoming property. We hear a voiceover from his father asking what it really means to follow God and meditating on having a child follow in your footsteps.

It then launches into the blistering 105-second song. As an aside, this is definitely one of my top-five Kanye songs. The song is compelling as hell for a Kanye fan who appreciates when he revisits his old musical styles. "Follow God" is like a throwback to his mid-2000s, early 2010s sound and, lyrically, it makes me fall in love with his wordplay all over again.

In juxtaposition to Kanye's father's words, in the video, Ray is following *Kanye* and listening to *him.* It's almost as though Kanye is saying, "I tried things your way, now we're going to do things my way." This image echoes his political choices and radical statements. For decades, Black voters have walked in the steps of those who chose the Democratic Party, but as Kanye has said many times: I am trying a new direction because what's been done before no longer serves me or us as Black voters. Regardless of whether the video's message is that direct, it's clear it's a meditation on his relationship with his heritage and past—what he owes to those who came before and how he'll choose his own path forward.

The video ends with the written words: "My dad came to visit me at one of our ranches in Cody, Wyoming. He talked about his love for fishing and how we would like to come here in the summers. It took me forty-two years to realize that my dad was my best friend. He asked me, 'How many acres is this?' I told him four thousand. He replied with these three words: 'A Black man?'"

Four thousand is likely a reference to the forty acres Black people were supposed to receive as reparations and start-up seed investment after the US Civil War, reparations that were never fully distributed. It was the first systematic attempt to right the sin of slavery through property and wealth redistribution, a policy Dr. Henry Louis Gates, Jr., calls "astonishingly radical for its time, protosocialist in its implications." But the failure of the Union to make good on this promise of opportunity for all, and the ensuing post–Civil War land grab, further concentrated power in the hands of oil, steel, railroad, and sugar barons. It launched a Gilded Age that created massive wealth inequalities that we wouldn't see again until the twenty-first century. Kanye seems to be saying we never got our forty acres, but on my own, I amassed one hundred times that amount—something that holds particular significance, considering his family history.

In the early 1900s, Kanye's family was located in Oklahoma—a land of opportunity for Black people. When Kanye's grandfather, Portwood Williams, was born, Oklahoma had fifty all-Black towns, more than existed in any other state. All-Black towns became a way for Black people to become self-sufficient, circumventing the economic and societal barriers erected post Reconstruction.

At the center of this land of plenty was Tulsa, home to what Booker T. Washington proudly proclaimed "Black Wall Street." The title made sense; it was founded by one of the first Black self-made millionaires—O. W. Gurley—and was widely considered to be one of the wealthiest Black neighborhoods in the south.

In 1921, when Portwood was a child, the idyllic Black Wall Street was attacked by an angry white lynch mob in what came to be known as the Tulsa Race Massacre. More than three hundred Black people were murdered, and thirty-five blocks and the businesses on them were burned to the ground, including the *Tulsa Star,* the Black newspaper that served the community. This would have surely left an impression on Black people in the region, including Kanye's family. In the years that followed, many of these all-Black towns would be economically destroyed and erased, one way or another.

But the ethos of the region had already been ingrained in Portwood. As a young boy, he worked shining shoes, bringing home his money to help pay the bills but also keeping a little for himself. He endured racial abuse and taunts and raced home after work to make sure he didn't get caught outside once the Oklahoma sun hit the horizon. As an adult, he launched an upholstery business, finding success and ultimately being honored as one of Oklahoma City's outstanding Black businessmen.

In 1958, Portwood took his young children to what became a three-day sit-in at the Katz Drug Store lunch counter in downtown Oklahoma City. It wasn't enough just to quietly build his own success; he had to move beyond self-interest and make demands for broader power as well. He wanted to show what it meant to be successful—on one's own terms and with autonomy—as a Black man. Portwood and his wife, Lucille, had four children: Shirlie, Klaye, Portwood, Jr., and Donda (Kanye's mother), in whom they would instill a strong work ethic, steely determination, unshakable faith in God, and a commitment to civil rights.

When you consider this history, Kanye begins to make more sense. The Williamses' legacy is one of a family persisting toward a vision of autonomy even in the face of overwhelmingly violent racism. For Kanye, it's led him down a path of seeking agency and power through often iconoclastic methods—the "we're going to do things my way now" mentality from the "Follow God" music video. It's why those four thousand acres mean so much to him and his father.

But this movement is bigger and older than Kanye. In 1895, at the Atlanta Exposition, Booker T. Washington gave a speech that would become known as the "Atlanta Compromise." In front of a mostly white crowd, Washington urged Black people to avoid confrontation with white people over segregation or political or social equity and instead focus on building independent Black economic security. His argument was this: Black people needed to create their own fate and fortune, independent of their white surroundings.

More than a century after that speech, this DIY framework of Black economic autonomy has persisted in Black political thought. In few places has this been clearer than the resurgence in surprising online spaces of Thomas Sowell, a prolific writer and a leader of conservative-libertarian thought. Central to his ideology, economist Thomas Sowell sees the combination of federal aid and racialized rhetoric as a gateway drug to neutralize the working class and compromise Black family values, community economics, and sustainability. The enemy is not conservatism, Sowell proclaims, but liberal intellectuals, celebrities, and politicians who hide behind platitudes and create ivory towers around public knowledge and free exchange of thought.

He has been name-checked by people ranging from January 6 insurrectionist Nick Fuentes to—you guessed it—Kanye West. Kanye's tweets about Sowell have been a gateway to modern alternative Black conservative thought anchored in a pro-Black agenda. And this was something, too, that he voiced that day on *The Breakfast Club* after the *TMZ* incident: "Yeah, it's not talking about economic power. You can complain as hard as you want [about racism], but it's not scary [like talking about economic empowerment]."

While most Black voters are well aware that racists occupy both sides of the political aisle, 90 percent of us have chosen to take our chances on the less obvious racists in the Democratic Party, hoping their need for our vote can help rein in their racism. But Kanye is a part of a growing group of Black voters reminiscent of the political identity of those who sought to build the Black Wall Street. That Booker T. Washington shit. That Thomas Sowell groove. The political identity of those optimists who left the South in droves, looking to build a new community free from the tyranny of a Confederate government and believing they could do so without interference from white people.

Under what seems like misguided and inflammatory bluster about Trump and slavery, Kanye is offering a radical vision for the future: one premised on the idea of building our own wealth, valuing our own intellect, and cultivating our own sanctuary for Black creativity and power. In other words, "WHEN YOU TRULY UNDERSTAND CULTURAL SETTINGS, BOUNDARIES, AND OUR MODERN DAY [*sic*] CASTE SYSTEMS, THEN YOU CAN FEEL THE GLORY AND PAIN FROM THE DAYS OF KINGS IN AFRICA TO THE NEW KINGS OF THE MEDIA."

Maybe the new Kanye isn't so different from the old Kanye after all.

It's a grand idea, albeit a vision coming from someone whose musical ingenuity allowed him to surpass certain disadvantages that plague people with fewer resources who might try to emulate this approach. But it's a thought that's far less cynical than what people might come to expect, given his ever-growing list of diatribes and publicly displayed grievances.

Like most people, I will never fully understand everything Kanye West says and does. I don't support many things he does, or at least the way he seems to go about them. But sometimes, I do. Sometimes, it speaks to a part of me that feels the same way. And regardless of its flaws, the sentiment about DIY Black economic empowerment is a line of logic that comes from a deep family history and from a powerful response to persistent anti-Black violence.

It's a story many of us have and one that is beginning to lead Black people in different political directions. Kanye West is one man. For all his bombastic nature and headline-making statements, it takes more than opinions and musical bangers to get millions of Black voters to suddenly exit stage right from the Democratic Party. But I do think Kanye is a canary in a coal mine, an example of an emerging party-ambivalent Black voter base that could upend expected Black voter norms in the coming years.

At the Vanguard

On August 30, 2015, Kanye West was presented with the MTV Vanguard Award. The lifetime achievement award goes to artists and video directors with long careers of innovation and influence, and he deserved it. Kanye West is one of the most influential individuals today.

On that night in 2015, he electrified the crowd, reminding them why he had stayed prominent for so long. In front of an enthralled audience, he gave a speech that would later be called "incredible," "blunt," "poignant," "blathering," and "incoherent." Polarizing is as polarizing does.

He talked about being confident and believing in himself. He talked about the legacy of Portwood Williams, who had passed away two years earlier. Kanye told the crowd that moment, and the moments that lay ahead of us, was about people with ideas and people who believe in the truth. "I'm confident. I believe in myself. We the millennials, bro. This is a new mentality. We're not gonna control our kids with brands. We not gonna teach low self-esteem and hate to our kids. We gonna teach our kids that they can be something. We gonna teach our kids that they can stand up for theyself [*sic*]! We gonna teach our kids to believe in themselves!"

He left the crowd with this: "And yes, as you probably could have guessed by this moment, I have decided in 2020 to run for president."

The audience went wild and social media lit up. It was a speech that encapsulated so much about Kanye and his contradictions—his thoughtfulness, his absurdity, his maddening desire to provoke. Naturally, I thought back to my Google chats with David about Kanye and his capitalized blogs:

> **ME:** my favorite part is, "I CAN HEAR YOU SCREAMING 'COLOR INSIDE THE LINES!!!' WELL FUCK YOUR COLORING BOOK, COLOR BY NUMBERS APPROACH TO LIFE."
>
> **DAVID:** Yes . . . he is one to forget about caps lock
>
> **ME:** I love how he just goes off on a rampage about how now that even though Barack is president, black people should still like fur, fried chicken, and red leather.
>
> **DAVID:** I don't really see that many black people wearing red leather
>
> **ME:** My mom has red suede pants, does that count? My sister dated a guy once that wore black leather pants to our thanksgiving dinner. My dad hated him.
>
> **DAVID:** i don't really get what he's saying? Is he like "just because a black man is president doesn't mean you have to give up on stereotypes just yet!"?
>
> **ME:** He's basically saying be who you are and who you want to be and don't give into the status quo. If you like red leather and fried chicken don't give that up because someone told you that you have to define yourself by their standards of what is "dignified."
>
> **ME:** Also he's saying Black people make the culture and we break the systems so the only thing we can be bound by is our imagination.
>
> **DAVID:** Oh. That makes sense . . . why couldn't he have just said that?

6

Hard Times

Reflections on the Possibilities, Pitfalls, and Inevitability of Populism

Whose fucking idea was it to buy a 55-inch television and carry it up three flights of stairs in a row house we're staying in for less than a week?"

"Your idea. It was your idea. I wanted us to just watch it on my phone, remember? Why are these stairs so narrow?"

"And you just know that pay-per-view is going to suck; they all suck now."

"Brandi. Can you chill for a sec? I've already been driving for hours, and I want to just get the damn TV upstairs."

"Well, you don't have to be sassy about it."

"Sorry, I think I'm just delirious at this point."

The road trip David and I took when we relocated from Oakland, California, to Baltimore, Maryland, was one for the ages. With our *Atlas Obscura* in hand, we drove fifty hours cross-country, visiting several quirky roadside stops, museums, and restaurants, and meeting up with family and friends. We had traveled through the southern region of the country, taking the slow way but with urgency because we needed to hit Baltimore in time to watch . . . WrestleMania. Yes, WrestleMania.

Like a sign from God guiding us on our righteous journey, during that trip we saw legendary wrestling heel Vickie Guerrero in a random gas station in the middle of nowhere, Texas. I was so starstruck, I hadn't even been able to go up to her. I just stood behind a shelf of pork rinds, wondering if I could get away with taking a photo of her without coming off weird. Then in the car afterward, I obsessed over the likelihood that Vickie fucking Guerrero had seen me being weird by the pork rinds.

Wrestling has been one of the great loves of my life. I love the cheesiness of it all, the superheroes of various shapes and sizes. I love how wrestling plays into the perception that David can beat Goliath. I love that you can be a villain one day and redeemed the next.

Which is why, on our first night in Baltimore, before our moving truck arrived and before we even had the keys to our apartment, we bought a TV and carried it up a steep flight of stairs in a row house we were subletting. All so we could watch WrestleMania.

I am aware the judgment is coming hard and fast right now, but I refuse to feel shame about the enjoyment I get watching oiled-up people in costumes pretend to beat each other to a pulp. Circle of trust, here.

As a Black World Wrestling Entertainment (WWE) fan, I'm actually not alone in my fandom. Surprisingly, around 23 percent of WWE fans are Black, and 50 percent are people of color. Perhaps predictable given these demographics, WWE fans are more left leaning than most sports fanbases, save for those of the WNBA, NBA, and European soccer. I also follow, like, virtually every Black female wrestler on Twitter or Instagram.

But being a WWE fan hasn't always been easy, especially when, for many years, the WWE has functioned as an oligarchy, cornering the market on wrestling in the US. Because of its TV deal, online accessibility, and integration into mainstream pop culture, it has existed for many years as the only game in town for casual wrestling fans for all intents and purposes.

That can make being a fan painful as hell. Watching a five-hour pay-per-view that doesn't even start until 8:00 p.m. on a Sunday can be an agonizing chore. You just know the company is going to make some ill-advised choice. Like having the longest-reigning world champion be a part-timer with low-level mic skills who wears shorts emblazoned with the Jimmy John's logo on it. Or cutting a problematic as hell ten-year deal with Saudi Arabia to host two pay-per-views a year that require bringing back from the dead some wrestler who was once popular in the eighties. Suffice it to say, one of my most masochistic relationships has been with wrestling and the associations and stereotypes that come with being a member of the wrestling fandom.

I know I shouldn't be supporting WWE, and yet, despite these issues, it was harder for me to break up with our subscription than it should be for a grown, Black, leftist woman. This is why our subscription had followed David and me from Oakland, California, to our new home in Baltimore, Maryland, where we would watch WrestleMania.

Despite the masochism, I'm also prone to self-reflection. What is it about the brand that compels me to subject myself to both the WWE's shitty programming and shitty business practices? Maybe it's because deep in my heart, I don't believe I deserve better; I don't have a right to demand higher standards.

I think the answer lies in the fantasy that wrestling has planted in my mind from a young age—a populist fantasy that imagines a world where the good guys win, and the rich and powerful guys lose. I relish the clarity and catharsis of it so much that I have allowed myself to give in to it, even when I know the fantasy is being manufactured and manipulated by WWE execs. I am still chasing the high—the simplicity of good and evil—that made me love wrestling as a kid.

Today, populism is associated with right-wing, white nationalism. But it wasn't always that way. At its core, populism is the idea that everyday people can come together and challenge the elite—those bathing in the trappings of conspicuous wealth who are disregarding their concerns. As Thomas Frank documents in his book, *The People, No: A Brief History of Anti-Populism,* American populism began as a left-wing farmer labor movement in the 1880s and 1890s. At the time, it was a radical call for large-scale government intervention in the economy on behalf of ordinary, working-class people—a far cry from the brand of populism we are familiar with today.

The simplest way to understand populism is through the framework that political theorist Ernesto Laclau laid out in his seminal work *On Populist Reason.* In it, he breaks down populism into three essential components: Us-Group Formation, Other-Group Formation, and Popular Demand.

Us-Group Formation is the coalescing of the aggrieved segment of the population—the everyday people who feel ignored by those in power.

Conversely, *Other-Group Formation* is the creation, in the minds of the *us-group*, of an antagonistic group who is responsible for the *us-group*'s difficulties. So, for everyday people, the *other-group* is the group of elites in their ivory towers. And finally, *Popular Demand* is the set of policy demands from the *us-group* it feels will solve its difficulties. So most essentially, populism is a collective push to reform or challenge capitalism in the interests of the real (or perceived) majority. And it is this core version of populism that WWE performs so intoxicatingly.

Sociologist Dan Glenday has called wrestling "a culturally embedded spectacle," a turbocharged version of the tensions playing out on the national stage. Wrestling, with its exaggerated narratives of good, evil, and the struggle of the everyman, is the perfect way to understand populism—its pitfalls and its undeniable draw. To do this, I'm going to look at one of the greatest populist left-wing speeches I've ever heard. Naturally it wasn't delivered by a politician, but by a wrestler: Virgil Riley Runnels, Jr. (October 12, 1945–June 11, 2015), most commonly known as Dusty "The American Dream" Rhodes.

There Is No Honor Among Thieves in the First Place

The American Dream represents many things to many people. For some, it means the possibility that anyone can break the barriers in front of them with goals, purpose, and fortitude. For others, it means the right to be a billionaire and buy everything one could want in life. And for others still, it means the right to live in an America where everyone can have a basic, healthy standard of living and quality of life.

But when I think about the American Dream, a different image comes to mind. I think of a sturdy and rugged individual who stood six-foot-three and weighed 289 pounds. Someone who moved with agility and had verbal game like Muhammad Ali—a beautiful combination of athletic prowess and savage MC skills.

I am talking, of course, about Hall of Fame wrestler Dusty "The American Dream" Rhodes.

For casual wrestling fans, the late Dusty Rhodes may be remembered because of his mentorship and leadership of some of the biggest stars in wrestling today, including his two sons Cody and Dustin Rhodes, both becoming executives and wrestlers at All Elite Wrestling (AEW). Some casual fans may remember Dusty Rhodes as the World Wrestling Federation (the precursor to WWE) creation "The Common Man," a moniker conjured up by WWE owner Vincent McMahon who meant to conflate "common" with "simple." They may remember him as a mid-card wrestler known for doing comical and oddly bizarre skits as a plumber or coal miner while dressed in a somewhat unflattering black leotard with yellow polka dots.

But the real ones know before that Dusty Rhodes was—and will always be—the headliner and iconic people's champ known as "The American Dream."

As I said before, part of wrestling's appeal is that it is an unapologetically populist endeavor. It sets up a dynamic between the elites and the heroic wrestler, the people's champion. The hero is a leader who isn't afraid to call out the rigged systems working against them. They represent the values that we as viewers embrace as our own. And the promos they cut—the short sound bites that end up plastered on T-shirts or replayed on YouTube—often pull from reality: news stories, politics, societal trends. The best promos are ones that resonate on multiple levels. They apply not just to the wrestler and their current story line but also to a broader collective consciousness and shared public sentiment.

The American Dream (or The Dream) is one of my favorite wrestlers of what's been called "The Golden Era," of wrestling (1980s–early 1990s). And in 1985, he gave *the* speech—an urgent, unapologetically political speech during a wrestling closed-circuit television event, a poetic harangue that, in my estimation, could be one of the greatest recorded leftist populist speeches of all time, referred to by wrestling fans as the "Hard Times" promo.

But before we get to the speech, here're a few wrestling terms I'm going to be using throughout this chapter:

Wrestling Lingo 101:

- **Promo:** A dialogue or monologue, usually in the form of a promotional interview (hence promo). It's usually scripted, and it's a plot device used to advance an angle.
- **Angle:** The plot or story line that kicks off or moves forward a "rivalry" between two or more wrestlers

- **Shoot:** Going off script on a promo, which gives the viewer the sense they're watching something real and spontaneous unfold in front of them
- **Face:** The hero you're supposed to root for
- **Gimmick:** The wrestler's distinguishable style or persona
- **Heel:** The clear villain you're supposed to boo
- **Kayfabe:** Preserving the illusion that wrestling is not scripted. An example of this may be two wrestlers beefing on Twitter despite being friends in real life
- **Work:** a scripted speech or dialogue

Returning to Ernesto Laclau, we can easily map these wrestling terms to his framework to see why WWE is so perfectly constructed to present a populist fantasy.

So, first up, there's the *Us-Group Formation*: this is the *face,* the victimized hero who represents the voice of the disgruntled masses. The *face* gives voice to all the trials and tribulations you are experiencing in your personal life, and places it in the broader context of group struggle.

Next, there's the *Other-Group Formation*: this is the *heel,* and the company in general, who represents the source of the angst not just for the *face* but for society broadly. The *heel* is the source of your trials and tribulations and the barrier to the group overcoming the struggles to success.

Finally, you have the *Popular Demand*: this is the *promo* or *shoot* moment that lays out the possibilities for a new normal where the *face* defeats the *heel* and ensures prosperity for all.

OK, so back to the "Hard Times" promo.

Let me set the stage for you. The American Dream had a short, permed, bleach-blond mullet. It resembled a dried-out Jheri curl, like he had haphazardly picked it out without putting some oil sheen on it first. Like he had been on the road for a while and left his Care Free Curl and shower cap at home. If you're wondering why I can speak so intimately about this, yes, I had a Jheri curl around this same time and I make no apologies.

And you just knew that although he was white, he would be comfortable at a table full of Black people animatedly playing spades—a Bill Burr vibe, if you will. If you brought him home, you knew he might say some wild stuff. He would probably have some race jokes about things you could only know if you had authentic relationships with Black people beyond the workplace or school. You didn't have to worry about that slightly uncomfortable feeling that comes over you when a white person starts getting too familiar and you begin to worry they may say something particularly out of pocket.

In the "Hard Times" promo, The Dream—who is the face—steps up to the mic to cut a promo for his ongoing feud with Ric Flair, a flamboyant and cocky heel known for wearing bedazzled $10,000 robes and swapping out his extensive Rolex watch collection on a whim.

As part of his gimmick, The Dream is wearing gold aviators with brown lenses. He has on jeans, a light gray pinstripe suit jacket with matching vest, a light pink dress shirt with the top button undone, and a navy paisley tie that is slightly askew around his neck. I don't want to say he looks vaguely coked out, so I will just leave it there. He was billed as "the son of a plumber," and this wasn't just kayfabe. In real life, his father was a nonunionized plumber who made $3.50 an hour and worked overtime to make sure his family was provided for. In his autobiography, The Dream contrasts that against the plumbers "of great wealth" who made $12–$14 an hour. He was raised in Austin, Texas, in a community predominantly of Black and Mexican Americans.

The promo starts like a standard monologue. He thanks the fans and his promotion company for standing by him and sending get-well-soon cards. The angle here is that he had beef with Ric Flair after the heel wrestler intentionally broke his ankle, putting him out of commission. He then makes it clear how he feels about Ric Flair, saying, "There is no honor amongst thieves in the first place," which, when taken with Ric's callous wealth, is almost too on the nose in its critique of late-stage capitalism.

And this is where the shoot picks up. The Dream looks directly into the camera, and it zooms in as the passion picks up in his voice: "He put hard times on Dusty Rhodes and his family. You don't know what hard times are, Daddy. Hard times are when the textile workers around this country are out of work; they got four or five kids and can't pay their wages, can't buy their food."

Suddenly, despite the pure absurdity of the scene, despite the intense breathing and how distractingly tiny the sunglasses are on his face, you're drawn in, because you realize The Dream isn't merely cutting a promo but delivering a populist sermon that not only reflected the times, but also was damn near prophetic. The country *was* freefalling into hard times, driven by corporate greed, deregulation, and growing disillusionment from years of civil unrest and economic decline. The speech served as a dire warning of the hard times that could befall a community that didn't stick together.

When the Dream gave his speech in 1985, the United States had recently gone through two recessions. Automation was beginning to displace low-wage workers across the country, and in the Midwest, auto workers were being hit especially hard. So it resonated when The Dream said, "Hard times are when the auto workers are out of work, and they tell 'em go home.... Hard times are when a man has worked at a job for thirty years—thirty years—and they give him a watch, kick him in the butt, and say, 'Hey, a computer took your place, Daddy.' That's hard times!"

Sound bites like these are the reason why up until The Dream died, people of all ages would come up to him, thanking him for honoring their plight. A cynical person could dismiss the speech as a *work*, especially without the context of his modest upbringing. In the promo, The Dream is not wearing a struggle outfit. As the top face on the roster at the time, he was probably making significantly more than the viewer watching him at home was. But regardless, you still got the feeling he understood you and you understood him.

Defining the "we" in a multicultural society is always a challenge. But in The Dream's promos, he always defined the "we" as a collective that cuts across racial boundaries. Whether you identified with John Wayne or Run-DMC or Flaco Jiménez, you knew Dusty Rhodes was holding a spot for you in his version of the American Dream and standing against a universally understood "them."

This is the reason why the "Hard Times" promo still stands alone as the greatest wrestling promo in history decades later. For three minutes in 1985, The American Dream cut to the heart of America: both who we are but also who we could be. What lives on forever is that for that moment, he made people forget their individual concerns and believe this country is capable of doing better by its people.

Listening to the promo, it's impossible not to draw comparisons to political rhetoric. The Dream was a man who knew how to give a political speech, and his "Hard Times" promo still serves as a template from which anyone seeking election should consider drawing. The Dream made you feel like him winning wasn't about him alone; it was about all of us. He made you feel like you were with him and, despite the shittiness of the world, maybe, just maybe, something different was possible if we were willing to take a leap of faith.

Sound familiar?

I don't know what The Dream's political affiliation was, but in a way, that's what makes the promo so great. Because there was a clear, broader critique of those holding power at that moment, it didn't matter which party was in charge. It was a sentiment that would continue to apply through many administrative swing shifts. While populism today is often associated with conservative politics, The Dream's speech uses a potent rhetorical tactic that has been deployed effectively for movement building by those on both sides of the aisle. Every time someone in power tries to say everything is fine, there will always be a group of people who feel like it's not. Who will see it's not. This is an inherent byproduct of capitalism, which intrinsically relies on an economic caste system that will always produce a disempowered group at the bottom and an entitled group that believes its own hype at the top.

A populist leader's success, therefore, is determined by their ability to activate the disgruntled masses for political gain. Because of this, a powerful leader, if not a demagogue, will always be the most effective—someone who can bring together the discontented group with a rallying cry. Dusty Rhodes, who often referred to himself as the John Wayne of wrestling, made for a good leader for the times. But the problem with populist leaders is when you're dealing with the best ones, it's hard to tell if a promo is a shoot or a work. It's hard to tell the difference between a powerful leader for the people, a demagogue, and a convincing perpetrator.

On television and in stadiums around the world, we are trained to respond to what's directly in front of us, not what's behind the stage. We're trained by the live audiences and the wrestlers themselves to understand who we're supposed to root for—the hero who fights his way to the top and beats the odds, pulling himself up by his bootstraps and manifesting his own version of the American Dream, much to the chagrin of the powers that be. And so even though we all know the game is ultimately rigged backstage, we remain active participants in the machine. The narratives are that powerful.

It took me a long time to question my love of WWE. Moments like the "Hard Times" promo transcended the gimmick. And those moments in wrestling are what hook you, what keep you paying your monthly subscription. In those moments, it feels larger than wrestling and larger than the theatrics. But at its core, the WWE is still a corporation, leveraging audience emotions and compelling narratives for a profit. And, like Pavlov's dogs, when nostalgia rings like a dinner bell, we're conditioned to come running.

To Be the Man, WOOO, You Gotta Beat the Man

"Left-wing populism doesn't work."

"Left-wing populism is the only thing that can work."

Most married couples fight about things like how or when to do the chores, terrible friends, overbearing in-laws, how to raise the kids, or how not to find your genitalia in the wrong place. But with David and me, our most throw-down, drag-out, "I want a divorce" fights tend to be about politics. We're not an ideologically diverse household. We've both been pretty left or at least progressive for our entire relationship. We agree on what policies the country needs, which politicians we like, and which politicians are the mega heels.

But where we collide is on populism and its ability to be a rhetorical tactic and tool for the Left to communicate a set of core values that speak to growing disillusionment. Marginalized communities and those who feel they are left out of dominant frames have long fought globally to be heard and to participate fully in shaping democracy and economy. Much of that has meant organizing in highly visible ways, often using the framework of populism and disillusionment with the status quo as the tool to try to effect change. But at the same time, we've seen right-wing populism take hold around the world, often anchored in a form of anti-immigrant nationalism, sometimes anchored in straight-up white nationalism. For David and me, our misalignment often stems from whether left-wing populism can ever work.

"We've been fighting for half the day about this," I said tiredly, my hands balled into fists.

"You know what happens when people get whipped into anger at others. Populism only works if people stay angry, and so populist leaders have to rely on keeping people angry even when you become 'the establishment,'" David responded, his face looking equally tired.

"I don't see how we get things like the New Deal, the labor wins of the early twentieth century—we don't get that without populism."

"You also don't get Trump without populism."

"People need to feel angry to make change." And people should be angry. People have a right to demand something better; we have the right to demand policies and leaders who can move the country from reactionary to visionary.

"If two high-profile populist movements are working at the same time, right-wing populism will win out because the one that has more control over the messaging platforms will win. This country is about 'rugged individualism'; that's how it was built. The people with the communications platforms are the people who cater to rugged individuals, and that's what pulls people toward the right wing. You know this."

"Bernie is a populist; he was able to move people using leftist populist language in service of something greater than rugged individualism."

"And guess how he was shut down? By mainstream publications drumming up fear by saying that Bernie is no different than Trump. I don't see how a populist left-wing agenda gets around that kind of bad-faith messaging."

Usually, David and my arguments end in stalemates. I'd like to think it's because neither of us is completely wrong or right. Online we've seen younger generations seeming to embrace populism more and more, both strands of it.

On the right, there's the presence of that younger, activated voting bloc that came out for Trump in 2016. In 2016, Trump surpassed expectations, winning one-third of young voters. More important, his younger voting base was more excited by the prospects of his presidency (32 percent) than young Clinton voters were about their candidate (18 percent).

But while populism is an effective way to activate a base of voters, it can be more difficult to lead from it. When a populist leader wins an election and becomes the establishment, they need to be able to show they're either making people's lives better or there's a greater enemy that still poses a threat. In the case of Trump, as unemployment rates skyrocketed and three COVID stimulus packages failed to make it to the community, it turned out that Make America Great Again worked a hell of a lot better as a slogan than Keep America Great. Moreover, particularly for younger voters of color, the 2020 Black Lives Matter protests made it easier to peg Trump (and not just "the powers that be") as a major threat to their lives and safety. Despite this, the January 6, 2021, insurrection at the United States Capitol showed right-wing populism isn't going anywhere anytime soon.

On the other hand, polling has shown Generation Z and millennials are more left wing. They grew up with parents saddled with student loan debt, they came of age during the 2008 recession and the housing crisis, and they don't want that for themselves. They want medical and health care systems to work and not just be a source of profit for private corporations. They want their institutions across the board to work.

It raises the question: Can multiethnic/racial populism actually be successful? That's hard to answer. There are signs it has worked in the past, but it hasn't proven sustainable. The power of capitalism is its ability to shift just enough chips around to make just enough people think it works for them, inevitably creating a wedge.

This can happen even within marginalized groups. I think about this in relation to the populist underpinnings of the twentieth century's civil rights movement and where things went wrong (or to the right). When the work of enforcing civil rights wins and antidiscrimination policies became the purview of businesses and corporate entities via human resources strategies and diversity initiatives, poor Black people were increasingly deprioritized. Labor fights took a backseat to fights for representation in boardrooms and "breaking the glass ceiling" as opposed to lifting the floor for all—even more so as the Reagan and Clinton eras took a sledgehammer to unions.

Ultimately, the movement ended up being steered more by a Black middle-class vision of prosperity mirrored in cultural products like *The Cosby Show*—which eschewed populism and embraced respectability and bootstraps politics—than by the poor Black economic conditions that had been the source of populist uprisings in the 1960s. As the racial wealth gap, which had been steadily closing since the passage of FDR-era New Deal policies, began to widen again in an era of deregulation and corporate consolidation, the Black middle and upper classes also concentrated resources. Identity politics became more about dressing up neoliberalism in a coat of many colors than leveraging Black culture and organizing to win economic power at scale.

Inevitably, anti-Black racism is such a permanent part of the American imagination that we are considered disposable in multiracial movements on both the Left and Right. At the same time, no leftist wins in this country have happened without us. So, are we permanently stuck in a draw?

You Can Call This the New World Order, Brother

"There's an AEW pay-per-view on tonight."

"Oh, nice, order it up. I'll get the pizza."

David and I were sitting out on our roof deck. That TV we had carried up the stairs after our road trip hadn't been big enough, so we had bought a projector to have one hundred inches of wrestling on our wall. But despite this, we had finally gotten rid of our WWE subscription. There comes a time when the mental gymnastics you have to do to make peace with something get to be too much.

No one could ever accuse the McMahon family of being heroes. For decades they have relished being greedy, shameless villains in wrestling story lines. But at a certain point, their offscreen villainy became harder and harder to ignore. Several incidents kept piling up. We had long known the McMahons were Republicans. But it was one thing to know that and another to watch Linda McMahon leave her position at WWE to go serve as Trump's administrator of the Small Business Administration from 2017 to 2019. It was yet another to see documented reports of the WWE's abusive behavior grow. It simply got too hard to subject ourselves to both the WWE's shitty programming and shitty business practices. The line between real and kayfabe villainy became too thin to ignore.

I was reminded of this during our cross-country road trip. We had basked in all the Americana our route had to offer. We visited the Steinbeck Museum in California and I saw the Grand Canyon for the first time. We stopped in Tombstone, Arizona, and learned Wyatt Earp and Doc Holliday don't come off nearly as good in real life as they do in the movies. We walked under the world's largest rose tree, which felt like a little slice of heaven. We sent photos to our parents to let them know we were OK. Feeling all-Americana, of course we had to put on Creedence Clearwater Revival and turn the volume all the way up.

Heading out of Arizona, we cut through New Mexico and made our way toward El Paso, Texas, and then hit State Highway 9, which snakes along the Mexican border. We were so close to Mexico, our phones kept threatening to charge us international roaming fees. For a long time, we saw only border patrol cars. The officers inside stared us down with walkie-talkies at their mouths, their eyes roaming to confirm the number of people in our car stayed the same with each car we passed.

We saw yellow crossing signs, many of them shot up with bullet holes. "For target practice," David said. I didn't have to ask who the shooters were practicing for. We both knew.

"Uh-oh," David said, glancing up at the rearview mirror nervously.

"What?"

"White nationalists, incoming."

I looked out the side window. A caravan with Michigan license plates drove up alongside us. Black SUVs, all American made.

I slumped down in the car; neither of us wanted to make eye contact. David pulled over to let the caravan pass us. All white dudes. In sunglasses. Stalking the highway like predators. It felt like the beginning of a horror movie, when the bubbly couple gets unceremoniously slaughtered before the opening credits begin.

As the SUVs drove past, we saw white nationalist stickers and slogans peppered the back of each of them:

> A Blue Lives Matter sticker
> A Reclaim America sticker
> An "All Lives Splatter" sticker, with the picture of an SUV
>   running over stick figures

In that moment, despite my hope for the potential of leftist populism, despite the promise of the "Hard Times promo," despite what The Dream always has and always will mean to me, I was reminded that the danger of populism is that in the wrong hands, it can be a tool for decimation.

Interlude: Because We Are Not Who They Say We Are . . .
Why It Matters Who Tells Your Story

CBS Studio in Downtown Chicago:

STEVEN BARTELSTEIN: This morning at 4:30, more gunfire captures a busy night in the city, including the shooting death of a sixteen-year-old boy.

SUSAN CARLSON: The gunman remains on the loose right now. This shooting happened just before 10:00 in the 3700 block of South Albany. Police say a sixteen-year-old boy was shot to death in a drive-by. The victim's identity has not yet been released.

Over time, I have learned to understand the power of story: the ones we tell ourselves, the ones we tell others, and the ones that are told about us. And, as my friend Joseph Torres, coauthor of the book *News for All the People,* often says: when other people tell our stories, they often get it wrong.

In media and in storytelling, framing is everything. This is what I mean when I say "frame." Have you ever posted a photo on social media? Have you ever added a filter to make the photo seem brighter or darker? Have you ever done some photo retouching to get rid of circles under your eyes from partying the night before? Have you ever chopped out an ex or someone you don't really fuck with anymore?

That's you framing that picture for your audience—friends, family, exes, strangers who care. It's how you craft the narrative you want to put into the world.

Every day, the media is framing the content we receive. That's true in newspapers, online, and on local and national news. Oftentimes, those framers are telling stories about communities they're not even from, and I don't just mean that racially. Many news anchors travel around to different affiliates, and where they end up getting jobs is not necessarily the community where they grew up. It is problematic that the media operates as the gatekeepers of our shared history and the key narrators of our stories.

Most of us, whether we want to or not, form our opinion of what's real and true based on what we see in the media, and yet the power and mechanics of framing—and the biases they stem from and perpetuate—are often absent in journalism training. This was something I saw firsthand when I interviewed Maya, a Gen Z journalism student. She's a smart, happy-go-lucky girl and Black (in case you hadn't guessed). She was raised in a DC suburb, and I interviewed her over video as she sat in her parents' backyard with her dog playing behind her. I've known her since she was a little kid and, like me, she always liked the news and politics. In addition to studying journalism, she recently picked up a political science minor. The journalism school where she's studying is in the top ten percentile ranking of journalism schools in the country, which is why I was astonished to learn how they address bias in their curriculum.

> **BRANDI:** In journalism school, how do they teach about bias? What's considered bias?
>
> **MAYA:** Yeah. So, like, in journalism school, bias, they've taught us, includes interviewing friends and family members, having connections with the people who you get your information from. So that's, like, a big no-no. If I'm doing a story on Black Lives Matter protests where I live, I can't interview my friends; that'd be considered bias. And also issues you have a close connection to . . . They tell you if you feel really passionate about something, maybe it's not best to write about it because your opinion just gets filtered in with facts and stuff like that.

BRANDI: Do you learn anything about how certain words, tone, and framing can impact how people receive information?

MAYA: In journalism school? Not really. Honestly, I feel like I learned about this more in my political science classes than in my journalism classes. Recently, we learned how local news stations have an impact on government policies . . . the way it frames crime and how they may only show primarily Black people as suspects involved with violent crime. Or even that all crime is necessarily violent—like drug use. We learn how, in turn, voters and policy makers will go and support more punitive policies, which expand the carceral system. So things like that, the way the media frames issues and the impact on the public, that's stuff they don't go into in journalism school.

BRANDI: It seems like if you're a journalist and not a political science person and you don't get that information, then you can really miss out.

MAYA: For sure. In my poli-sci classes they're always, like, "Watch the media; be careful in how it frames things." And in journalism it's, like, "Don't be biased," but they don't really talk about how or why framing matters.

What Happens When They Get It Wrong . . .

CBS STUDIO IN DOWNTOWN CHICAGO:

BARTELSTEIN: Meantime, two teenagers are wounded on the city's South Side. It happened at East 74th, where an eighteen-year-old man and sixteen-year-old girl were hit while standing on the sidewalk. The male's in good condition while the girl is expected to recover. And kids on the street as young as four were there to see it all unfold. And [now for] a disturbing reaction.

> *Video footage cuts to a young, Black four-year-old on the street being interviewed by an anonymous reporter.*

FOUR-YEAR-OLD: I'm not scared of nothing.

ANONYMOUS REPORTER: When you get older, are you gonna stay away from all these guns?

FOUR-YEAR-OLD: No. (*shakes head and crosses arms*)

ANONYMOUS REPORTER: No! What do you want to do when you get older?

FOUR-YEAR-OLD: I'm gonna have me a gun.

FOOTAGE CUTS TO A YOUNG WOMAN (POSSIBLY A TEEN-AGE GIRL) LIVING IN THE COMMUNITY. SHE'S BEING INTER-VIEWED IN A DIFFERENT LOCATION.

YOUNG WOMAN (OR GIRL): I live right here, and I don't want my family members to get shot.

Camera cuts back to the news studio, where Bartelstein is shaking his head sadly.

BARTELSTEIN: That is very scary, indeed. So far, no suspects are in custody.

CARLSON: Hearing that little boy there, wow!

Chicago CBS affiliate, 2011 (footage captured by
Maynard Institute)

It's a familiar refrain to me: some version of "If you care so much about Black lives mattering, you should tell that to the people on the South Side of Chicago who are killing each other." Bartelstein, with his somber "that is very scary, indeed," in one sentence telegraphs a whole story about Chicago and about Black people on the South Side of Chicago. The story? That we're all born to fail. We raise babies who are monsters and from the age of four, they have murder on their mind. The punctuation by Carlson—"Hearing that little boy there, wow!"—rings to me of condemnation of Black parenting. It's a very familiar frame, one I've heard laced into the reactions to the various communities I've called home throughout my life.

I've lived in quite a few places. Three of them—Chicago, Oakland, and Baltimore—are widely considered scary places. I don't think it's an accident that they're all etched in our minds as being very Black places.

Your family's from the South Side of Chicago . . . that's a tough place.

—*ANONYMOUS FRIEND WHO GREW UP IN OAKLAND, CA*

You live in Oakland now! That's like crack rock city, right?

—*ANONYMOUS WORK COLLEAGUE THAT GRADUATED
FROM JOHNS HOPKINS UNIVERSITY IN BALTIMORE, MD*

You're moving to Baltimore? They shoot people there, don't
they?

—*ANONYMOUS FAMILY MEMBER CALLING
FROM THE SOUTH SIDE OF CHICAGO, IL*

Buried in those reactions to my home cities, current and past, is an inherent indictment of Black people and our "uncontrollable urges" to kill each other. People don't even need to say *Black*. When they're talking about Chicago, they're not talking about the Italian and Irish mobs run by Al Capone, James "Little Jimmy" Marcello, or Dean O'Bannon. They're talking about Black people.

Beyond the obvious flattening and generalizing, what's missing from these reactions is the nuance that civil unrest doesn't just come from one triggering event but rather a series of grievances layered on top of one another until it becomes a powder keg ready to explode. Police practices, underemployment, ineffective political structures, and the inadequacy of federal programs all play a role in driving a community to the brink. And in an ironic full circle, failures by the media to tell a complete Black story often play the biggest role in creating barriers to advancements and community revitalization efforts.

Harmful pathologies about Black families run rampant across media, derailing conversations about social safety net programs. And studies have repeatedly shown that Black political candidates—particularly Black women—receive coverage that's more about their race than their issue platform.

Media narratives reinforce the idea that Black people have failed within the system when the truth is the system has failed Black people. Racism is often rendered invisible while the question of accountability goes unanswered.

Our stories are often told without our consent, our voice, or our context. This was reinforced for me when, during the BLM summer of 2020, I watched in horror as social media circulated a video of my little cousin being tased repeatedly and dragged out of his car by Atlanta police during a protest. As the video of the incident went viral, different videos were released without his parents' consent or knowledge, including previously unreleased body cam footage.

Headlines and stories speculated on his background, minimizing him and his life story. Many of those stories ran without the reporters ever talking to him, members of the family, or even eyewitnesses. On the same page or within minutes of telling his story, mainstream outlets followed up with feel-good stories that glorified the humanity of police officers even as people watched videos of his humanity being stripped away. And it doesn't feel fair. Not at all. It feels infuriating, in fact.

From the moment we're born, can walk, can talk, Black people are seen as menaces to society. That's the frame we live in and work to break out of. And every day, the media perpetuates that.

What's most devastating about this is Black people consistently exhibit the highest levels of trust for local and national news and are among the most avid news consumers. According to Pew Research Center, in 2019, a third of Black adults said they trusted information coming from the local news, and 80 percent of Black adults said they expect national news stories will be accurate. Black people are also more likely to feel connected to their main source of news and are more likely to view members of the media as necessary watchdogs that provide a check and balance to political leaders.

This means that often, as Black people, we absorb the damaging stories told about us. In absorbing those stories, we run the risk of internalizing the same pathology non-Black people have about us. We start to feel disconnected from certain Black people because we begin to look at them as they are presented via the news. This has become even more of an issue as we've seen a rapid decrease in Black-owned and controlled news spaces on- and offline. All of those people who shared with me their respective negative associations of Baltimore, Chicago, and Oakland? Those were Black folks.

So let's rewind back to the CBS footage. As a refresher, a four-year-old boy is being interviewed in Chicago after a shooting in a South Side community. He tells the onsite reporter he wants to get a gun. But it just so happened that someone in the news station wasn't down with the editing, so they tipped off the Robert C. Maynard Institute for Journalism Education, which got hold of the original footage. And here's how the conversation really went:

> **FOUR-YEAR-OLD:** I'm not scared of nothing.
>
> **ANONYMOUS REPORTER:** That's what I like to hear; you ain't scared of nothing. Damn. When you get older you gonna stay away from all these guns?
>
> **FOUR-YEAR-OLD:** No. (*shakes head and crosses arms*)
>
> **ANONYMOUS REPORTER:** No! What do you want to do when you get older?
>
> **FOUR-YEAR-OLD:** I'm gonna have me a gun.
>
> **ANONYMOUS REPORTER:** You are! Why do you want to do that? Do you know what happens to these—?
>
> **FOUR-YEAR-OLD:** (adamantly) I'm gonna be the police.
>
> **ANONYMOUS REPORTER:** OK, well, then, you can have one.

So, now a story about this four-year-old monster is actually one about a little boy who is bound and determined to make his community safe. We can dissect the choice of law enforcement as the best route for that. But putting that to the side, the story reads quite differently with just one more sentence: *I'm gonna be the police.*

There's not a parent in sight; it's not even clear the reporters got approval to interview a four-year-old. But if that parent was there and heard their child say they wanted to be a police officer, I think they would've been proud of that. In fact, they may have been horrified to see how the media then went on to reframe their child. Also, WHY THE HELL ARE THEY INTERVIEWING FOUR-YEAR-OLDS? Beyond that, we never learn anything about the people who were shot. There are no interviews with their family or friends. We don't even know the victims' names. They're just dead bodies that serve as props for a broader frame about violent Black children on the South Side of Chicago being groomed to kill.

When the unedited footage came out, CBS scrambled to issue an apology. But I can pretty much guarantee you that the number of people who heard about the apology doesn't even come close to the number of people who watched the original airing of that story. It makes me wonder how often that happens. It sends a chill up my spine to think about how many Black stories are reworked just like that.

As Napoleon is rumored to have said, "History is a set of lies agreed upon." I want to add to that: history is a set of stories agreed upon that have been told and shaped by those with the means and power to enforce that story.

We live in a society where three quarters of white people don't have any nonwhite friends. Even if people have a more diverse friend group when they're younger—in elementary school or even through college—by the time people get into adulthood, they begin to settle into a permanent social circle that's more homogeneous.

That data point means most of what non-Black people understand about Black people tends to come from how Black people are shown in cultural products and how they are seen in the media. And perhaps even worse, much of what Black people understand to be true about ourselves is based on how we're reflected in media not owned or controlled by us. As a result, we often receive and accept warped programming about who we were, who we are, and who we can be.

7

Hood Vampires
Making Magic in Dark Surroundings

"You made a movie?" I asked excitedly, turning to Vic.

He nodded seriously. "*Hood Vampires.*"

We were sitting on the couch at my cousin Eric's apartment in Washington, DC. Eric, or Skillz Ferguson as he goes by, makes hip-hop music. We had recently reconnected after too many years had gone by without much more than a passing "like" on Instagram. Most recently, he had left a comment that just said "BARS!!!" under a video I had posted doing a corny freestyle rap about net neutrality for work.

After my dad died, we had started talking more, and he told me about how much he loved my dad, how seeing my dad, growing up around him, and being able to call him any time had been a source of inspiration to him. It had reminded him that he could experience a life that wasn't confined by the boundaries of the projects. One night, we found ourselves talking about drill music, which I had started listening to in the last months of my dad's life because it soothed me. It was a place to channel my inner rage in a more constructive way.

"I have a friend that does drill," Eric said. "Want to meet him?"

"Yes! When?"

"He's in town this week, if you want to come through."

Two trains and a bus ride later, I was in DC, where I proceeded to wait another two hours in Eric's lobby because my family stays being late all the time. But soon enough, we were in his apartment, eating a late dinner and talking to his friend Vic. Vic is from Chicago and was part of the early scene of what we now call drill. He's tall, Black (in case you hadn't guessed), has a quiet presence, and always seems to be observing his surroundings, taking everything in, processing the life going on around him.

If Black skinheads had a soundtrack, drill—a subgenre and culture of hip-hop—would be one of the top contenders. Similar to goth music, it is a camp performance of mourning and hyperrealism. Also like goth, it delves into themes of depression, disillusionment, and has flirted with the occult at times. But instead of white suburban kids cosplaying in Victorian attire, drill casts working-class youth—mostly Black, Indigenous, and people of color—in the role of the mourner. As I watched my dad die, I found it was the only music that I had an appetite for, because it was the only sounds that encapsulated my mounting frustration, anger, and overwhelming sadness. Drill was one of the few anchors I had that kept me from engaging in more destructive behavior.

It's also a uniquely modern creation of the post-2008 global recession that has been made possible through new forms of technology and communications platforms like YouTube. In the 1980s, Public Enemy's Chuck D famously said, "Hip-hop is Black America's CNN." And, to a certain extent, that is very much true. But in many ways, it's not. Or at least the kind of news that rap is shouldn't be read or processed in the same way you may process the actual CNN.

Rap, even when it was party music filling the dance breakdown in a disco song, has always been a direct reflection of the immediate environment that surrounds it. It can be as mundane as going to your friend's house for dinner and "the macaroni's soggy, the peas are mushed, and the chicken tastes like wood" (The Sugarhill Gang's "Rapper's Delight"). Or you could be talking about playing basketball last week and your game was so on point you "fucked around and got a triple-double" (Ice Cube's "It Was a Good Day"). OR you could be talking about feeling so paranoid and unsafe in your community that you are not able to sleep at night and you see "candlesticks in the dark, visions of bodies being burned" (Geto Boys' "Mind Playing Tricks on Me").

Within various hip-hop movements, we've seen signs of the Black skinhead, the disillusioned political outlier who tells the story mainstream media is missing. An extension of the African diaspora, hip-hop is anchored in an immigration and migration story of people from the Southern United States; Caribbean; South, Central, and Latin Americas. It was made by people whose paths initially converged in the predominantly Black, economically depressed South Bronx in the 1970s before spreading across the different New York boroughs and beyond. Together they forged a new world and shared a cultural identity. In the hands of the community, rap is an art form of interconnected folktales drawn from the everyday highs and lows of life. But that is the thing about rap and hip-hop. It is as much a folktale as it is a reflection of reality. It is not CNN. It is not the Channel 9 News. It tells an untold story, yes. It can tell an important truth. But, like any other art form, you're meant to glean the lessons or be entertained by the story, not give it a literal reading.

When we listen to folktales, we automatically assume there's a bit of truth, a bit of hyperbole, and a bit of fantasy. Take "Little Red Riding Hood," for example. Embedded in the tale are all the stories of little girls who are stolen in one way or another, never to be heard from again. Of the "wolves" that prey on them. But nobody above the age of five thinks this broad is actually talking to a wolf. Nobody thinks that wolves are out here dressed like Grandma trying to get some blueberry muffins or whatever the little girl had in her basket. Nobody thinks the Brothers Grimm cosplayed as wolves and murdered little girls so they could tell the story "authentically." We all understand this to be *just* a story.

But often, the folktales of rap are taken verbatim. The frame placed on rap music focuses on the perceived failures of a culture. We don't read and process the music in the same way we would, say, a violent Quentin Tarantino film or every country music lady's song out here talking about killing motherfuckers. Instead, in the absence of other narratives about Black people, the literal interpretation of rap serves to activate the middle class's moral panic and, specifically, white people's. This frame simultaneously feeds into the damaging narratives we saw earlier and ignores the truth rap contains, corrupting an art form and a culture that have long been a crucial form of resistance for Black folks against these very stories.

Though hip-hop culture has working-class roots and still is a draw for working-class artists and creators, up until the internet age, much of what made it to the centralized airwaves like MTV and radio stations was dictated by a small group of mostly young, Black, middle-class males working in concert with record producers, executives, and publicists. The music then started being tailored toward a mostly white, suburban audience whose interest in rap, in the words of hip-hop scholar David Samuels, "rested in its evocation of an age-old image of Blackness: a foreign, sexually charged, and criminal underworld against which the norms of white society are defined."

I'm implicated in this, too. As a young, middle-class kid, I totally fed into the whole Tupac-versus-Biggie debate and cosplayed as someone who was really about that life when I knew damn well I wasn't. But, I mean, really, who hasn't lost their phone and going-out privileges for a significant period of time because your middle-class ass was dumb enough to send a roll of film to Walgreens that contained photos of you and your friends casually posing with guns. Who hasn't been so stupid, they didn't even bother to put their gun cosplay photos under a different name, so when your parents went to pick up their photos from the Tennessee family reunion, they witnessed your lame attempt to recreate an early '90s music video? Who hasn't come home to your mom yelling at you for being *a dumb bitch out here playing recklessly with guns?* Just me? I'm alone in this? Cool.

In my own defense, I also knew it was a fantasy life that wasn't indicative of Black culture. But under the white gaze, it became exactly that. Hip-hop and its creators became the boogeyman disturbing Middle America, monsters that rose up out of the swamps from the hood with a need and want to destroy America. But the reality is that a culture built on several elements, including urban folktales, was stripped down to its most base elements and leveraged as a means to indict Black people, Black product, and Black culture. And through that, it became a billion-, probably trillion-dollar-plus industry. And its storytellers, like Vic, became increasingly targeted for police surveillance.

With hip-hop and rap music, the songs and their artists are often read as an indictment of a corrupt Black culture and degradation of the English language. They're never just read as a constitutionally protected art form. The language of hip-hop is never seen as a beautifully encrypted preservation and observation of street life. The music, to the extent it should be dissected, should be seen as an indictment of society and the policies that devastate Black communities.

Instead, we criminalize the storyteller or the rapper, turning them into the malignant Black skinhead who needs to be suppressed, surveilled, and incarcerated. Just like how (as discussed in a previous chapter) a Chicago local news outlet took a little boy who wants to be a police officer so he can protect his community and turn him into a little sociopathic monster who should be feared and surveilled. What we're served up as the broad representation of rap and hip-hop culture is defined and framed within a very narrow scope.

Crazy Story

From a product standpoint, hip-hop can be divided into four distinct elements:

- DJing, which includes beatmaking and turntablism;
- MCing, also known as rapping, cyphering, or rhyming. In its original form, MCing was a form of spoken word that would tie-in to contemporaneous issues;
- break dancing, also known as B-boying or breaking. A freestyle, more physical form of dance that was both influenced by lindy hop acrobatics but also breaks from the traditional norms of partner dancing;
- finally graffiti art, which reimagines and designs urban environments by turning any space into a canvas.

Writer The Black Dot, who wrote the book *Hip-Hop Decoded,* posits that these four elements can be read as a sacred art and culture that comprises a type of religious and cerebral experience: the sacred word, drumbeats, dance, and a master of ceremonies. In my own words, I understand The Black Dot's description of hip-hop to be like Captain Planet, made up of earth, fire, wind, and water. The heart flows through all of it. Now, full disclosure: The Black Dot would also be considered by many to be something of a conspiracy theorist, because of his espoused beliefs in the Black Illuminati. But I want to stay with this idea that hip-hop culture and its power comes from its complete experience.

As hip-hop culture has become increasingly commodified and whitewashed for public consumption, the four core elements are often broken up and exist in their own bubbles. Sometimes they overlap, but they are often consumed separately in a way they were not consumed in the beginning. The Black Dot says the breaking of this sacred Black experience allows a subculture that was meant to be a tool of resilience to be turned into something that can be weaponized against Black and working-class people.

In the 1970s and 1980s, as hip-hop culture was forming, several laws and policies were put on the books that would both physically isolate the collective elements of hip-hop and individually criminalize people within the genre, muting this form of Black resistance. The Noise Pollution and Abatement Act of 1972 initiated a federal program of regulating what was called "noise pollution." Over the next decade plus, local legislation and law enforcement practices would develop that gave police officers and prosecutors permission to break up public gatherings in urban areas and criminalize DJs under the guise of protecting "human health and minimizing annoyance of noise to the general public."

In 1982, as hip-hop and its expressions were becoming increasingly public, criminologists introduced into the public lexicon the "broken windows theory," which posited that visible signs of "crime, antisocial behavior, and civil disorder," create an urban environment in which people become savages. They didn't frame it exactly that way, but this is the gist. That theory was used as a way to pass a series of legislations and develop police enforcement practices that were aimed at minimizing "vandalism," which targeted graffiti artists, and "loitering," which targeted street performers like B-boys and girls.

These regressive law-and-order practices, when taken in their totality and combined with a much-amplified media narrative of Black lawlessness, helped cultivate an atmosphere of fear and political retaliation that was used to disrupt Black community spaces. And community responses to aggressive acts of policing and harmful policies were channeled through Black music, especially in the emerging youth music of rap.

As I write this, I'm thinking about both of my parents, who worked to give me the comforts of an environment where police officers felt called to protect the community, not terrorize it. I think about the stories of their own experiences with law enforcement. Ones that were unfamiliar to me.

My dad recounted a story to me of when he had gone to a burger place after basketball practice one day. He would spend hours practicing basketball, his primary focus getting out of the projects of Syracuse, New York. He barely had any money, so that burger he bought was his main meal of the day.

> I had gotten that burger, and I remember I was starving. A police officer almost immediately stopped me; he pulled a gun. I knew I couldn't move a muscle, or he would shoot me. He snatched the bag out of my hand and riffled through it. I wasn't doing anything but trying to eat. Seeing that there wasn't a threat, he pulled out the burger and just threw it on the ground and walked away. I was so hungry I thought about whether or not to pick up that burger, but I didn't want to give that police officer the satisfaction of seeing me crawl.

His voice, which for a second drifted away, got deeper again.

> There are things that have happened in my life, but I was so used to being treated a certain way that it didn't bother me as much as it should have. I just got back in the game and kept going. But now looking back and thinking about things that happened to me, my friends, my family, the bitterness is still there.

My mom talked about growing up on the South Side of Chicago and always seeing the police as a looming threat instead of a force for good. City laws were created so three or more people standing out on a corner and sharing the same physical space could be considered gang members. They used this shit to just go after Black kids—kids who were out here not doing anything wrong. Just trying to find a place to go. She used to go out to do the family's laundry with her brother, and in the summer, it would get so hot in there because of all the dryers. They would go outside to talk to friends and stay a little cooler and, as she tells it . . .

> The police would just show up to harass us.
> They would make us go to the dryers and point out which ones were ours and tell them what our clothes looked like. They'd be going through our underwear in the washer, just violating our

space like it meant nothing. That's what they still do to these kids out here. We don't get to be kids. Look at Tamir [Rice], you can't even let your kids play with a toy gun like all little boys do without worrying about your child being murdered. What the hell is that?

But on the public stage, that's not the main story. Instead, the dominant public narrative is framed squarely on Black people's lawlessness. And the violent posturing of hip-hop and rap culture is used to reinforce a story that justifies violence leveraged on Black communities.

For me, hip-hop culture still feels deeply embedded in that Black experience and feeling of shared struggle. Like sampling in hip-hop— taking pre-existing recordings and layering them together to create a completely new piece of music—Black culture has a wide range of influences and origins. But when woven together, it creates something that is uniquely ours.

And listen. I know there are white rappers out there offering their authentic expressions and experiences. They're fine. This is not about them.

On the Corner

For hip-hop artists, the music is not just an outlet but also a way to make magic. At least that's how my friend Vic, the drill artist, tells it. Not just the magic of spinning a folktale that reimagines your everyday realities, but the magic of producing literal capital that can make the illusion of a different world real.

Drill music is very aggressive, chaotic, and rude. When they talk about spraying or peppering people, they are not talking about doing that with water or seasoning. Lyrically, it's probably made up of a lot of things that offend my values and senses in virtually every other setting. To be honest, I can't say I recommend it unless you're desensitized to violence. But after years of having to look at and analyze videos and media coverage of Black people in various stages of being killed or tortured by law enforcement and racists not in law enforcement, I am sufficiently desensitized.

I mentioned earlier that drill is a modern creation of the post-2008 global recession that is made possible through new forms of technology and communications platforms like YouTube. Here's what I mean by that: it's a global phenomenon. YouTube is populated with reaction videos of people doing drill from all possible corners of the world telling their own community stories. Reaction videos have become a way for the content to circulate, as it's often censored or algorithmically smothered on platforms at the request of police who work in nebulous ways with social media companies to monitor, surveil, and suppress the music and related cultural pieces.

But the culture behind it is too strong to be totally stamped down. Drill music puts a sound to the disillusionment of a city or community deprived of capital and investment. It feels like that experience of watching a horror movie with your hands covering your face and your eyes peeking through your fingers. It's a performance of camp pain and expression that feels more authentic to me than the goth or gothic music and subculture that appealed to me when I was a middle-class teenager in Middle America. It's something that globally resonates with people who experience the crushing weight of policing and the cutting off of resources to their community. People who have made magic in the darkness of their everyday surroundings.

There are many casual listeners who will swear it is from the UK or New York City. But nah, it's from Chicago.

The first decade of twenty-first-century hip-hop was dominated by club anthems and the second wave of consciousness music. An outsize amount was being produced or shepherded by Kanye West. In the 2000s, Chicago had seen an explosion of rappers like Lupe Fiasco, Rhymefest, and rapper-philosopher-turned-actor Common. In many ways, their music more reflected both the levity and pressure of Black life, particularly during the rise of President Obama. The duality of the moment would even play out among the Chicago artists themselves. Both Kanye and Lupe would become outspoken critics of President Obama, while Common's invitation to perform at an "Evening of Poetry" event at the White House would be weaponized by the right wing as a sign of Obama's horrific thuggery.

Common is already objectively nonthreatening unless you find incense, Black love, and stylish attire threatening. But compared to the new crop of drill rappers, he is altogether wholesome. Drill is inspired by clique-based gang life. The videos often look like something filmed on a Nokia flip phone with, like, a hundred dudes throwing gang signs, most with their faces covered. I'm sure many of them in 2020 videos are simply trying to be considerate about COVID. However, some drillers do it because they're under surveillance and are not allowed to be seen with their friends. They're assumed to be gang affiliated, and, let's be real, some of them are. But why gangs may exist in a community is as important a question to ask as what and who are perceived as gang members.

I see gangs and community organizing as flip sides of the same coin—organizational structures operating outside the realm of traditional politics. Both are responses to failures or gaps in societal institutions and infrastructure. One is considered legal, the other isn't, but both have long operated under surveillance.

It is not an accident that drill and its affiliated culture emerged just as people were feeling the impacts of the 2008 recession. In the early to mid-twentieth century, Black people arrived in Chicago in droves from the South, looking for new opportunities and new lives for their families. Homeownership was crucial to building wealth in Cook County, where Chicago is located. Even when many people began to leave the city in the 1980s and 1990s, families settled into disproportionately Black suburban areas in the southern portion of Cook County. But in 2008, a devastating number of Black people lost their homes, losing their wealth and equity. Median house prices in the northern (white) part of the county continued to hold steady, recover, and rise while the median house prices in the southern part of the county plummeted.

At the same time, Black-owned businesses, cultural spaces, and community centers closed en masse. By 2013, fifty Chicago public schools in mostly Black and Brown neighborhoods were closed. Any resources or options that people had to pursue better options or ways of life drained out of the Black city and suburban neighborhoods. This triggered a massive exodus—or a reverse Great Migration—of Black families out of Chicago. A record 181,000 Black residents left the city between 2000 and 2010, more than any other city besides Detroit.

It was under these conditions that the sound of drill began to emerge from the streets of Chicago. In 2011, the song "I Don't Like" would make then sixteen-year-old Chief Keef an instant Chicago legend. How could it not be; what was more Chicago than talking about all the shit you don't mess with? His album *Finally Rich* introduced the world to a new wave of Chicago sounds, rappers, and producer Young Chop. They weren't like Common. These were people who would probably never be invited to the White House, and they were fine with that. They might be too tempted to blow it up (like Chief Keef had threatened to blow up New Jersey) when they got there anyways.

Drill in many ways is like a musical riot, it is the language of the unheard, and—like it or not—the lyrics and sounds forced America (and eventually the world) to hear and see the things many had failed to acknowledge. It became a channel for the stories of people who were not the face of the Occupy movement that would pop off in September 2011 but were experiencing the crushing weight of what it meant to be at the bottom of an economic caste system that works for so few people.

By 2011, we had a Black president. A Black president from Chicago. Black people should've been feeling like we were winning. But as is often the case, despite having a Black president from Chicago, Black people were losing, and that felt particularly acute in the city.

That was something Vic saw up close and personal. He watched as libraries shut down, replaced by alcohol and clothing stores—none of which were owned by Black people. He saw all the places where kids could go and be kids disappear at an alarming rate. Drill music, he said, helped him make sense of it—the anger, the disappointment, the disillusionment. The music helped him stay sane and productive. See why I call it the soundtrack of Black skinheads?

No Rules

The American Dream (as long as you aren't into WWE) is the belief anyone, regardless of where they were born or what class they were born into, can attain success. The American Dream promotes the idea that upward mobility is possible for everyone.

Hip-hop culture challenged the ways the American Dream could be attained. You could get there through hustling, drug dealing, or other means. But eventually, you would still go legit, and you would get the house in the suburbs. You would scare the good white people in your new hood. And though you never forgot where you came from, ultimately you were supposed to want to be away from the community. You were not supposed to want to stay where you were.

As hip-hop became absorbed into the mainstream, the media began to reflect the story of the kid who makes it out of the hood and becomes the new version of the American Dream. When watching the NBA or NFL Draft or any of the games, inevitably there's a human-interest story about the kid who made it out of the hood, achieved the American Dream, and became something. But that story—that anyone can make it if they just work hard enough—is the true illusion.

A study released in 2015 found Americans routinely overestimate prospects for upward mobility by an average of 23 percent. In general, Americans tend to think it's easier to pull out of poverty than it truly is, potentially leading them to downplay the severity of economic inequality—which is getting worse by the year. Prior to 2010, the middle class owned more wealth collectively than the top 1 percent. But since 1995, the share of middle-class wealth has consistently declined as the top 1 percent's share has increased. In the 2010s, the top 20 percent held 77 percent of the total household wealth, more than triple what the middle class held. And lowered prospects for mobility correlate directly to race.

Unlike traditional hip-hop, drill is not about chasing society's commodified vision of the American Dream. Drill is about staying in the community, recognizing those who may never leave the community. It's not just about repping your block, but also staying on your block, protecting your block. It's also a gothic story depicting the current conditions of urban decay, policing, and the fight for survival. It's the natural successor of early hip-hop forms by artists like Grandmaster Flash and the Furious Five, and late 1980s hip-hop groups like N.W.A.

Despite it all, Black imagination survives. This is the beauty of drill, even with all of its so-called ugliness.

Make a Movie

When I asked Vic what he would do if I could make millions of dollars appear in his hand, he answered without hesitation:

> VIC: I would invest it, the whole shebang. I'd invest in more businesses for the community. In the schools. I'd bring back a library and make sure the kids could get computers and stuff. Nursing homes. Parks. And I'd do a record company, make music, make movies with a drill

soundtrack. Probably a cop movie. I'd want to do something that could generate money and resources for centuries so we wouldn't need the crooked politicians anymore.

BRANDI: Wait... why a cop movie?

VIC: I like the way the uniform looks. And I want to show them doing what they're doing. (*laughs*)

After my conversation with Vic, he sent me the movie *Hood Vampires,* which he was involved in as a writer and actor. It is an admittedly obscure cultural artifact, either suppressed by YouTube's algorithms or not very well tagged for easy searching. I would consider *Hood Vampires* to be a hip-hop product, and, I must say ... it's not that bad. In fact, I rather enjoyed it. The film has suspense. It has a full story arc. It had some comic relief in the form of two hood vampire slayers who just want to play cards but can't finish their game because they have shit to do—specifically, go hunt some vampires. I mean, it's great. I can honestly say that it is about as good as any student arthouse film that I've seen. And you can take that for what it is.

Now, is it Oscar-winning material? Well, what is? The Oscars are bull-shit; all of that is subject to mostly white definitions of high and low art anyways. But it actually is quite good—even more so when you think about the ways they had to pull together a lot of resources and work to make scraps out of nothing. They weren't dealing with a million-dollar budget. They weren't even dealing with a hundred-dollar budget. They made it purely for their love of film, wanting to tell a story about vampires. And I loved it. I loved watching it. I would sit through that again sooner than I would any Gerard Butler film.

When I asked Vic about *Hood Vampires,* I wanted to read all sorts of subtext into it. I wanted the movie to be this broader critique of capitalism and neoliberalism. I wanted it to be about trying to break free from the infrastructure failures of the hood by becoming a vampire. I wanted it to be about how capitalism and economic segregation force us all to be bloodthirsty, to aspire to the trappings of capital and material gain, and to long to fly like a vampire bat from the South Side of Chicago to the North Side where all the rich white people are. That's what I wanted him to tell me this movie was about.

But no, it wasn't. It was just a movie about vampires in the hood. Most of the dialogue was improvised on each day of filming. Vic and his friends had never seen a movie script before, so they had no idea how to go about writing one. When I asked him why vampires, he said, "Why not? People like vampires, so I wanted to tell my version of a vampire story."

And you know what? I enjoy it that way. I prefer being able to watch it without having to overthink all the potential hidden subtext and clues, without the framing we're so used to. I prefer to take it in as a future hood classic . . . after some significant rewrites and location shoots.

Hip-hop is the most policed art form in modern culture. It is also the most commodified art form in modern culture. These two truths live side by side to feed a moral and social panic that plays out in regressive policies and practices that maintain systems of oppression levied on the backs of working-class and marginalized communities globally. The narrators of that moral panic are news journalists who regularly traffic in race play under the pretense of neutrality to tell a hostile story about those people—a story we as Black people, particularly those outside of certain neighborhoods and communities, are primed to accept as the truth.

But sometimes, I see the other stories that manage to slip through the cracks of that frame, the stories that tell a more complex and nuanced and full tale of Black life. The stories that make you laugh out loud, remind you of people you see on the block, and make you think of home as something more than what others make of it. Stories like Vic and *Hood Vampires*.

I remember sitting in bed with David, watching the film on my laptop, filled with joy. I turned to my white husband, and I said, "Do you ever have a moment where you just love your people?" And he looked at me incredulously and said, "Well . . . no." Fair enough, sir. I guess it's a good thing that he doesn't have those moments of *Oh, I am just really into being white,* because if he did, it would probably be in context of something like watching the January 6 insurrection at the Capitol.

But in a way, I feel sad for him because I find so much joy in seeing Black people be artistic, liberated, and free. I love seeing my people doing some stuff that's unexpected. I just think it's so cool. It's not just that it feels cool or looks cool, but it makes me proud to be Black, to be a part of this culture. It makes me proud of the resilience that is being Black. It makes me proud to see people who can take restricted resources and use them to make something priceless. And I felt that while watching this film. It felt like magic.

8

The Bay Area Hustlers
Believing in Your Own Hustle, Community Resource Building, and the Dangers of Losing Black Space

Going to see a Black movie on opening weekend is one of my favorite pastimes. There's something about the energy of it—how excited Black people are about seeing representation on screen. It's a beautiful experience. If it's a good movie, I'll often have to go see it again because that first time, there's so much talking over the movie that I miss some lines or crucial plot points.

There are things you're going to have to shrug your shoulders about and say it is what it is. People are going to be late. A family of five might walk in and turn on their phone flashlights to try and find space in the dark in a theater already damn near packed to capacity. At some point, you will find yourself crankily asking yourself, *Why is this two-year-old at an R-rated movie, or even at the movies?* If you're some place in Oakland or the Bay Area, where I lived for nearly a decade, or, depending on the movie in general, someone might spark it up mid-movie. I don't want to say this only happens during Black movies, but I'm just saying it's important to be prepared.

Based on observing some cranky white people at the movies, I've learned there can be a different set of decorum, customs, and norms when you go to see a Black movie, especially on opening weekend in a Black-ass city. For me, it's the ultimate moviegoing experience.

Going to see a Ryan Coogler movie in the Bay Area is especially electrifying. With him being a son of Oakland, there's an immediate feeling of pride in seeing one of the films he wrote and/or directed. The theater is guaranteed to be jam-packed, be it a more arthouse film like *Fruitvale Station* or a sports-themed blockbuster like *Creed*. One way or another, all of his movies somehow manage to feel like a love song to Oakland and California culture. The Bay loves him right back, and he's become an instant legend in the region.

Every little nod he makes to Oakland, the audience gets it. For example, in *Creed II,* one of Donnie's boxing opponents, Danny Wheeler—played by another Oakland son, boxer Andre Ward—gets into an altercation. In the scene where the altercation is being discussed on ESPN's *SportsCenter,* the news ticker at the bottom of the screen shows the Golden State Warriors have beaten the Los Angeles Clippers, the Oakland Athletics are on a baseball hot streak, and there's another nod to a son of Oakland—American football player and future Hall of Famer (I said what I said) Marshawn Lynch. That scene damn near got a standing ovation from the audience, definitely more applause than the movie's climax.

As an aside, on more than one occasion, I've seen Marshawn casually chilling at my Oakland Starbucks, talking to anyone who stops through and wants to chat with him. He's truly a man of the people.

So, with all of that context, you can imagine what the energy was like in the East Bay on opening weekend for the cultural touchstone that is *Black Panther.*

I don't know if this is a race thing or Marvel fan versus non-Marvel fan thing, but for some reason, David's (non-Black) friends were totally unprepared for how hard *Black Panther* was going to hit. But I knew from the moment the teaser for the movie dropped during the NBA Finals in 2017 that this was going to be a cultural experience for the ages.

The Huey P. Newton–inspired movie poster, Photoshop challenges aside, was yet another ode to Oakland. In the poster, Chadwick Boseman, dressed in the full Black Panther suit, is seated on a regal throne, staring directly into the camera. It bears a striking resemblance to an iconic photo of Newton, who was the cofounder of the Black Panthers, a Black Power political organization that started in Oakland. The curves on the side of the Black Panther throne are reminiscent of the curves in the chair from Newton's photo. The resemblance was unmistakable. It was full-on Blackity-Blackness, and I was here for it.

If you ever want to see true Black joy and love, do yourself a favor and go on YouTube and look up "Black Panther | Teaser Trailer-Reactions Mashup" by the account "Elijah." The video is a supercut of reaction videos from Black people around the world watching the teaser trailer. It's two minutes and change of pure happiness, and one of the few videos that consistently brings me out of even the deepest of funks. I do not know who "Elijah" is, but I am deeply grateful to them for pulling it together.

Black Panther revolves around T'Challa (Chadwick Boseman), who is the Black Panther and heir to the throne of Wakanda, a super-advanced kingdom in Africa that the Wakandans have kept hidden for thousands of years. As T'Challa was taking the throne (spoiler alert), his long-lost cousin, Killmonger (Michael B. Jordan)—who grew up in Oakland instead of Wakanda and is the film's villain—returns to Wakanda to claim the kingdom for himself. Killmonger's goal is to distribute Wakandan weapons around the world, arguing it is Wakanda's responsibility to reveal their existence to the world and share their advanced technology—a stance that threatens Wakanda's long-held secret existence. Ultimately, T'Challa defeats Killmonger but decides Killmonger wasn't entirely wrong, ending the movie by building a community center in Oakland and revealing Wakanda's existence to the world.

Now that we've covered the basics, back to opening weekend in East Bay. I loved the movie. I loved the theater's energy. I loved seeing everyone dressed up in their African outfits at the theater just outside of Oakland. People crowded the nearby Barnes & Noble and Fuddruckers and spilled out of the garage, everyone ready to get whisked off to Wakanda. How could you not love it all?

"Brandi, I don't hate the movie. I love how it makes many Black people feel. I don't want to take that away from them. BUT there's some problematic things that go down."

My friend Jade was the first Black person I knew who had a less-than-glowing opinion of the movie. She was reluctant to talk about it because it's *Black Panther*, and no one wanted to burn it down. It just felt wrong. But eventually she got going . . .

So the story line is a man from . . . like . . . a wealthy African country. He goes to the United States, has a secret kid. Leaves the kid. The kid grows up in the hood in America. In Oakland. No food. No community centers. No lights. Meanwhile, he grows up knowing, because his dad told him, that there is a whole nation of Black people with lots of money, endless resources, cutting-edge technology. And yet in America, Black people don't have shit. And he's the bad guy for wanting them to share the resources globally. BRANDI! Crazy, right?

While watching the movie, I had found myself relating more to Killmonger than Black Panther. At the time, I hadn't exactly been able to put my finger on why besides the fact he was an American character from my adopted hometown of Oakland. But as Jade started running it down for me, I was like, *Oh, yeah . . . OK.*

Michael B. Jordan wants to democratize and bring access to technology to all oppressed people in the world and *he's* the villain? I was just, like, wait. Oh, hold on. And THEN, at the end of the movie, it turns out the CIA is, like, a part of the whole caper. Dude is killed. Then, at the end of the movie, they do some trickle-down economics stuff and put a community center in Oakland. Like the real Black Panthers did, but with the community? They might as well have created a Wakandan task force on American relations. BRANDI, ARE YOU SERIOUS RIGHT NOW??

Having the CIA be the heroes was an odd choice for a director who grew up in Oakland, the home of the Black Panthers, since the Panthers were heavily surveilled and targeted by the CIA and FBI for disruption because of their Black political organizing and global solidarity movement work. It's also a strange choice because the CIA has long been rumored to have been heavily involved in cocaine trafficking into Black communities, something many Bay Area rappers like Too $hort have talked about. This was an allegation that to many seemed like a crazy conspiracy until 1996 when a newspaper series by reporter Gary Webb in the *San Jose Mercury News* (a Bay Area–based newspaper) detailed allegations that the CIA's drug trafficking had played an important role in creating the crack cocaine drug problem in the United States. As an aside, the CIA used the release of *Black Panther* as a promotional tactic, repeatedly tweeting about it from their official account. They do weird things like that. Weird, insidious, messed up, whatever you want to call it.

So, I don't disagree with Jade. In fact, I actually think Ryan Coogler told this twisted Black fairy tale intentionally. Call me a conspiracy theorist, but my hunch is that he got a movie deal with Disney and had to Disney-fy his work, but that he left nuggets of truth buried inside the art. To me, the film's power lies in Coogler's deft navigation of this fine line.

Unlike other villains, you're supposed to feel sympathy—or even empathy—for Killmonger, despite the fact he bears all the traditional markers of a Hollywood villain (kills his girlfriend; tries to kill his popular, well-liked cousin; etc., etc.). Even the ending—Oakland being left with only a community center in a rapidly gentrifying city displacing its Black people—feels like acknowledgment.

Superhero movies have a magic to them. Often, they are the realm of heroes who have limitless access to infinite resources across galaxies they can use to make the world right and just for all. But the *Black Panther* universe is a zero-sum game in which the image of Black unity is coupled with the idea that it's OK to let other Black people struggle to protect yourself. And even to the extent you let other Black people in, there are limits. Because of this, to me, the movie feels like a warning.

It's a warning that it is not enough to do trickle-down economics saviorism. That we have to work together—not against each other—to build the resources needed to sustain our community. We can't rely on external forces to distribute resources equitably in a community. We have to build a radical collective community that understands structural inequities while also tapping into a vision for the future.

I think *Black Panther* is a story about the need for cooperative economics and mutual aid models that involve collaborating with and listening to communities about what they need. It is not optimal for the haves to control and dole out resources to the have-nots—to build shared resources and support that can create economic opportunities for our community at scale. It's about the need to bring into the community even those who skirt the edges of what's deemed acceptable or respectable in society. Failure to do that means we lose our souls. We become trotted-out tools of those who have actively harmed our communities.

I'm sure that's the movie's point. After all, Ryan Coogler is an Oakland son, and nowhere serves as a better example of this warning than Oakland.

DIY

> **BRANDI:** How did growing up in an all-Black community shape you or your values?
>
> **KAMILAH:** I don't think I actually recognized the value when I was growing up in it. To be honest with you, I probably only recognized it was a privilege a few years ago. But it was and is a ... *cocoon* is the only word I can think of right now ... being able to be yo' Blackity-Black Black self, and then also see examples of excellence at the same time. I don't know if it makes sense.
>
> **BRANDI:** It does, I completely understand.
>
> **KAMILAH:** Whereas I felt like I was able to be my true, full hyphy, 'playing loud music in the neighborhood' person, do you know what I mean? Just like ... going from braids to weaves and being able to yell, sing, and dance on the street and also have that be protected and not judged.

Blackety-Black Kamilah was one of the first people I knew I wanted to interview for the book. We instantly connected on the experience of growing up in all-Black spaces around Black people of different classes and the comfort that can offer as you're coming of age, particularly in a world that looks to define you one-dimensionally. There's something about the freedom to just exist that is so crucial to thriving. When Kamilah talked about that feeling of being your Blackety-Black Black self, I related to that so much.

I met Kamilah (I'm going to start calling her Kam) around 2014–15 when I lived in Oakland, California. Immediately, I felt like she was a girl after my own heart. In 2009, Kam had started a streetwear and women's empowerment apparel line called Princess Punk, which she then renamed RICH + RIOT and expanded to become a network of women entrepreneurs sharing resources, experiences, and opportunities. It's a whole vibe.

The first thing I bought from her was a BLACK FEMINIST shirt, which incorporated the iconic logo of the band Black Flag. The whole punk-rock aesthetic, being modeled by women of color in all shapes and sizes, projected power—all the hustle and grit flowing through Black girl DNA.

Kamilah is Oakland to the core. Like Oakland, she has a chill confidence about her but also a fiery energy and hustle. She doesn't take a color-by-numbers approach to life. She doesn't just march to the beat of her own drum; she builds the drum and reconstructs the sound. Then—if the situation calls for it—she may just play that drum in your living room.

It's something she attributes to growing up in an all-Black, middle-class community in Oakland, as well as the city itself more broadly.

Oakland is known as a very Black city and has been responsible for the spread of a lot of Black culture around the world. It's so Black that it has—along with South Central Los Angeles—convinced people California is more Black than it really is. Don't let the sounds of G-Funk and hyphy fool you: California is less than 6 percent Black. An anomaly, for generations, Oakland was nearly 50 percent Black.

Droves of Black people arrived in Oakland starting in the late 1890s with a major influx occurring between 1940 and 1970 during the wartime military and civic economy. At the time, it was, quite literally, the end of the line: where the railroads and highways ended. With people associated with a military economy came a more regimented and revolution-minded style of community organizing, which accelerated during the Vietnam War and its aftermath.

As the Blackest place for hundreds of miles in any direction, the Bay Area community had to band together, leading to a vibrant tradition of community building and resistance that would shape the city's identity for decades to come. At the same time, many Black multimedia artists and business owners converged on the region, helping to tell the story of Oakland through unique cultural products.

Kam's mom, Mrs. Richardson, moved to Oakland from Dallas, Texas. In the 1960s, she had gone to Merritt College alongside members of the Black Panther Party (BPP cofounders Bobby Seale and Huey P. Newton both went to Merritt). The Panthers were creating in Oakland and across the country what they called "Survival Programs," focused on mutual aid. These programs involved caring for children while their parents were at work, doing chores and transporting elders to the grocery store, offering culturally relevant schooling curriculum, and building a pipeline of Black doctors, scientists, and educators. The city's energy inspired Mrs. Richardson, who had studied sociology and gone into recreational therapy. For her as a parent, it was important to ensure her children grew up feeling safe and surrounded by community care and pride—something she saw in Oakland and the all-Black neighborhood Kam grew up in.

Oakland definitely has an identity and city pride I haven't seen in many places—and that's coming from someone born into an extreme amount of Chicago pride. Game recognizes game. But while Chicago remains one of the most segregated cities in the United States, with a bunch of different micro cultures and nations that make racialized divisions more exploitable, Oakland is a place of multiracial counter-cultures, subcultures, and radical politics. There is a history of distinct cultural, racial, and ethnic fights as people organize in and for their communities, but there has also been strategic allyship and alignment around shared targets, systems, and issues (e.g., education, housing, and anti-surveillance, etc.).

One time in my Downtown Oakland office, I overheard a group of kids from the Asian Youth Promoting Advocacy and Leadership office next door: *"We march all day, dog; it doesn't stop. We march to the bathroom up in here."*

I imagine they're still marching. In Oakland, the marching truly never stops.

I Did a Lot of Shit Just to Live This Here Lifestyle

Oakland is one of the major hubs of streetwear fashion in the United States, and perhaps because of this, Kamilah grew up really into streetwear. As an adult, she wanted to make apparel that catered to women. So, in addition to designing and printing her own products, she began working at a local printshop to learn the business.

As Kam recounts, the printshop owner's health started failing, and though it wasn't the transition he'd hoped for, he knew he would have to step back from the business's day-to-day management soon. In previous conversations, he had told Kam that he wanted to give the business to her, his top and most loyal employee. And so, Kam expected he would start making moves toward transitioning the business to her. But when the time came, he brought in someone new, who he called a family friend, someone who had never been involved with the business but who the owner now said he wanted to take over the shop.

Kam was, in her words, dumbfounded. He had been telling her for years that he was going to give her the business, but when the time came, he told her point blank that he felt more comfortable with someone that was "like him."

When he said, "He's just like me," he didn't mean they had similar business styles because Kam's business style was like his; her work ethic was strong, and her commitment was strong. When he said, "Like him," he meant someone who was physically from the same community as he was. Hearing those words was life-changing for Kam. She realized she had spent years building someone else's business for someone else's community, and now she had little to show for it. She had given her all to something that could never belong to her.

Kam left the printshop and went to work under a woman who designed apparel and women's sports uniforms, but she knew there was a shelf life for this job, too. She had to do this shit herself.

> September 11, 2015—I'll never forget that day. That was the last day I got a paycheck in my hand from a full-time job from someone else.

Hearing Kam's story, I was reminded of a conversation I had with Nenna, another Oakland entrepreneur. Nenna Feelmore—née Joiner—is the founder of the Feelmore Adult Gallery in Oakland. Nenna is a renaissance person. She makes and produces independent porn movies, teaches and hosts sex education courses, and builds out tech platforms. She also used to be in the pimping game.

I remember when Nenna's brick-and-mortar retail store opened right down the street from my offices. I had never seen so many classy-looking dildos and artfully designed vibrators in my entire life. When I went there to help a friend shop, I was blown away by the levels of inclusivity and intentionality applied to the environment. But before she had her store, Nenna got her start by selling sex toys and videos out of the trunk of her gold 1993 Toyota Camry on Downtown Oakland street corners. Nenna wanted to be at the top of the sex game; that was her approach and hustle. Seeing the template that had been laid out by successful musicians like Master P, E-40, and Too $hort, she made her way from Las Vegas to Oakland. Being in Oakland helped her see the ways in which place and space can be reimagined.

What struck me was how Nenna viewed her car. She talked about all the things a car can be: a house, a music store, a grocery store selling fruits and vegetables out of the back. For Nenna, this view of a car was part of her philosophy of reimagining what you already have instead reaching so far into the future that your current situation disappoints you. Instead of just dreaming about getting the money needed to buy a sex shop or relying on someone else to front the money, Nenna believed in making the car she already had into her sex shop and then using the income from her sales to get capital, reinvest in herself, and keep moving toward her goal.

When she talks about a car being your home, your space, your land, there's a resonance to that that ripples deeper than the current state of Black wealth. It's about branding, ownership, and control over your own content, image, and future.

This philosophy is something that Nenna and Kam share. It's a quintessential Bay Area vibe. When she started out, Kam spent nearly every weekend selling her apparel at markets, events, and conferences. She even worked holidays, since holidays meant people wanted to shop. But the silver lining was that during those markets and events, she met other Black women entrepreneurs. As they sat in booths next to one another, they would share tips and support each other—through times of personal pain and moments of national crisis.

The group's bond solidified when Philando Castile and Alton Sterling were killed by police officers on the same weekend in July 2016. They started to meet up more regularly, and together cofounded Just Be, a business community with the express goal of building up Black women business owners and sharing resources. Together, they started organizing pop-up markets around the Bay Area.

The largest of these—*For the Culture*—became the largest all-Black women's holiday market in the United States. The painful lesson that Kam had learned as a young, upstart entrepreneur helped fuel her drive to not only start her own business, but also to pay it forward. There's the hustle that's about getting over on your community, and then there's the hustle that's about sustaining the community. For Kam, it wasn't just about building her own shit, it was about working—both in name and literally—"for the culture."

Kam's story is an experience that feels true for many Black people. Her story of resilience and building a women-driven entrepreneurship community in the marketplaces of the Bay Area is one that feels very global, even if her Rich + Riot aesthetic and Black punk posture has an Oakland twist to it.

Black-owned independent businesses have historically provided avenues of upward mobility for generations of Black Americans—not just for owners, but for those they hire as well. Black-owned businesses are more likely to employ Black employees, especially those considered unemployable by the larger society including those with criminal records. They are also more likely to be in and serve predominantly Black communities and are more likely to provide a community service beyond the original business function.

Black communities add access to resources and keep tax dollars within the local economy. Black financial institutions help support the next generation of businessowners and forge pathways to homeownership not often afforded by non-Black financial institutions. And on a larger level, Black-owned businesses have supplied critical leadership, spaces for organizing, and financial support for civil rights movements then and now.

Pimp or Get Pimped

Kam is an example of someone who has built out a business hustle that's legit. But there are other avenues for accruing wealth, too.

Oakland is *the* home of alternative economies. Some, like the 1930s co-ops, were tied to leftist organizing for community resilience. Others are guided by the hood principle: **pimp or get pimped.** *The Mack,* the 1973 Blaxploitation classic, was one of the first highly visible cultural products to reimagine the Oakland pimp as an all-American antihero.

There are several quotes from the movie that really sum up the Oakland DIY hustle:

> This system was not originally . . . designed with Black people in mind . . . And it definitely was not prepared for Black people to, in the end, begin to demand their rights and an equal share in this country which [*sic*] they've died for . . . Hey—and we definitely are not going back to Africa. . . . We ain't going back! For us to exist in this system, we must first of all realize that we have got to form our own Black America, within—but without— white America.
>
> —*THE MACK,* 1973

Chicago hustler Al Capone once (allegedly) said, "Capitalism is the legitimate racket of the ruling class." Oakland's pimping, music, and drug culture is a continuation of alternative economic systems that have been built throughout American history by those who are not immediately privy to entering the gates of national power. These systems work outside of the boundaries of American governance to build and circulate capital in marginalized communities denied access to resources, thus circumventing dominant, white gatekeepers in the more "respectable" corporate hustle.

Chill, friends, I'm not saying that to romanticize the violence, misogyny, or ruthlessness that can come with that. But I am saying these alternative economies are a direct byproduct of the violence, misogyny, and ruthlessness that have maintained a larger economic, racial, and political caste system in this country. In the *pimp or be pimped* challenge to deeply embedded societal norms, there are two possible directions short of all-out revolution: replicate capitalist systems from the outside or work to disrupt capitalism from the inside. Frankly, one is easier than the other. Here's a hint: it's not the *disrupting capitalism* route, which gets even harder as more and more Black residents and their businesses are getting pushed out of the city.

Centuries of racism and economic disparities have required the creation of a distinct culture built around Black businesses as a safe space for survival and self-determination. But decades later, we are still pushing up against a system that's not tryna work for us.

Overall, working-age Black Americans have become far less likely to be their own bosses than in the 1990s. The per capita number of Black employers declined by some 12 percent just between 1997 and 2014. While we have seen a boom in internet businesses and start-ups, clear barriers to Black people in these spaces still remain. And in the first two months of COVID-19 alone, when one in fifty businesses shut down, that number was one in five for Black businesses.

This increasing loss of Black-owned businesses has been unbelievably devastating for the prospects of building Black economic power and autonomy.

For us, "do it yourself," or DIY economics is based on the idea of leveraging government policies to accumulate the increased distributed wealth and resources to ultimately create our own independent infrastructures free from the tyranny of white supremacy. But we cannot forget that in addition to businesses, we have to fight for government policies that help build labor and lift the floor for all Black people, not just some. Rich Black people are 1,382 times wealthier than poor Black people. Despite the ending of *Black Panther,* that trickle-down economics shit doesn't work, y'all. This is where Ryan Coogler's warning starts to really resonate.

The Oakland that Kam, Nenna, and Ryan Coogler grew up in is rapidly disappearing. As wealth pours in, not even a Black Panther–backed community center can stabilize the community.

As Boots Riley discusses in the *Vanity Fair* article "*Sorry to Bother You* Director Boots Riley Takes a Ride Through Oakland's Changing Landscape," since the 1960s, cultural spaces like pool halls, roller-skating rinks, and parks that were gathering spots for people of color have either been shut down due to exorbitant price hikes or become increasingly policed with a variety of nuisance laws being used to surveil, track, and target youth.

Over time, this had impacted the music and youth subcultural scene, forcing much of it to go underground and find innovative ways to thrive. When bars and music venues in Oakland refused to book hip-hop performers or parties for younger people of color, they rented union halls, restaurants, and warehouses. When the city banned permits for those kinds of events, they took to the streets. This is where hyphy culture came from—in part from creating a party while driving from one side of town to another.

Once, Oakland had been a home base for hip-hop icons such as Too $hort, E-40, Mistah F.A.B., Mac Dre, Keak Da Sneak, Boots Riley, and 2Pac. It held the kind of energy that swirls around visible signs of art, activism, youth culture, entrepreneurship, and radical education, preserving a unique type of homegrown hustle that just flat-out doesn't give a fuck. It's like OK, you're gonna shut down our community spaces? Fine, then we're gonna ghost ride that whip and make our cars the entertainment space.

But while Black residents made up nearly half of Oakland's population in 1980, by 2010 that number had dropped to 28 percent. By 2020, it had dropped even more as a record number of Black people continued to leave the Bay Area, driven out by rapidly rising housing and rent prices. For decades, working-class people have had to fight to maintain space in Oakland as business interests and the tech economy have accelerated gentrification and displacement even while Oakland continues to brand itself off of that rebellious, multiethnic history.

This is a common story for many cities across the United States. Take for example roller-skating rinks, which have long been sacred and safe spaces for Black culture. Roller-skating rinks in Black communities across the US have been meeting grounds and neutral territory for intercity groups at odds. They have been places where Black people of all ages could have fun and incubators of hip-hop talent ranging from Queen Latifah to N.W.A.

According to data shared with me by the team that produced the 2018 documentary film *United Skates,* more than 1,200 roller rinks were shut down across the country between 1980 and 2018—ten in Oakland alone. This is not just about the loss of economic power, this is about the devastating mass loss of spaces that were once our cultural, social, and spiritual homes. And when these spaces disappear, so does the Black culture and identity they have been instrumental in maintaining.

But You Know and I Know It's All about Survival

It wasn't until I was writing this book that it occurred to me that Black as a shared story is something of a twentieth-century creation. Because

I've always conflated Blackness with the creation of race as a social construct—which predates the twentieth century by a good little bit—it's hard to imagine a time my people didn't see themselves as Black. But the idea of being Black, embracing Black as an experience, and understanding Black to be a culture? Well, that started more recently. There are many people still walking this earth who were there when it happened. It was still evolving and solidifying when my great aunt Velora was born, which may be the reason she still says "colored."

Black culture was built in a time when Black people of mixed economic status lived side by side. Resources were distributed through mutual aid and co-ops, and power was built in these shared spaces. Today, data shows that income segregation has increased, meaning that poor and nonpoor Black people are less likely to live within the same neighborhoods as they did in 1970. As Patrick Sharkey found in his paper, "Spatial Segmentation and the Black Middle Class," there is a growing divide between the fortunes of the Black middle class and majority-Black communities. This points to a weakening link between progress leading toward the reduction of racial inequalities at the family or household level, and progress leading toward the reduction of inequality across communities at scale.

The implications across the board are alarming.

In early 2020, a Pew Research Center study found 75 percent of Black people in the US were significantly more likely than other groups to say Black is central to their identity. But this headline doesn't tell the full story. Four years earlier, that number was around 81 percent, which means the number of Black people who closely identify with Black is decreasing. In addition, Black adults younger than thirty years old were less likely to say race was an important part of their identity. Finally, the study found a correlation between identity and both family income and education level. The higher your income and education attainment were, the more likely you were to feel a heightened sense of Black identity. Those numbers could mean nothing, or they could mean everything.

I see a direct correlation between limited economic access to remaining Black-owned and controlled spaces and the loss of cultural identity. We saw this in the media space with the disappearance of Black-owned media outlets, and in Oakland, we can see its physical counterpart as well. The top 1 percent of Black people hold more than 70 percent of Black wealth. The digital racial gap is growing. More than half of Black people could be underprepared for 86 percent of jobs by 2045. When access to technology and capital development are more and more concentrated in the hands of a few, then who is the culture really for? Who can it really be for?

When I talk to middle-class Black people and ask them where things have gone wrong for Black people, the number-one answer I constantly hear is integration. I hear it so often, I don't even get surprised by it anymore. They (well, me, too) are out here living like T'Challa, impervious to the nation of Killmongers being created through economic starvation, unaware of the growing economic divides in the Black community and the people—and shared culture—now left behind.

If Black culture is only the realm of the elite, how do we survive that?

9

Basement Politics
Black Women Fighting on the Front Lines of the Sex Industry and Rejecting Respectability Politics

My first understanding of sex and sexuality came from flipping through old *Playboy* magazines in my grandmother's basement. That's a common story for a lot of kids of a certain age, I suppose. But maybe less common is that some of my most radical politics were formed down in that basement as well.

I used to spend my summers in Syracuse, New York (DeWitt, to be more specific). When I was a baby, my grandmother's youngest brother, Alex, lived out of her basement. By the time I reached adolescence and was spending my summers in DeWitt, Great Uncle Alex had died. But the basement was like this strange time capsule. His room had been almost perfectly preserved as it had been when he died, with 1970s and early 1980s shag rugs, beaded curtains, mini Buddhas—the whole nine yards. I'm pretty sure I found weed down there, though I didn't really know at the time what to make of the smelly, dried bag of weird-looking dirt. I would wander down there when there weren't any more shows on PBS or network television that held my interest. I always had to sneak down there, as there was a chair in front of the door and my grandmother would tell me to stay upstairs. But as soon as *Guiding Light* came on, or she would go upstairs for her nap, I would make my way toward the magical door.

In the dark, cobweb-ridden basement I found what seemed like endless stacks of *Playboys*, at least a decade's worth. We should've saved them because some of those editions have to be worth something today. Although, some of them were quite worn.

But as I flipped through the tattered pages, I found myself less interested in admiring the women's physiques than I was in actually reading the articles. As unlikely as it seems, I think I can safely say that my politics, radical as some people may find them, were shaped in part by the carefully crafted words on those pages in between the 1970s bushes.

The Lost Art of Reading *Playboy* for the Articles

Though *Playboy* is most frequently associated with the Playboy Mansion in LA, *Playboy* as an institution and Hugh Hefner as a figure have to be placed in the context of the radical politics of Chicago, where Hugh Hefner was born, came of age, and launched his empire in the 1950s.

Chicago is a city where a lot of money can be made. It's a city that's always hustling, a city of affluence, a city that knows the power of a good promo. For Hugh Hefner, that energy and a mission to put play and pleasure into an American (and Chicago) lifestyle that had a more puritanical attitude was part of what drove him to carve out a career in the sex industry.

Much of what's discussed in relation to *Playboy* as a cultural artifact is Hefner's role in the sexual revolution, and there is no doubt the questions posed by broader counterculture movements of the 1960s and 1970s shaped Hugh Hefner's worldview. We could make money as capitalist beings in constant pursuit of material gain, but could we enjoy it? What would it mean to allow ourselves the pleasures of affluence's trappings? And what were our obligations to one another as self-interested people?

But he was also influenced by Chicago's Black radical politics, which pushed him toward a progressive ideology. In Hefner's own words, he valued what he called a more "socialized capitalism," a far cry from the social conservatism often ascribed to *Playboy*. "International law instead of warfare to control the possibility of nuclear holocaust. An end to racism. An end to poverty around the world. [To] the population explosion. [To] the pollution of our natural resources. Then, all that remains is disease. If we spent our money on these things instead of war, by the year 2000, we could be moving into a real golden age."

Hefner brought on a slate of journalists, editors, and staff who shared a similar worldview. Through both the written content and the deliberate construction of the pictorials and artwork throughout the magazine, he used culture and the lure of sex as a vehicle to challenge the status quo on all fronts.

Though this may seem strange to people who see *Playboy* as a very white institution (which it is), we can see evidence of Black radical influence everywhere in the artifacts of the magazine and Hefner's political inclinations. Many local progressive thought leaders, including the late great Chicago mayor Harold Washington, would be introduced to national audiences on the pages of *Playboy*. *Playboy* gave these progressive leaders a platform in the way that right-wing thinkers were being amplified at the same time in *Reader's Digest*. Hefner also financially supported Mayor Washington and other progressive candidates (including many Black candidates and other candidates of color), hosting fundraisers at the Playboy Mansion. In *Playboy,* articles, forum letters, and interviews unapologetically offered a progressive critique of institutions that had failed younger generations.

Playboy had diverse hiring practices in its clubs, on its television show, and in its magazine—both on the pages and behind the scenes—years before civil rights legislation required companies to evaluate their hiring and payment practices. *Playboy* was a venue for not just Black visuals, but also Black thought, art, and culture in a way that was unapologetic and challenging.

Hefner created space for the Black radical politics that informed him. Even as a kid, I could sense this, and it was what kept me sneaking down to the basement to flip through the dusty, old magazines.

Playboy's subversive nature lay in Hugh Hefner and his editors' willingness to showcase the good, the bad, and the ugly in politics. The magazine allowed for competing schools of thought in ways that aren't seen in other print publications even today (kind of like *The Breakfast Club*). In-depth interviews with Black Panthers like Eldridge Cleaver, Huey P. Newton, and others would run, followed the next month by tersely written letters to the editor from aggressive white men complaining about intellectually inferior Negroes desiring their women. Alex Haley's no-holds-barred interview with American Nazi George Lincoln Rockwell lives in the *Playboy* archives alongside James Baldwin's stirring long-form essay on race, class, and poverty—"The Evidence of Things Not Seen"—in Atlanta, as played out during the Atlanta Child Murders in the 1980s.

Hugh Hefner's long-standing commitment to free speech often comes with having to wade through a lot of uncomfortable hot takes. Sophomoric humor intertwines with the more cerebral reflections in a way that can give the reader whiplash, especially if they're getting themselves off and all of a sudden have to stay up while reading *Playboy*'s "History of Assassination in America," critiques of capitalism, and references to Karl Marx. It's a roller-coaster experience, to be sure.

This is not to say that *Playboy* is an uncomplicatedly misunderstood publication that has only a positive legacy. Feminists have charged that the magazine has never shown women in their full humanity. Some women who have modeled for the magazine have said later that it came at a cost to their personal lives and relationships with their families. Most disturbing, some of Hugh Hefner's former partners and models who worked with the company have alleged he was violent, emotionally abusive, and manipulative.

And there are many critiques that could be made about *Playboy* in terms of body and aesthetic representation. But for all its blond bodaciousness, *Playboy* magazine did also show Black women as beautiful. While *Playboy* reinforced Black women's role in the public discourse as both sexual objects and dominants, it also portrayed Black women as empowered sexual agents. Part of that was reflected in the magazine's selection of models and celebrities, which even included Blaxploitation goddess Pam Grier. And part of that was through showcasing Black women with natural hair in a time when white beauty magazines (and even some Black magazines) were slow to do so. Morgan Jerkins, for example, traces the story of Darine Stern, *Playboy*'s first solo Black cover model:

> Years before American *Vogue, ELLE,* and *Harper's BAZAAR* had a Black woman grace their cover, *Playboy* became a maverick. In fact, in 2005, the American Society of Magazine Editors listed this feat as one of the forty most important magazine covers of the past forty years. . . . For the cover, she wore an afro wig and the seat behind [*sic*] which Darine posed was designed right on the set. While other magazines were struggling with how to properly light and photograph darker skin, her image was taken behind [*sic*] a black background to contrast both her skin color and afro.
> —"WHAT HAPPENED TO *PLAYBOY*'S FIRST
> BLACK COVER GIRL?"

Naturally, various figureheads of second-wave feminism ranted against the publication, with Gloria Steinem once saying, "There are times when a woman reading *Playboy* feels a little like a Jew reading a Nazi manual." I can't speak for all women, but I've read *Playboy,* and I've seen a Nazi manual; they feel fairly different. *Playboy*'s interrogation of class, identity politics, and institutions made it a more comfortable home for a Black feminism more like my mom's (and later mine) than the broader feminist movement.

Over the years, *Playboy* has moved into various multimedia venues, including calendars and video, before ceasing print publication in 2020 and going fully digital. In keeping with its traditional radical edge, the platform has increasingly featured models with a wider range of body types and before going all digital rolled out a cover featuring actor Ezra Miller as a gender-fluid Playboy bunny. In keeping with its history of centering more Black radical politics, in 2021, Playboy announced the platform had brought on Grammy-winning artist and rapper Cardi B, as their first official creative director in residence.

Prominent Bernie broad and proud Afro-Latina Cardi B, a long-standing advocate for sex workers and racial justice issues, wasted no time bringing in a visually and culturally diverse array of pornographic actresses and content creators to help usher in this new era for the legendary outlet. Her fame and influential social media presence has helped shine a light on harassment, exploitation, and victimization in the sex work and adult work industries. But by talking about it through her personal experiences, she also challenges the idea that sex work has to be a source of shame and secrecy: "People say, 'Why do you always got to say that you used to be a stripper? We get it.' Because y'all don't respect me because of it, and y'all going to respect these strippers from now on."

As I was writing this book, I wanted to capture all aspects of what it means to be a Black skinhead, a political outlier that moves outside of the mainstream lane of Black thought and perceived politics. And because of the double edge of respectability politics, Black woman who are employed in sex work occupy this space more than almost anyone else.

The Sex Work Revolution Will Not Be Televised

Sex work and labor in the tech economy are part of the unresolved political issues that underpin Black feminist fights in the twenty-first century.

For the first wave of feminism, the fight was around access to the ballot box and property rights for women. The second wave of feminism was about critiquing and reforming male-dominated institutions and cultural practices throughout society, particularly in the realms of workplace equity and reproductive rights.

Though those movements have always involved and relied on women of color and Black women in particular, white women and assumptions about white women's frailty were often centered in those fights. And where white women have been able to make notable strides across several metrics, the workplace and reproductive justice fights of the second wave have not borne as much fruit for Black women. Black women are the most educated racial demographic across the board, yet they still earn significantly less money at work, in entrepreneurship, and in venture capital. Black women are also three to four times more likely than white women to die from pregnancy-related causes, and they generally die at a higher rate from lack of accessible or adequate reproductive care.

The default "woman" in most spheres of media and public life is a middle-class, cisgender, straight, white woman. If someone says woman and they don't put a specific race, ethnicity, sexuality, class, or other quantifier in front of it, one assumes they are talking about a certain type of white woman. And this carries over to the "women" included in feminism. Because of how much mainstream feminism has been dictated by respectability politics, feminism has typically only included women who perform a certain kind of womanhood. This means Black women have often been ignored by feminism but so have sex workers, who are continuously viewed as performing womanhood in an unpalatable way. And for Black women involved in sex work, it is all the more compounded.

The United States' approach to dealing with sex work (even consensual) and its legislation have historically been underpinned by the idea that precious white women are in danger of being trafficked. The 1910 Mann Act, one of the first modern US antitrafficking laws, criminalized Black men in relationships with white women, claiming that it was forced prostitution. It was literally called The White-Slave Traffic Act. It was 1910; they could've just called it the Slave Traffic Act since slavery was supposed to be outlawed by this point, but they wanted to be clear who they were concerned about.

That's the type of racial hostility and anger that drives the narratives that lead to puritanical policies. And this hysteria obscures who's really at risk. In a two-year review of all suspected human trafficking incidents across the country, 40 percent were Black and 24 percent were Latine. Native American women were also dramatically overrepresented in certain states. And yet, most legislation doesn't actually *stop* sex trafficking or keep people safe from sexual predators. It is largely centered around criminalizing prostitution—which criminalizes the sex workers themselves—punishing legal forms of sex work instead of focusing on "johns" (or buyers). Immigrant communities are targeted in particular. The outcome of these laws is that those most criminalized are the trafficking victims, which makes it nearly impossible for them to get help for fear of legal retribution.

This is to say nothing of consensual sex work. There are many pathways into sex work. Often, the story is framed as one of trauma or economic survival. Certainly, that is an aspect of entering into informal economies. But there are many people who enter into sex work to pursue the pleasures and joys of sex or just because it can be a viable and legitimate form of income enacted without coercion. The result of our country's melding of trafficking and consensual sex work—and the legal stigmatization of the latter—is that those involved who are in most need of support are left particularly vulnerable because of a lack of legal protections. Sex workers face barriers at every turn, limiting their ability to grow their businesses and build capital.

This was something that became super clear when, in 2018, Donald Trump signed into law a package of bipartisan bills: the House bill FOSTA, the Fight Online Sex Trafficking Act, and the Senate bill SESTA, the Stop Enabling Sex Traffickers Act. The legislation meant publishers and digital platforms could be held accountable for third-party ads for prostitution—including consensual sex work—on their platforms.

The rules had a chilling impact on all forms of sex work and content creation in many online spaces. A big reason why is because the legislation and surrounding rhetoric routinely conflated sex trafficking with consensual—and even legal—sex work. Opponents argued not only would the bills be ineffective at stopping sex trafficking, they would actually put victims of sex trafficking and sex workers in *more* danger.

The rules compelled companies to close down forums where sex workers could exchange vital information about dangerous "johns" and places sex traffickers frequented, and they prevented sex workers from being able to conduct negotiations online, forcing some people out onto the streets where the risks of experiencing violence and nonconsensual interactions rise significantly. The laws also had the impact of blocking people from taking care of themselves financially through engaging in legal forms of sex and adult entertainment work like cam modeling, escorting, and video content generation. All of this disproportionately impacted Black sex workers, who studies indicate are more likely to have their bodies overly censored and accounts taken down due to "false positives"—content incorrectly flagged as being in violation of platform rules—and are less likely to have the level of "fame" or "influence" that would allow them to push back against companies.

But there's something even deeper at play. The relationship between sex politics and the creation of a racial caste system in America collides in grotesque ways. The moral policing of Black bodies in particular is tied to a continued perception of ownership not just of our bodies, but of our labor, our expressions, and even our spirits. It's a continuation of the perverse abuse that was taken out on our bodies for centuries in the name of slavery, procreation, and caregiving.

When you consider the structural racism that exists in economic legislation—from the criminalization of sex work, to the criminalization of marijuana, to who's allowed to get married and what constitutes a legitimate marriage, to why restaurants are allowed to have low-wage workers hustling for tips and barely making ends meet in the finest Michelin-starred restaurants in the world—there arises an untold story of the racism and xenophobia that underpins all of it. So, while we work to disrupt, reform, and dismantle those systems built on our backs, we also have to create a vision for ourselves of what healthy Black communities can and should look like. And from my vantage point, that has to involve moving with urgency to destigmatize alternative economies. As a Black feminist, to me it means seeing all of our people, including and especially those involved in sex work, in our full potential.

So, what would it look like to be seen in our full humanity? What if, as Ntozake Shange hoped, we really did find God in ourselves and loved her fiercely—not just as a tagline but as a truly embodied principle? To me, that would involve imagining a space where sex work could be economically sustainable or about unapologetic pleasure. Imagine if we actually worked to keep our communities safe by creating broader accountability mechanisms instead of forcing those who engage in consensual sex work to function in secret due to fears of criminalization, abuse, and censorship. That would look like a political agenda guided by a human and civil rights framework, not one based on moral policing and white supremacy gift wrapped in the false pretense of progress.

What would it look like to have a broader economic conversation about what it means to respect and legitimize informal economies that have been built by and for Black people? Data has shown there are more than one million women engaged in what's currently considered illegal sex work. Tax revenue generated by the sex industry could account for potentially an additional $20 billion per year, money that could be routed into education, housing, and job skills training programs to create viable alternative economic opportunities for people who do want to leave sex work but feel like, for many restrictive reasons, they can't.

Back to *Playboy*

"Well, I was modeling for *Playboy* back then, so I used to go to the original Chicago mansion for my workouts and exercise."

My eyebrow rose as I looked up from furiously handwriting notes at my mom on the computer screen.

This took a turn, I thought to myself.

My mom is always doing things like that—casually throwing in facts about herself that completely recalibrate my understanding of her as a person. Before she got hired by the airline, my mom was a model. That part I already knew—she still has her modeling portfolio and photos framed on the wall. But the modeling for *Playboy* part . . . was new information.

"I was registered with their agency. They had a modeling agency. I only got the local stuff like the clothing and fashion shows. But, I never got print with them other than the hand ad that they ran for a nail polish and salon one time. It was a trade magazine. . . . Their headquarters were in Chicago, and they had a mansion here. They required all the models to exercise and do yoga and stuff like that, so I would go to the mansion."

"Oh."

My mom looked at the expression on my face. It must have reflexively twisted up at the memory that popped into my head: a story a friend told me about going to the Playboy Mansion in California and seeing a (now) A-list celebrity sitting by the pool with his dick out of his pants.

"There was nothing funny or shaky about it. I mean, it was straight up. I was just there to work out and network. It wasn't what it is now."

"Oh."

But I didn't really know what would make my mom even apply to Playboy's modeling agency, particularly during a time when she was heavily involved in local leftist Black politics, labor, and housing fights. In some ways, it initially seemed to me to be contradictory. And when I asked her about it, she was pretty chill about it all. For her it was just kind of one of those things.

A friend of the family was a cook at the Playboy Club, and she used to go there as a visitor. She admired the scenery of the city and the lifestyle, and her family friend and others had nothing but positive things to say about Hefner. So she basically thought, why not?

> It was so long ago, my darling. I really couldn't tell you what I was thinking, to be honest. Not long after that, I started at the airline. But I didn't really care about what the white women had to say about it because feminism was their fight anyways. Besides Shirley Chisholm. I liked her feminist politics. She was a super intellectual woman. I thought that she stomped her foot just enough and she carried the right stature and status. She said what she had to say, and I think she had our concerns. I think they gagged her a lot because that's what they did in particular to Black women.

When I was a child, my mom was the president of the Chicago Local Union of United Airlines flight attendants. I remember accompanying her to labor strikes, and some of my earliest memories involve helping make the posters and doing chants while standing among a bunch of well-styled people who all looked like they could be part-time catalog models. Some of them were wearing artfully fitted T-shirts that said pithy things like, "Flight attendants are here to save your ass, not to kiss it." One time when she was on C-SPAN, the interviewer asked Mom what a lawyer was doing working as a flight attendant. Laughing haughtily, she shot back, "Doing union work."

My mom had been a flight attendant since the early 1970s, back when they were still called "air hostesses" and had to look like part-time models. For most of her career, up until the 1990s, she still had to meet a certain weight requirement to be cleared to work. She told me she was hired specifically because they were looking for smart Black women they thought could represent the airline in a desirable way to passengers. On the surface, she fit the respectability politics mold Black people are often required to fit ourselves into.

They didn't think they were getting someone who had spent years organizing in her community against economic segregation, redlining practices, overpolicing, and discriminatory hiring policies—a background she brought to union organizing at United Airlines, much to the chagrin of United executives. And they *definitely* didn't think they were getting someone who would go back to school and get a master's in labor and industrial relations, as well as a law degree from the University of Illinois Urbana-Champaign, in part to negotiate labor contracts for her union. But that's my mom. Even in retirement, she wants to go work at an Amazon warehouse so she can do union organizing there.

When the manager at United Airlines told my mom "she didn't fit the profile" of someone they usually hired at United, he meant it as a compliment. When she asked him, in what I imagine was her uppity way, "What do you mean by that?" He replied it was because she just said what she wanted to say and was always out in front of ideas.

> At that time, I didn't even know they had a profile. I said, "You're joking." He said, "No, I'm not." I asked, "What profile—for women, period, or for flight attendants?" He said, "No, for Blacks." I was really quite surprised to hear that. I had no idea they had some profile. When I got hired, the girl that [sic] hired me, she and I were both Brownie leaders. We never talked about the airline. We only talked about what we did with our Brownie troops and stuff like that. It didn't occur to me they were looking for docile Black women.

Moreover, they wanted someone who looked like they could model for *Playboy* (or at least their clothing line) but knew how to stay in their place. They wanted superwomen who, on the surface, fit traditional perceptions of femininity and respectability politics, as if to mitigate the ways their presence in the labor force was starting to challenge that. Women who checked the diversity box of Black, as long as they didn't look *too* Afrocentric BLACK. After all, that would make customers uncomfortable. And they wanted women who maintained at least a pretense of being demure even while they were routinely being propositioned as though they were sex workers—and in ways one should not ever approach a sex worker—whether they were open to that or not.

But it wasn't in my mom to stand back and watch injustices unfold, especially when Black women and Black people in general are the ones who have to face the brunt of policies created to reinforce social, political, and economic castes. Similar to my mom, *Playboy*'s creative director in residence, Cardi B, continues to leverage her power and the resources at her disposal to work against systems that weaponize respectability politics and moral policing. In the aftermath of the passage of FOSTA-SESTA and crackdowns on platforms like OnlyFans, she rolled out the announcement that *Playboy* was launching a new, creator-led, digital platform called CENTERFOLD. Like OnlyFans, it would allow content creators and those working in the sex industry and adult entertainment to interact directly with their fans and build out their own commerce businesses in the name of creative freedom, economic empowerment, artistic expression, and sex positivity.

Playboy has always been seen as a secret shame, something you should hide in the basement or under a mattress. A dirty magazine. Maybe that was because of the nudity, but maybe that was also America's natural response to articles and interviews stridently affirming the dignity of people not traditionally seen in roles of power, even if in a limited container. In a post-Hefner era, *Playboy* has become an online venue that not only makes room for alternative political thought, but also explicitly empowers Black women and others on the margins to create their own spaces on their terms. And the good news is now that *Playboy* is digital, we can experience that without having to pull apart the sticky pages to get to the good stuff.

Interlude: Awkward Adventures on OnlyFans

Some of the biggest twenty-first-century fights that cut across race, gender, and technology are the interconnected fights for autonomy, safety, representation, and anticensorship that are taking place in and around the sex industry. I knew I couldn't tell the story of outsider Black feminists just through the pages of *Playboy*. I also wanted to bring in the voices of sex workers who are operating on the frontlines of these issues.

I decided to shoot my shot with one of my favorite porn content creators, Lotus Lain. I had seen her talking often about Black Lives Matter, free speech, technology, and how it all relates to the sex industry. She is also the industry relations advocate for Free Speech Coalition, the trade association of the adult entertainment industry.

After a super awkward outreach on OnlyFans that involved me accidentally offering to "make things weird" for her, thanks to a bad cut-and-paste job, she agreed to meet for an interview.

I spent a lot of time worrying about what I was going to wear. I changed, like, three times.

"Do you have something that doesn't look like you're going to a funeral?" my friend Jay texted me after insisting I take a photo of each outfit.

No. No, I didn't. I was also staying in my parents' basement during COVID, my dad had just died, and I was working on this book. Most of my clothes gave off the vibe that I had given up on life.

"Just brush your hair, put on red lipstick, and do your recording in the room with the leopard print carpet and the good lighting so you create ambiance, darling," my mom helpfully suggested.

"Don't forget to drink your water out of your mom's Waterford crystal glass so you look classy while staying hydrated," my husband jokingly added.

After a jam-packed interview, I then agonized for a while over how to synthesize it. She had made so many wonderful points. Then, I decided instead of overthinking it, I should just do it *Playboy* style and give it to you straight, no chaser.

So, in honor of everyone who's ever read through the stuck-together pages of a magazine because you really *were* interested in the articles, I'd like to present you with 10 Questions with the lovely Lotus Lain.

(Yes, I know normally it's Twenty Questions, but space is at a premium in this book since economy of words is not my strong suit.)

10 Questions with Lotus Lain

When you saw my message, did you think about not responding?

LOTUS: I was kind of surprised at first. I thought, "This sounds like some bullshit," because, like, I've gotten weird, long messages before. But it was people being scammer-ish or trying to fish for information in a weird, convoluted story that they made up. When I saw your message, I also wasn't sure I wanted to respond, especially unless you were willing to do my full rate. It's exhausting—all the conversations and asks to do free panels about racism in porn. It can be really emotionally draining.

Well, thank you for responding. You had a different career before you moved into the industry. Why porn?

LOTUS: I joke around and say, "I always felt like *Total Recall* because every time I would have sex or a random hookup, I'd hear, "Damn, girl, you should be [in] porn." At first I thought, that's crazy. But after more than five people said it, I made a secret pact with myself that if I still wanted to do it when I was thirty, I was going to just do it. When I had my kid at twenty-five, I had the realization that I hadn't really fulfilled a dream that I always wanted. I was a pretty conservative young person besides just hooking up. I realized that I couldn't raise someone to be everything they want to be if I hadn't done that myself. I would be a hypocrite. And maybe it also started out as a social experiment with myself to see if I could do it. Once I got into it, I found my community. I didn't have to feel like my approach to relationships and sex was abnormal. I felt so isolated growing up, so different. But going into porn, not only did I find people like me, I found myself.

Love that. OK, switching gears. So much about the entertainment industry is about categories based on perception versus self-identity. What's that like?

LOTUS: It was weird to be thirty, and I came into the industry, and they're immediately, like, putting me in the "old bitches" category. Not bitches, it was nicer than that, but same energy. And, yeah, being multiracial, I got into the industry, and it's, like, your ass is Black. But they don't even understand what Black means to or for us. So, it's not just that you're Black, it's "you're Black, you must twerk on command." That was a shift. I've learned to find comfort within my Blackness, my strength. Yeah. That comes from my family. But also amongst my peers, you know. I found my best friend, Ana Foxxx. And it's a real Black girl friendship, someone I could be my worst self with. Someone I could be my best self with. We challenge each other to be better. We've seen each other grow, and I don't think I would ever have this type of friendship in another field. So we relate to how messed up the industry has treated us as Black performers, but also we can say, well, we're still gonna be fabulous. We're still us. There's a lot of girls that [sic] get bitter. But we lean on each other, and we say fuck it: we're mad, we're bitter, but we're going to change this shit. We're going to be here. They're not going to kick us out. They're not going to make us go off and be secret escorts. We're going to be running so much shit that they're going to hire us, whether they like it or not.

Do you feel that solidarity is across the board among Black performers?

LOTUS: No, not across the board. There are girls that [sic] are beautiful, they're popular, but their behavior is the worst toward fellow Black people. They don't feel solidarity. There's [sic] girls who will just do any type of porn, and that's a problem for me because I feel like, value yourself and value us, you know? Because when you don't, it hurts all of us. It makes rates lower; it allows these companies to degrade us without having an obligation to change. Plus, it's still very cliquish. The Black porn industry is so vast—there's mainstream, there's the independent route, there's the LA scene, then more down South or New York based, and they have their own cliques. I even recently saw a new social media group with Black porn actors. I didn't know any of those people. I was surprised, but also that was really cool to me. Because that means more Black people feel comfortable jumping in the mix. And it's not just because you know someone or because someone put you on, but you're doing your own thing, making your own way. And that's exciting. Hopefully, we get along when we finally meet each other. That's always the goal.

Can policy create change?

LOTUS: In theory, it should make positive change. *Does it, though*, is the question. I feel like the exact moment we knew things were stalled was the [January 6th] insurrection. No shit happened from that. It just went down the way it did, super casual. Everybody was able to go home. It re-affirmed, "Oh, no one actually gives a fuck about all this sacred America shit." The whole thing, like I knew, was a farce. All those lawmakers, all those Republican lawmakers that sit there and come up with all these fake-ass ideas like FOSTA-SESTA. It's not about creating positive change.

Porn is supposedly a health risk. That's what all these different conservative lawmakers say. But they're the main ones that supported or fanned the flames of the insurrection. I just can't even wrap my head around it. You guys are saying that sex is what's killing our country, and you literally have these people with bags of feces, COVID, all kinds of nasty-fucking germs and disease—you let them up into the Capitol. And the same people who say they're so worried about saving our country, they don't want to charge anyone? They don't want to help. I'm, like, *you guys* are the public health crisis.

White supremacy is the public health crisis. It's always been. Things could be different if they weren't so set on being supreme. If they were chill with progress and equality, we could actually reach the goal of America as this great place that we envision. But greatness doesn't come with keeping others down or ignoring injustices against one group. As far as in our industry, too, after BLM and public conversations about pay inequities, it was almost business as usual before 2020 even ended. People started making movies again. As soon as I told one production company my full rate, if they wanted me to be production manager, they ghosted me. We're back to the typical jokes and high jinks and bullshit, you know.

How much does it cost to be a successful Black porn star?

LOTUS: Well, start with taking an Uber to a set, some, like, basic shit like that. And then what most people don't take into account are all the things that a Black woman has to do to be deemed desirable at a baseline in the industry. Even if white girls get extensions put in, they can either take them out the same night, [or] they can glue and staple them in. They're easier to manage. Ours have to get done more frequently, especially in porn, because jizz is flowing everywhere. If you're [a] Black girl, you have to be on point, you can't get the cheap ones. You've got to get the good ones. Sometimes five hundred dollars or more. And with all the fluids, they don't last for several scenes. Nails are a big one. White girls can show up with, literally, like grown-out nails or busted toenails that are chipped and not painted. It's "alternative." But a Black girl, you literally have to be on point because there's already an assumption about you and your personal maintenance just because you're Black. You have to come, like, goddess level—Beyoncé level in their mind—you know.

Makeup, you have to have a backup makeup bag because you don't know what the artist will be like. And again, it has to be good makeup because there's stuff flying at your face. I had one makeup artist that [*sic*] had me looking like the Joker, like she just did a paint by numbers on my face. My friend, I remember her being really upset. She had flat ironed her hair to the point where it was all breaking off because that's the thing with Black girls. You have to have straight hair, especially if you're, like, a 4c chick. You can't have a natural 'fro unless that's the theme of the shoot.

Pubic hair. That's a whole thing. If you shave, the razor blades can cause razor bumps and all sorts of stuff that doesn't look great when there's a close-up. So then you have to afford a laser treatment, and there's only a specific kind of laser that works only on Black skin. And you have to go to a practitioner that [sic] knows how to work with dark skin, or you'll get burned. Everything is extra time, extra research, just extra everything in order to be on a bookable level.

If people only knew how expensive it can get—because if you don't look good from the beginning to the cum shot, you get hired less, and you're already working with less money to do stuff, less opportunities to do big-budget shoots.

What do people misunderstand about the ho life?

LOTUS: We are not fucking scammers. The people that [sic] are scammers aren't real hoes. Real hoes don't scam, real hoes make money. Non-ho people think, "Oh, I could jump on this ho train real quick, scam money." But that's not the way we really are. This is a business—we work out, we take pictures, we promote ourselves, we interact with our fans. All of that is a business. We're not scamming people; those people are not a part of the industry. It's the same thing with sex traffickers. They're not a part of the industry. They're doing something else completely.

How do you see your legacy?

LOTUS: I hope it would be that we really made people aware of the injustices in our industry, not just racial, but the treatment in general, and we didn't get off the necks of those in power until they changed, you know, because we're still in the middle of it right now. There's [sic] still people who we have to meet with and let them know about themselves and things that are going to get called out. I have a passionate spirit about all kinds of social justice issues, but I can see that I'm having an influence in this space. Not just in my own advocacy but [also] in having conversations with other people and getting them activated. I just hope people don't feel like they have to accept the way that other people choose to see them, whether it be . . . a dumb porn star, the angry Black woman, a stupid Black bitch, or the "do-nothing" single mother.

That could have been what people saw in me, but I won't let that be my legacy. People don't have to let all the things that others think make them feel like all of this is hopeless.

Do you worry about getting blackballed for speaking out?

LOTUS: I knew that could happen, but I was ready to let it happen because even if porn got taken away from me, I know I could do something else with my life. This is my favorite thing that I'm choosing to do with my life. So, yeah, that would suck. But if I have to lose my career over calling out these motherfuckers, then so be it. They have been here for twenty years, proud of what they've done, proud of complacency. It is mind-boggling. And you have to, like, throw it back in their face and let them know what they're saying. You're saying you're *proud* of a legacy of denying people opportunities? Because you keep picking a favorite based off of data and data that's based off of who you keep putting on because that's who people keep seeing in the front. I feel really passionate and powerful about what we are doing because we could be, like, fuck this, we could do some something else, but no, we're going to be those Black women who we wanted to see when we were new in the industry. And we're going to put other Black women on and give them their moments to shine because no one's going to do it but us.

Any companies or performers that you would want to lift up that are down for the cause?

LOTUS: Mike Adriano Productions is one of the best for the hardcore people out there. People get on his ass because he doesn't shoot with as many women of color, but he employs nothing but women of color behind the scenes. I'm one of them. I've helped write captions for him. Even down to the makeup artists. That's what I'm talking about. People want to do public service announcements, tweet things, look good on social media, but they don't want to do the work that it takes to change things. You can be like Mike and quietly do your thing behind the scenes, or you can be more vocal and push for tangible changes, but do the work.

Thank you to Lotus Lain for an awesome interview.

10

An Abomination of Obamanation
The Rise of the Pro-Black Conservative Movement and the Implications for Future Voting Patterns

How did your meetings go?"

"Meh . . . you know how it goes with Congressman [redacted]. Talks a good game, but we both know that . . . what the unholy fuck??"

"What just happened? Brandi, are you OK??"

Have you ever had one of those *Twilight Zone* moments that just fuck with your head? One of those moments that you find yourself revisiting over and over again because there's a disconnect between what you're witnessing and what you believe to be true?

I've had several of them.

But there's one moment that fucks with my head more than any of the others, and it's the moment that sent me on the journey of writing this book.

The year was 2018. It was a bright and sunny fall day. I was in Washington, DC's Union Station. I had just gotten through an exhausting slate of meetings on Capitol Hill and was on the phone debriefing with my colleague before jumping on the train.

All of the sudden, I saw them.

Hundreds of jubilant teenagers streaming past me. All in MAGA hats.

In hindsight, there may have been twenty of them, max, but it seemed like hundreds. Thousands, even.

Because they were Black. Black, I tell you. Black AF, as a matter of fact.

I thought for a second that maybe they were in costume since it was close to Halloween. But they didn't really seem like jaded teenagers doing group cosplay as a legion of Kanyes. They seemed very giddy about their Black MAGA pride, rocking their red MAGA hats with all the flex and attitude that a kid with Jordan 1 sneakers would have had in the 1980s.

I paused with my mouth open, my conversation forgotten. They walked, ran, and skipped out the door, and I almost broke my neck craning it to follow them. I half expected them to walk outside and disintegrate into dust as though they had never been there.

But they were just as real as me.

My colleague on the other end of the phone called me back to attention, asking me why I had stopped mid-rant about Congressman [redacted]. As I sped up to catch my train, I tried to explain what I had seen.

"There was a Black MAGA teen apocalypse. They were everywhere in red hats. Being happy and shit."

"Are you sure they were MAGA? Maybe they just like red hats. Maybe you're just tired; you've been on the road a lot."

Part of me wanted to believe I was hallucinating, but those teens were real. As I sat on the train heading home, I had only one thing on my mind: those kids.

Who the hell were these unnaturally happy Trump-supporting children in our midst? Where did they come from? Were they even old enough to vote? Where were their parents? I needed to know everything.

So Here's Where They Came From . . .

In the next two chapters, I'm going to look at who I call right-wing Black skinheads. These are people who are currently underrepresented in mainstream and right-wing media discourse and who reject their societal value or cultural identity being defined by their willingness to vote for the Democratic Party. And to do that, I'm going to start with their leadership—or at least, those purporting to be their leaders.

From the moment I saw those Black MAGA young'uns, they held my curiosity. I would learn later they were part of the inaugural Young

Black Leadership Summit, which had been put on by Turning Point USA (TPUSA), a conservative group that had been taking over college campuses and recruiting people for years. That week, a few hundred Black MAGA people would go to the White House to meet with Donald Trump and would also hear speeches from then secretary of housing and urban development Ben Carson, actress and resident conservative vampire Stacey Dash, and others.

TPUSA founder Charlie Kirk fed the energy of the group that week. "The fakers say you don't exist," he told the crowd as they cheered, chanting "USA!" and "Trump! Trump! Trump!" It was the moment that any white person who's been inspired by movies like *The Help, The Blind Side,* and/or *Cool Runnings* would kill for. This white man had led Black people to the promised land, off the so-called Democratic plantation and into Trump's gilded tower.

So here's the deal on Charlie Kirk and TPUSA. Charlie was born and raised in a 90 percent white suburb just north of Chicago. Naturally. He grew up obsessed with the godfather of neoliberalism, economist Milton Friedman. Naturally. And from a young age, he was obsessed with getting into politics and aspired to rule the world, or at least the United States. Naturally. As a teenager, he wrote a piece for Breitbart called "Liberal Bias Starts in Economic Textbooks." As I understand it, the gist of the article is that unionized teachers and left-wing economists are pushing a liberal agenda for "equality," and that's bad. He's the one who put "equality" in quotes. I read it a couple of times, and that basically seems to be what he's saying.

Around 2012, Charlie met Bill Montgomery, a wealthy restaurateur, marketer, and conservative who saw promise in Charlie. He dropped out of an online university to start an organization that would rival progressive internet-based grassroots (aka netroots) group MoveOn.org. Started in 1998, MoveOn is the pioneer of email-based petitions, online advocacy, and targeted advertising. They had turned out volunteers, activists, and online voices for President Obama's 2008 and 2012 campaigns. Charlie wanted to see a youth-led machine that could reinvigorate the Republican Party, recruit on campuses, and develop a pipeline of future conservative leaders and media spokespeople.

Soon, Charlie and Bill Montgomery had donors lined up, including US Supreme Court Justice Clarence Thomas's wife, Ginni Thomas;

Home Depot cofounder Bernard Marcus; and others. Turning Point USA was off and running.

While the Left Sleeps

This strategy of replicating liberal and progressive institutions is part of a long game the Republicans have been playing for quite some time. Conservatives have gotten quite adept at copying what works on the Left. They secure dark money funding from rich, right-wing donors and then build out what appears to be a credible grassroots movement with what's really a bought-and-paid-for machine. This is a practice known as astroturfing, or fake it till you make it, as they say.

In 1995, internet pioneer, academic, and mysterious recluse Dr. Phil Agre pointed out in *WIRED Magazine* that over decades, right-wing funding had been filtered into building out a network of parallel institutions that were meant to mirror and challenge mainstream liberal media, public interest, think tank and political institutions. The *Washington Times* mirrored the *New York Times*, the American Center for Law and Justice mirrored the ACLU, and The Heritage Foundation mirrored the Brookings Institution. The right wing countered the center-left political philanthropy space occupied in the 1950s to 1970s by private foundations like the Ford Foundation with the corporate-backed, right-wing American Legislative Exchange Council.

This web of institutions, Agre said, marked the largest and deepest shift in US political institutions since the New Deal, and all this was happening while the Left slept. He maintained that liberal institutions had been slow to really pay attention to the alternative institutions being developed right under their noses. Their world has been stable for so long that they couldn't wrap their heads around how changing political conditions could lead to a wave of cultural and financial resources going to these new institutions.

He suggested we were all existing in an internet space that had been shaped and framed by a set of actors using alternative media vehicles. These conservative and libertarian figures had the production, material, and relational means to hijack populist and leftist rhetoric and repurpose it to consolidate their own power, amplify their own message, and erase its original meaning. Conservative raconteurs had adapted language like "elites" (a term that no longer includes bankers but does include journalists) and "political correctness" (a term once only used seriously by sectarian Leninists but is now routinely employed to conflate social dissent with political repression). Mind you—he was saying all of this back in 1995.

This is the roadmap Charlie Kirk was following. He wasn't just replicating MoveOn or being a youth-driven PR machine for the Republican Party, he was setting up real estate on the internet that allowed the Right to jump on internet trends and co-opt and reinterpret internet language.

Charlie was doing his thing, the energy was popping—and then, 2016 hit. Initially, Charlie didn't really like Trump. He felt Trump was divisive, but Charlie was a party-line Republican. So when Trump won the GOP (Grand Old Party) party nomination, Charlie knew he had to be a good soldier and bring in that youth vote he'd been promising since 2012.

Being the internet guy he is, Charlie saw the populist center of gravity building around Trump on the right-wing side of social media. Since Charlie was on campuses, he got brought on to back up Donald Trump, Jr., on the campaign trail and build his brand among younger voters. He dirtied up Jr.'s talking points, helping him get extra sassy on Twitter so he looked hip to the youth.

So when the dust had settled after the election and it became clear Trump had overperformed with youth voters, Charlie was looking like a boy wonder.

Then Charlottesville happened.

The establishment Trump base was rocked. TPUSA was rocked. They couldn't believe people thought they were white nationalists. Just because they hung out with white nationalists, used white nationalist dog whistles, and some TPUSA staffers texted each other lovely things like "I hate black people. Like fuck them all . . . I hate blacks. End of story," it didn't mean they were white nationalists or racists, right? But now they had a brand problem, especially after they fired their only Black employee. On Martin Luther King, Jr., Day. To be fair, Charlie Kirk has said that he does not condone white nationalism.

Charlie also knew the demographics of America were changing, and after Charlottesville, the winds were blowing a different way. He had to be able to tap into a diverse pipeline of young conservatives and fast.

He knew he needed some Asian people and some Latine people, and he really, really needed some Black people. But since Charlie is from a really white suburb of Chicago, he didn't know how to attract nonwhite people. He needed a Black Moses.

And in the whitest move ever, he got Candace Owens.

The Polar Bear and the Arctic Fox

Candace Owens can best be described as a YouTuber-turned-political-pundit who simultaneously demonizes "identity politics" for white conservative audiences while using her own identity as a Black woman to launder Far Right ideology. She started off as a feminist progressive journalist/part-time model who got a little too into the idea of doxxing people and then got canceled. But like a lot of people allegedly "canceled," she didn't stay canceled and instead made a hard pivot to the Right.

To give you a sense of this shift, in 2015, she had been running an anti-Trump, anti-conservative website that had launched a tongue-in-cheek investigation into then-candidate Trump's penis size, deducing it was very small. By the time of the 2016 election, she had had a whole internet makeover and emerged as Red Pill Black Girl, a Black Trump supporter going against the grain and escaping the "Democratic plantation."

You can't make this stuff up, kids.

She gained some traction, and Charlie Kirk noticed. He hired her to recruit Black young people into the TPUSA movement.

The problem was she was a burgeoning social media influencer, and that's very different from being able to get boots on the ground.

So Candace was spinning her wheels, tweeting and being all in her zone. She may not have known how to round up Black people offline, but she definitely knew PR. And she caught a break. A huge one. A video of her went viral. In it, she's yelling at Black protesters at the University of California, Los Angeles, calling them "privileged Americans" obsessed with "shouting about slavery." Of course, it got the attention of Kanye "I can make you a celebrity overnight" West, who tweeted out to the world: "I like the way Candace Owens thinks."

His tweet raised a lot of questions in the public sphere. Namely: Is Kanye OK? Where were his friends? Why doesn't someone take away Kanye's phone?

But far and away the biggest one was: Who the fuck is Candace Owens?

Trump saw what was up and followed the wave, calling in to *Fox & Friends* to say Owens was "the hottest thing out there right now." Candace got even bigger.

Before this moment, the most prominent Black MAGA influencers were Diamond and Silk, two older Black women whose performative Trump videos came across to *some* as more of a Stepin Fetchit vibe (I'll let y'all look that one up) than the more alluring visual of a young, Black, fly MAGA movement. Diamond and Silk hadn't even voted for Trump in 2016—that was how thin the Black MAGA spokesperson pool was. But now, the Trump team had Kanye, Candace, and the potential to attract a roster of young Black leaders they could call up to help counter the white nationalist MAGA narrative that had long plagued Trump, especially after Charlottesville.

Trump took a face-to-face, twenty-minute meeting with Candace and Charlie Kirk at the White House. Kirk later told reporters he and Candace talked to Trump about "Black America, Kanye West, and the intersection of culture and politics," and the "incredible progress being made for Black America by President Trump . . ." I wonder how the time was divided between talking about Kanye West and talking about the progress being made.

I had a dream once that I was a fly on the wall during that meeting and there were more N bombs dropped than at a 1960s Klan rally in Mississippi. Legal advised me to tell you that it was just a dream.

In any event, after the meeting, Candace was rewarded with a Trump tweet about the "big impact" she was having on politics: "so good for our Country!" She was put on, big, and she latched on to Kanye because she knew he was her golden ticket. He had given her instant credibility, an instant audience, and instant access to an untapped base of younger Black voters who were disillusioned with Democratic Party politics.

At the time, the relationship between Kanye and Candace was something like the symbiotic one that exists between polar bears and arctic foxes: one in which one species benefits from the relationship while the other is virtually unaffected and in some ways derives pleasure from being needed. You see, in the winter, when food is scarce, arctic foxes track and follow polar bears out on the hunt. The polar bear makes the kill and feeds until full, and then the arctic fox follows behind and dines on the scraps. The polar bear is fully aware of what the arctic fox is doing but remains unbothered.

In this metaphor, Kanye is the polar bear and Candace is the arctic fox. After receiving Trump and Kanye's support, she moved fast, seizing the opportunity to get fed. She and TPUSA quickly rolled out a really slick-looking initiative attempting to become a movement: #Blexit, or Black exit. It was a call to Black people to leave the so-called Democratic plantation and jump aboard Team MAGA. She made the media rounds, giving the strong impression that Kanye had been hands-on with developing the branding.

There was only one small problem: #Blexit was already being used. In 2016 it had been coined as a term by an economic justice movement looking to encourage Black Americans to explore community banking as well as other alternatives to extractive financial systems that engage in exclusionary and predatory lending practices. It was formed out of a set of community meetings after the police killing of Philando Castile in Minnesota.

TurningPointUSA steamrolled right through that noise, much to the horror of the Blexit founders, one of whom called the right-wing initiative "so counter to what we view as an inclusive future for Black people." No matter. With their dark money ATM, Candace and Charlie were able to ignore two cease-and-desist letters from the original Blexit movement and push paid advertising using stock photos of Black people across social media.

Really.

I just want to pause for a moment to really let that sink in—Candace Owens and Charlie Kirk took the name of a *real* burgeoning Black movement for independent economic power and changed its meaning. They bought up all the online real estate around Blexit and used it to push something so inauthentic they had to use stock photos instead of images of real supporters.

Just like the website photos, the TPUSA events were misleading as well. A Black conservative woman would be the one to expose how flimsy Candace's grassroots game was. YouTuber Tree Of Logic released a series of YouTube videos from #Blexit events showing that much of their flex was astroturfed, smoke and mirrors. Tree Of Logic uncovered the publicly reported number of attendees at live events was more than double the actual number, that the majority of attendees were white, and that many of the Black attendees had to be paid and bused in from other parts of the country to fill seating.

See, even Black conservatives can sniff out Candace's hustle because her disdain for Black Americans—and really anyone with half a moral conscience—is too obvious. I don't even know if she's trying to hide it. She gets really close to saying things like *white nationalism is a hoax* and *Hitler would've been fine if he had kept the concentration camps in his country.*

There's a video clip of Candace fighting with Steve Bannon about whether to put resources into local Black communities. In it, he advocates for spending money on tech skills development and education programs in major cities to grow the economy.

Proudly (and on camera) Candace responds, "And here's where I disagree with your assessment. . . . So the problem that you're facing is that, yes, Black Americans, Hispanic Americans should be competing, but do they want to? . . . [In Black Americans] you have people that are looking for excuses and looking to be victims, and it's being promoted in the culture."

If you had told me that in a conversation between a Black woman and someone who has to repeatedly deny being a Neo-Nazi and white nationalist I would be more on the side of the person who calls himself a "race realist," I would think you were nuts. But here we are. Welcome to my personal nightmare, where no one wins and we all go to hell.

The anti-Black sentiment dripping from some of her tweets was a turnoff to many Black Republicans who are concerned with matters of Black success and opportunity. It was not long before the jig was up and there was a very public exit out of the #Blexit movement.

Well, let me not call it a movement; that's a reach.

But Candace's high jinks were hiding something more important and more powerful: that there *are* a bunch of new Black right-wing leaders. Some may have refined and developed certain social media hacks by going through the TPUSA bootcamps, but there are many different entry points into conservatism that range from religious institutions to alt-right online message boards to libertarian spaces. These leaders all have their own savvy and swagger that they're using to build up a revival pro-Black conservative movement that doesn't shy away from identity politics and that allows them to spread their gospel in an authentic way.

I saw what I saw on that fall day in DC. Those kids were living, breathing, walking, wearing MAGA hats, everything. Some Black people somewhere were going to these TPUSA events, and a new group of leaders was emerging, ready to take their followers away from the Democratic Party. The question to me was, if Candace Owens and Charlie Kirk were all smoke and mirrors, is that what the actual Black conservative youth movement looks like?

Spreading the Gospel of Conscious Black Conservatism

> In keeping with my promise to elevate Black voices that deserve to be heard and are completely ignored by everyone else in the media, we have a follow-up tonight on a story we brought you back in May, a story of twenty-two-year-old King Randall. Now King's group, [The] X for Boys, has empowered his community of at-risk youth by not only giving them a safe space, safe place, but also through education. He's also not just teaching out of a textbook. King teaches his kids everything from how to change a tire to how to mow the lawn . . .
>
> —*FOX NEWS PRIMETIME* WITH LAWRENCE B. JONES III,
> NOVEMBER 10, 2021

I had been keeping tabs on the rise of young Black conservatism ever since that day when I saw the kids going to the White House in 2018. I had noticed they were gaining traction online, building bigger followings, and developing their own brand. But 2021, post-MAGA, seemed like a coming-out party for the Conscious Black Conservatives.

In December 2017, about four months after Charlottesville, one of the speakers for the TPUSA Student Action Summit was Lawrence B. Jones III. Jones had come to prominence in 2015 for raising money for a pizza shop that refused to cater a gay wedding and had since become a prominent voice in mainstream conservatism. In 2021, he was offered a role as enterprise reporter across the *Fox & Friends* franchise, and before the end of the year, he had landed a spot on *Fox News Primetime.*

Over the years, the pool of Black conservative Fox News pundits has been fairly lean and skewed older. They've also towed the line on GOP talking points. But in his new position, Jones wasted no time in promoting a number of the younger Black conservatives I had been following over the years.

In one week in November 2021, *Fox News Primetime* rolled out a who's who of the new Black Right, including Tea Party veteran Sonnie Johnson; political organizer and founder of the Conscious Conservative Movement and Network, Felecia Killings—who is widely credited with coining the term *Conscious Black Conservative* in 2018; and Olivia Rondeau, college wrestler and writer for the Foundation for Economic Education. They also featured Afrocentric alt-right Proud Boy media personality Hotep Jesus, who I don't really fuck with. He's a bit too much of an algorithmic clout chaser and conspiracy pusher for my taste. Even Joe Rogan has called him out for his weird shit about soy and damaging denial of the African slave trade's existence—which is saying something.

The clip that appeared to get the most traction on social media was one with King Randall, who had been battling with his local school board in Albany, Georgia, to open his own school. He was eventually granted the right to open a school.

> Children are failing at reading. Our children are failing at many different things in our local hometown of Albany, Georgia. But here we are trying to help our young men and push them forward. . . . These children just need to see possible, and so many of our children in the city of Albany don't get to see possible.

Notice the difference between Candace Owens telling Steve Bannon that Black Americans don't want to be successful and are undeserving of community investment, and King Randall saying just the opposite—that Black children deserve more than what they're getting from government systems. Randall notes he doesn't get paid by the national GOP (they hadn't at that point reached out to him). He was focused on the bigger picture beyond party alliances:

> I shun people who try to politicize my message. I've had a lot of people, even conservatives, get upset with me for maybe going to different spaces. . . . I had to go to these spaces to give the message. I have to go there and tell them the truth about what's actually going on in our communities. . . . I'm trying to make a unity piece where we're unified [across] many different groups of people. . . . We have the same issues. It's not within your race, it's not within the parties, it is within your government.

That week of FOX News programming marked the largest platforming of unambiguously pro-Black conservatives to date. I don't know how many of them were the kids I saw in DC, but these conservatives had arrived, and they had a different energy.

Conscious Black conservatives (CBCs) distinguish themselves from the Candace Owens and Diamond and Silk contingent of Republican thought, establishing their own vision for what the GOP could be for them and for other young people. They have been a crucial part of reshaping the post-MAGA conservative movement that has been building momentum since Trump's loss in November 2020. Many, even those who found their political footing as Trump voters, hesitate to call themselves "Republicans" instead of independent conservative voters.

Online, they are primarily composed of Gen X, millennial, and Gen Z Black voters and are universally against the messaging and leadership of #Blexit and Turning Point USA. They are also skeptical of boomer conservatives in the talk-radio sphere—people like Larry Elder—referring to these Black avatars for white conservatives as "Black Conservative Inc." They believe a historic realignment of Black Democrats back to the Republican Party is possible if white conservatives listen to Black voters. But they're also willing to talk across ideological lines to build power outside of the national GOP. Consistent points of alignment are opposition to gun control and unapologetic, full-stop capitalism—both in service of protecting and empowering Black communities.

CBCs are pro-Black, pro-prison and police reform, and open to real discussions about addressing the racial wealth gap and reparations. Many publicly voiced their critique of President Joe Biden specifically because of his role in the drafting of the 1994 crime bill, which had a devastating impact on their generation. Most that I've seen are socially conservative when it comes to sexuality, gender, and reproductive justice issues, and outside of basic social services, economically libertarian. They want Black people to be able to "pull themselves up by their bootstraps," but they don't lie about poor Black people not having boots to pull.

They're largely split on lightning-rod topics like critical race theory, with some accurately pointing out how most white right-wingers are pushing pro-white narratives while offering nothing material to Black people in return. They are equally split on Black Lives Matter—while many agree with many of the movement's demands, they critique their methods and the "Marxist" core of the movement, and some take issue with BLM's pro-LGBTQ+ stance. They are increasingly adopting terminology and frames to articulate a nationalist/nativist conservative/libertarian Black political identity. Some, in fact, would hate my use of identity politics, but they are undeniably articulating an agenda for Black people in America.

Their content is largely socially progressive on racial issues, and they don't engage in swarm-like activity to attack critics; more focus is placed on developing a pundit class of CBC evangelists. CBCs organize proudly and openly on YouTube, Twitter, and Instagram, using streaming services or Clubhouse to reach wider audiences. Influencers in the movement use exclusively factual peer-reviewed materials in their claims, even engaging with critical leftist and antiracist scholarship to build their arguments.

Thus far, many have taken an active role in calling out disinformation operations and misinformation, actively debunking false narratives that arise in their community. That's not true of all of them, but it is important to note disinformation and misinformation spread can and has happened across the ideological spectrum because of failures of tech companies to rein it in. They're also pro-democracy, and not only encourage the Black vote but also campaign locally for candidates they are invested in. They share a restrictionist view on immigration that aligns them with many other American right-wing factions.

Personally, I don't agree with many of their policy stances, but I don't take issue with ideological differences. My beef is primarily with false-information peddling and digital echo chambers that can be exploited for violence, chaos, and hate-mongering. In my eyes, those things, and the power to amplify certain types of information and people over others, are the biggest threats to building an inclusive democracy. But everyone can and should engage in their own political journey, and, not for nothing, I would welcome a debate on what kind of policies can benefit Black communities. The Conscious Black Conservatives have something useful to bring to the table.

Who Got Next?

There is much to be said about this new wave of Black conservatism, but one thing that's clear is there is a growing group of Black voters who are reminiscent of the political identity of those who sought to build a Canaan in the West in Tulsa, Oklahoma—Booker T. Washington style. These were the people who were less concerned with fights for social and political equality. They believed the more pragmatic approach was to accumulate enough economic capital to build autonomous communities separate from white aggression and resentment.

In the upcoming chapter, "My Beautiful Dark Twisted Fantasy," I'll introduce you to more people on that same wavelength, but I want to close this chapter by introducing you to one of them: Reign. Out of every Black MAGA person I spoke with, he gave the most insight into the potential mindset of younger, under-thirty voters who are part of the Conscious Black Conservative movement. Here's why:

Most of the Black MAGA people I interviewed were emphatically against attempting to work with Black people on the Left. This was consistent with what we have seen across the country in general—an unwillingness to even consider bridging the ideological Left-Right divide. This was, however, a clear divergence from traditional Black organizing, which has taken place across ideology for most (if not all) of the twentieth century.

This was also different from many of the Conscious Black Conservatives I had been following who, unlike their conservative elders, had directly engaged online with self-identified Black leftists. More than anything, in CBCs, I see a fork in the road marking how algorithmically segregated political organizing is fracturing Black communities working in service of a better life for all of us.

Reign is a younger millennial from Chicago. He was born in the 1990s and is a fan of "old Kanye West." I had noticed a couple of times that while many Black MAGA people I spoke with talked in sweeping generalizations about liberal voters, he had politely but firmly offered an alternative take: that maybe Black people should be talking to each other across ideology in order to find shared values.

"What's your book called, by the way?" he asked. I kind of slow played the title, not wanting to shut down the conversation before it even started.

"Untitled, umm . . . but I'm leaning toward *Black Skinhead*."

"That's controversial for sure; it'll turn heads," he responded.

He talked about his political journey, discovering Chicago had not had a Republican leader since the 1920s. He had voted for President Obama in his first election in 2008, but didn't vote in 2012 or 2016. The 2020 election would be his first time voting for a Republican: Trump. He had been led toward Trump by the desire for small government and independent economic empowerment.

He pointed out that America is a capitalist country. It's about money: making money and economic power. His political ideology was evolving. Religious ideology wasn't a motivating factor for him, but Black people, and everybody in America, need money in order to live. And Trump, in his estimation, knew how to make money.

> Before you were a conservative, you were Black. Before you're a Christian, you're Black. When white conservatives look at the values of America, they say they want to go back to a time when everybody was safe, went to church, and prayed in school. We weren't allowed the freedom to do that. So to me, it's not about the past, it's about the future. I think that every Black person in America, if we can't agree on everything else, we can agree that it's time to get out of this system. We can all agree upon our history and the role of skin color in influencing our history. In order to even have a future in this country, we need to focus on our present economic situation to guarantee that we can have a future.

But he wasn't necessarily a committed Republican or even a staunch right-wing voter.

> Everything else, to me, is secondary. It doesn't matter if you go to church or not, if your church is going to get blown up. It doesn't matter if I want the right education if I don't even have the option to get *an* education. I'm not really tripping on conservative or whatever else; to me, it's about how to get the power to create something new.

Several studies in the last few years have challenged the very idea of a "swing voter," noting that the only choice that swings an election outcome is whether or not to vote at all. But more than most other ethnic and racial groups, Black voters have been nothing if not Democratic Party loyalists during the last several decades.

For voters under thirty, that appears to be changing. One study by American University found only 47 percent of Black voters under thirty say the Democratic Party is welcoming to Black Americans. Even fewer, 43 percent, say they trust Democrats in Congress to do what's best for the Black community. The door is open. But despite these Democratic Party failings, it remains to be seen whether conservatives can connect at scale on any genuine messaging to these distrustful Black Democrats.

If there's anything the TPUSA #Blexit fail shows, it's that despite outward appearances, Republicans do actually recognize that to stay relevant, they have to court Black voters on some level. When you listen to the Republicans' rhetoric, it's not a secret they have run all the numbers, and they understand that if they can get 20 to 25 percent of the Black vote, then it's over. They will win every time. And so, they know they have to find ways to convince Black people to their side—ideally without losing the base of Republican voters drawn in by racist talking points.

In 2020, despite hitting the 90 percent mark with Black voters, the Democratic Party had to overrely on Black voters over sixty to pull those numbers. Only 78 percent of Black voters ages thirty to forty-four went for Biden. Younger voters were slightly more, but still not the high numbers they once were. Those who had left the party didn't equal the magic 25 percent number Republicans are looking for, but that's also not really a trajectory the Democratic Party should feel comfortable being on, not when millennials and Gen Zers are less than two presidential elections away from dominating the electorate.

Trump lost Black voters in the aggregate, but those small percentages are creeping up in a worrying way. We are beginning to see signals that in the coming decades, Black voters could be looking at a voting realignment. But what that actually means for Black voter behavior is less clear. In 2021, we saw more Black Republicans in Congress than we've seen since Reconstruction. On the other hand, congresspeople like Cori Bush and Jamaal Bowman, who are members of the Democratic Socialists of America, have shown they're not in DC to play rec league softball. Moreover, younger Black voters are more likely than their elders to embrace socialism. We have a national Democratic Party that has placed a high premium on the voice and opinions of conservative Congressional Black Caucus statespeople and a Grand Old Party that would rather deal with a volatile Candace Owens than a Conscious Black Conservative. So which party (and which voter base) is in the best position to take advantage of the political moment?

11

My Beautiful Dark Twisted Fantasy
What Happens When a Black (Sort-Of) Leftist Meets Some Black (Very) MAGA People?

After my encounter with the Black MAGA kids, I was determined to learn more about Black MAGA supporters in general, so I turned to the one person I knew could help me—Lisa.

She was more than happy to help and asked me how many Black MAGA people I knew.

"Basically, just my cousin that [*sic*] watches QAnon and gold standard videos, in between listening to house music and tie-dying things. And now you."

"Would you like to meet some?"

"Yes. More than life itself, I would like for that to happen."

You see, Lisa is something of a social media influencer and connector. She had been holding regular meetings and moderating a Facebook group for Black Trump supporters, and she was down to let me crash a meeting.

I had been pretty open about my left-wing tendencies with Lisa, but I had gotten her to warm up to me enough to introduce me to the members of her Black MAGA Facebook group. I didn't know if Lisa had vouched for me as a well-meaning actor or if they just didn't care because they were open to bringing in anyone willing to listen to their perspective even if it could mean getting burned. Either way, I had hit the gold mine. Lisa and I arranged for a Zoom video call.

I was nervous. What would it be like? What would *they* be like?

I half expected it to be one of those situations where it's a Black event but there are only white people there. Like one of those Blacks for Pete Buttigieg fundraisers. But no, as the video started to populate with faces, I saw these were really Black people living their Black lives.

Now, I'm familiar with Black conservatives. There are quite a few in my family—we're a regular smorgasbord of Black political thought. But Trump seemed like a new kind of animal to me. Actually, that's not true—he seemed like a throwback to the old animals that used to burn crosses on Black people's lawns before returning to their offices to write policies to maintain economic segregation. So I couldn't really understand why Black people would be down to fuck with him like that.

I wanted to listen and truly understand what brought people to Trump. And what I learned was that for many of them, what had led them to conservatism or Trump was not conspiracy theories or delusions, but a commitment to their Black identity and to caring for their communities in a country they felt had failed them.

Things a Bernie Broad Learned from Black MAGA

When Lisa popped onto the screen that morning, I was greeted by a beautiful, vivacious woman with dark, almond-shaped eyes, bouncy curls, and a big smile. She had a charismatic energy about her, like one of those self-help gurus who has a head microphone pop stars wear.

She welcomed her group into the Zoom meeting, like the ultimate host, and helped facilitate the conversation. We talked for two hours, and many things came up. I worried people would have their guards up, and though some might have, they were also quite generous with their thoughts and time, and I was incredibly grateful for that. Our conversation was wide ranging, but by the end of the conversation, I had four main takeaways.

1. Conservative Black voters feel more empowered to break from the ranks of the Democratic Party than in recent years.

Black people have always held diverse political beliefs, but they almost always voted in service of equity and in response to and rejection of white supremacy—a unique tension at the heart of Black politics. In *The Loneliness of the Black Republican,* Dr. Rigueur explains that while Black

Republicans believed racial egalitarianism was in keeping with the party's principles, not everyone agreed with what direction the party should take.

What has long been true for those studying Black conservatism is there is no universal story of what draws certain Black people to conservatism beyond, most frequently, a pursuit of civil rights and racial equality. The mid-twentieth century was a time of turbulence for Black politics. In addition to growing fears the Republican Party did not support racial equality, the decision to nominate Barry Goldwater as the GOP presidential nominee in 1964 was considered a slap in the face for many long-standing Black Republicans. While some began to organize on a national scale for intra-party reform, by the end of the 1960s, the assassination of several key figures in the civil rights movement had left Black people reeling.

The National Black Political Convention that took place in Gary, Indiana, in March 1972 brought together Black leaders from across political ideologies to discuss what it meant to forge a unified Black political agenda after losing so many leaders. By the end, it was clear not everyone was, or ever would be, on the same page. But historians have stuck a pin in this moment, which marked a turning point in the consolidation of Black votes into the Democratic Party from the top to the bottom of the ticket.

The persistent conservative and neoliberal strands reflected in Black voter behavior within the Democratic Party are the direct result of Black Republican absorption into the party. The Black neoliberal turn of the party, Rigueur says, marks an ideological shift from traditional Black liberalism's emphasis on collective action and government intervention—which had powered New Deal-era Black rhetoric. Now, from a narrative and policy standpoint, there was a direct line drawn from economic success and hard work to "personal responsibility" and self-reliance—AKA the whole bootstraps refrain that's become a cornerstone of Capital D Black Democrat rhetoric: individual success and the building of independent Black wealth is the best way to uplift the collective race. No one cares about your grievances, just work harder.

Most of the people on the call had not always been Republican voters. In fact, most had voted for the Democratic Party for many years. But the dominant feeling now was one of frustration that it was always assumed they would vote for a Democrat. Moreover, many of them said that even when they were voting for Democratic candidates, they had considered themselves to be conservative thinkers. Lisa and her group wanted to be able to practice political agency through free choice instead of the pressure they had always felt to vote a certain way, especially since they felt the Democratic Party had often failed them:

> If I don't see a good candidate that really represents my views, then I just withhold my vote. I don't believe in that cliché that the ancestors died for you to vote. I'm, like, well, if they died for me to vote, then they also died for me not to vote, too, if I don't believe in a candidate. Voting is not the only thing you can do to change the community. I employ people, I give to my community, I do things to uplift my community. Uplifting my community is not voting for someone who doesn't care about my community.

Katina, a Generation X voter from Virginia, felt similarly. She became a Republican after Hurricane Katrina because of what she saw as failures of local Democratic leadership in New Orleans to build the infrastructure needed for the community. Similar to Lisa, she is a businesswoman and is focused on building capital for the Black community. "I think Black people need to learn how to critically think. I've never been one to want to force everyone into one party because that's what we have now."

To Katina, this didn't necessarily mean that allegiance to either party was better, but the ability to choose was imperative. "Republicans don't always speak for the Black community . . . but I don't agree with what the Left is doing: all the communism, trying to take away our individual liberties and make it hard for businesspeople. . . . When people understand how to make better choices first individually, then we can make better choices as a community, and then we can make better choices as a nation. And that way, especially with the Black community . . . I don't want blind loyalty on either side."

I do want to note here that online content in the run-up to the 2020 election falsely equated voting for Biden as a vote for communism. This was particularly used in Florida, where right-wing voices on social media target Cuban voters in Spanish- and English-language ads, with Red Scare–style messaging. President Biden himself is on record saying he sees communism as a failed system. The Communist Party also has not had a foothold in American politics since at least the collapse of Soviet communism. But I definitely agree with Katina on the piece about critical thinking and the dangers of unwavering party allegiances. Speaking of which . . .

2. [Some] Black voters on the Right also like the idea of third-party options.

I already knew there were Black independent voters, anecdotally and from national polling. For a long time, I had even been a registered independent voter before realizing that in California, "Independent" seemed to be code for weird survivalist white men who would make me uncomfortable if we ran into each other at McDonald's. Black people have a long history of working with, aligning with, and even creating their own political parties, like the populist Mississippi Democratic Freedom Party. But most of the efforts I knew about came from what today would be considered more Left, more progressive spaces, not from the Right.

Yet I saw this same desire to work outside the political establishment in the Independent Trump voters in Lisa's group. Tariq, for example, grew up in an independent-voter household. He voted for Obama in 2008 because of his anti-war stance, but in 2012 he voted for Ron Paul before becoming a Trump voter. Tariq had voted for Trump because he viewed him as a third-party candidate, not a Republican.

It was similar for Charles, a Generation X voter with a friendly demeanor who had been a conservative ever since the 2000 presidential election. He is from Gary, Indiana, and is interested in seeing Republicans develop on the local level and contest for power in both Gary and nearby Chicago, Illinois. He was also Team Fuck the Leftists, which I tried not to have a complex about, especially when I looked in the camera lens and realized I had either accidentally or subconsciously worn my "eat the rich" earrings.

"Really, you need more than three parties," Charles said. "Third party won't work. You need multiple parties." Like others, Charles's Independent standpoint was motivated by a dislike of both parties at the federal level. "They're all the same . . . they're all pro–big corporation and they all go in [to the Senate] middle class or upper–middle class and come out rich."

Maybe my earrings were fine after all.

3. Nah, man, local Black Republican politics is really where it's at, tho.

While some in the group were open to third or multiparty politics, for some of the people I talked to, the Republican Party in Black communities was an empty vessel that was there for the taking. They were less interested in immediate third-party options and more interested in a strong Republican party that could be rebuilt by and for Black people. Clifford, a Generation X union leader in Washington, DC, is also vice president of the local Republican Party.

He defines himself as a conservative across the board, a constitutional Republican and a proponent of individual rights and family values, which, to be honest, I find to be a contradictory mix, but it does ring true of traditional conservatism. He was a smooth kind of fellow; on video, he was wearing a suit and tie and posted up in his place, which looked like a 1980s R&B video that you would see on BET. He even had the DC skyline behind him. I was struck by his calm, cool demeanor. Clifford had spent years organizing the DC GOP, and for him, Republicanism offers the opportunity to build a Black power base within pre-existing political structures.

> I think the Republican Party is already a third party because we're just not there, but it's established. So in order to get a third party or fourth party, you're talking about years and years of getting it established to the point where it could garner enough votes nationwide to be viable.

Clifford pointed out that because of the voting laws in certain jurisdictions, the bar to build out a viable third party and get on the primary ballot is too high.

> When I say pick up the Republican Party, I mean that in the truest sense of the word. So, we're not asking the national GOP

to do shit. You see what I'm saying? We're not looking for the established Republican. We want to pick it up and make it our own here.

Businesswise, to me, that's the quickest route for Black people to get to the table. I'm not saying a third party isn't a goal or something we shouldn't work toward, but in the next two to four years, you're not going to have a statewide, citywide, established third party that's going to be able to compete as it is. But what we can do is pick up this empty vessel.

This was familiar to me. Earlier in the week, I had interviewed Reverend Eric Wallace, a Republican who, at the time of our interview, had been running for office for the Illinois State Senate. He pointed out something I also heard on the Black MAGA call, which is that often, Black Republicans don't even get the resources from the party that they need to run a competitive campaign, and that in major cities like Chicago, Democratic candidates run unopposed for several election cycles. From the standpoint of the folks I talked to, that meant the elected officials didn't have accountability to the community in the same way.

Rev. Eric Wallace: Black people with conservative values could find a place in the Republican Party, they just feel like [they still need to vote Democrat]. We're trying to change that. We are trying to say: hey, you need to be over here because you fit better over here; come help us change the Republican Party, so it can be a natural home.

Back with my MAGA group, Keith, a Gen Xer with an Oklahoma twang and Bill Pickett vibes, agreed with this. Like Clifford and Rev. Wallace, he is a true believer in the Republican Party and what it had to offer Black voters. Keith has a family history that is firmly entrenched in the "Booker T. Washington" brand of Black Republicanism and civil rights work that shaped the development of all-Black towns in Oklahoma.

There's too little on the Democrat platform that has anything to do with what we have historically and culturally valued, and

I think there's so much more that the GOP offers for us. I don't mean give us rights. It's "get out of my way and let me do what I'm able to do...."Allow me as an individual to exercise my rights as a human being and to prosper or at least potentially prosper.... Black people, we are entrepreneurs.

4. Religion and restoring core Black family values was important to many of them.

Though economic independence and Black autonomy was a core theme and entry point for most of my new Black MAGA friends, the traditional family values strand was still deeply embedded in many folks' consciousness on the call.

In general, one of the—if not *the*—biggest drivers of Black political identity is religion. Studies show 97 percent of Black people in the US believe in a divine power, and more than half say prayer helps guide their decision-making. And though millennial engagement in religion and churches has dropped, Black millennials remain engaged at higher rates than any other group within that generation.

But, contrary to traditional narratives that suggest having otherworldly religious orientation deflects attention away from politics or logic-based decision-making, Black religion has historically served as a resource for political mobilization and communal collective action. Black women, particularly, often work to organize and infuse more radical religious politics into institutional spaces.

In listening to people talk about the role their faith has in their politics, I found a strange unspoken kinship with my Black MAGA people—until they started talking about how we had anywhere from sixty-four to eighty genders out there now and this is what's wrong with society. They lost me on a few levels with that.

Still, for me, faith and religion are also drivers in my politics. I believe in God; I pray every night and sometimes throughout the day if someone is trying my patience. But my relationship to religious institutions has been shaky due to my anti-authoritarian tendencies and inquisitive mind.

I've only recently been able to reconcile most of my values within a religious institution, but my faith has always led me to a more leftist politique, a fundamental belief in inclusive community building and a revival of New Deal–era policies that today would be called socialist in America.

For many of my Black MAGA folks, their faith had led them into the Republican Party.

April, a Gen Xer from Georgia, had a sweet, lovely smile; short natural hair; and a fly red lip. Though she said she was initially brought into the Republican Party because of her desire for small government and a return to trickle-down economics, she had realized what was most important to her was to see Black people return to traditional family values. To her, the fundamental misalignment between Left and Right on the question of what makes a family was something she saw as a critical barrier in developing a Black consensus even outside of politics.

> In an ideal world, I would love to have this beautiful meeting of the minds. But at the fundamental level, I personally don't see that happening because there's a fundamental dichotomy in worldviews. We can't even agree that up is up and down is down. Men are actually men, like, at the DNA level, and women are women. Women have babies. Men don't.

So, there's that. I bit my tongue; it was hard to argue with the proclamation that our world views were quite different. As I was about to close, Lisa jumped in to offer a final thought: that Black people and/or Democratic voters are too concerned with past grievances and the opportunity is there for all of us to succeed if we are so inclined.

> So, I think when you talk to a lot of conservatives or Republicans, they are going to have a mindset of *get out of my way. I am in the land of opportunity.* There are people that [sic] come here [from] all around the world, across the world . . . to take advantage of this opportunity. And then you have another group of people who are born here but believe that someone has their foot on their neck. I'm, like, what is this invisible foot that you're talking about because I don't have any foot on my neck as long as I have the opportunities—which we do. They are available to us.

Intriguing, I thought to myself. At the end of the call, I contemplated whether Black Republicans with a pro-Black economic agenda would be able to influence the broader party moving forward. If the broader party was even ready to listen. And I kind of hoped they would listen or that someone was listening. It seemed like for the most part, people wanted to only listen to Candace Owens or people who were willing to read out whatever talking points were on the alt-right, all-white teleprompter. Then again, no one on the call was that bothered, because they were organized and moving forward whether the national party was ready for them or not.

I wondered where an organized pro-Black economic leftist movement was. I had friends and colleagues who thought like me, and organizations like the Action Center on Race & the Economy working at the intersection of racial justice and Wall Street (of which I'm a board member), but, to be honest, it didn't seem like we were working with as many resources or platforms as these Black MAGA folks were or as visible as a viable political base—at least online.

I support the vision of Black Lives Matter and the global fight to address the injustices that have fueled the disproportionate targeting, criminalization, incarceration, and state-sanctioned murders of Black people. This informs my Left-leaning politics. But at the same time, the tangible economic conditions of Black people in America seem to be getting worse by the day, and that feels like an unfinished fight that lacks the same cohesion. It feels like something that hasn't been fully captured and addressed by the Left. Even though I don't agree with all of their political and policy visions, I find myself, in a way, rooting for the Black conservatives. At least they have a plan. At least they have a vision for Black economics. Do we? Moreover, can we offer a more compelling vision for Black economics? How do you convince people that *more* government is the answer when it's been generations since the government has successfully moved a series of programs, public works projects, financial reforms, and regulations that provide tangible proof of concept?

Even if we do, I find I'm still not sold on the idea that one-party politics has proven beneficial to Black interests at scale. Historically, the most important wins we've had for radical Black politics have come from the ability to both develop a Black consensus and force political parties to contend with us as a voter base. But in the modern world, because

Republicans are not concerned with Black voters in the same way, it seems like the national Republican Party turns to voter suppression tactics, while instead of combatting that through policy-making, the Democratic Party focuses on turnout tactics but hasn't always been able to deliver on promises. Maybe these Black MAGA folks are right, that the two-party model isn't working for us.

Also, on a mental health and community resilience front, I don't want it to be an us (Left) versus them (liberal) versus them (conservative) dynamic. I want it to be a collective Black us, and I remain convinced that any chance we have to thrive relies on being able to come to the table to form a baseline consensus. Yet in an increasingly ideologically and physically disconnected world, it is becoming harder and harder to find each other.

The Loneliness of the Black Leftist

"These were your only takeaways from Black MAGA? You didn't challenge them on the communism stuff?"

I looked up from typing furiously on my computer. David was looking at me expectantly, awaiting my answer to his question. It was the eve of the 2020 presidential election, and though it seemed like Biden should win easily, we were all cautious, having thought the same about Hillary Clinton in 2016.

"I was just there to listen."

"Aren't you going to say more about how the conservatives are wrong? You know if Trump gets re-elected how devastating that would be. We're in the middle of COVID, people are dying, people won't get vaccinated. He doesn't fucking care."

"I know," I said slowly. I didn't want to have this fight right now. It was one we'd had before, and I knew where it was going. He looked down, hesitating. He didn't really want to have this fight either.

"I just feel like . . . I mean, this book can't only be an indictment of the Democratic Party. It just seems like sometimes you seem to be . . . I don't know . . . romanticizing conservatives just because they're . . ." He hesitated again.

Black I silently filled in for him. I sighed, squinting as I looked up at the ceiling fan that was in desperate need of dusting.

"What do you want me to say?"

"A conservative agenda is not what this country needs; we're already going too far Right as it is. When you look at the younger generations, they have nothing for them. All those comforts that older generations had—the ability to go to school without debt; have good, stable jobs they could work at forever; homeownership; business ownership . . . the reason why all those things are failing is conservatism. I don't see how you can justify it."

"I'm not justifying conservatism. But what am I gonna say? Black people need to do what we feel we need to do politically to survive. I don't know that I think one party having control over the Black vote is a good thing for Black people long term. Is that what you think?"

"No . . ." David sighed. "But you know as well as I do that Republicans in power don't give a shit about Black people."

"I know. But maybe Black people can make Republicans *have* to care. Parties are just containers; they can and have shifted over time. Maybe it's overdue for that now." David stared at me incredulously. I imagined he wanted to tell me how naïve I was being, and maybe he was right.

"I don't want to do this again," I said. "You don't know. You couldn't possibly know." My therapist would probably say shutting down a conversation in this way is manipulative, but I didn't have enough energy to do it in a different way.

"Fine, I'll let it go," he responded. "But if Trump wins in 2020 or loses but runs again in 2024, everyone's fucked, even the people who don't want to realize it."

I believe that to be true. Wholeheartedly. But I don't see a lot of signs that Black people on the Left are building spaces at scale for identity politics outside of BLM, and that makes it hard to see how we win when so many Black people, including me, see our identity as core to who we are and to our politics. White socialists and progressives looking to push the Democratic Party economically to the Left, or make viable newer third-party options, have routinely failed to successfully recruit and retain a large, long-term base of Black radicals.

This hamster wheel of failure is the result of decades of deprioritizing race, not explicitly addressing racial hostilities, and story erasure within the movement. Mega-platformed leftists like to proclaim identity politics as a hindrance to their cause. They make it too easy for the media and members of government to weaponize a "[white] progressives versus

Blacks" frame as a way to shut down critiques of those in power and once again negate Black Radical Left thought within and outside of the party.

That is not to say there are not prominent Black Left and progressive thinkers grappling with that. People like Briahna Joy Gray, Marc Lamont Hill, and Benjamin Dixon have used their media platforms to talk about the intersection of Black identity and leftism. Black voters have galvanized around electoral candidates like Nina Turner, Cori Bush, and Jamaal Bowman. We're definitely out here. I can't speak for them, but I see many of them as Black skinheads like me, disillusioned political outliers who are underrepresented in mainstream media discourse. Like me, they are fighting a constant uphill battle to be seen as a force the Democratic Party has to contend with, not seek to destroy or ignore.

In the Conscious Black Conservatives, I see right-wing Black skinheads who reject their societal value or cultural identity being defined by their willingness to vote for the Democratic Party during presidential elections. More and more they are finding their people, and though we have yet to see a seismic shift in Black voter patterns, there are signs that without a counter force, a Black right swing could be more imminent than many of us previously imagined during the Obama years. But moreover, the people I interviewed were mostly excited to talk about why they supported Trump. And if they didn't necessarily love Trump, they were excited to talk about why they saw the future of Black people in the Republican Party. When I talk to Black people on the Left, they don't have that same energy for the Democratic Party. The party is almost like a necessary . . . not evil, exactly—but kind of like a speed bump to slow the steady drive toward right-wing authoritarianism.

Generation Z and millennials are more supportive of socialist policies than previous generations. They want institutions to work. They want the government to work. They make many appeals to authority figures to do better. But they've also discarded all the mystery of authority, especially Generation Z, who don't think those in power know better than them. Finding a base of power, particularly with those who do value identity politics and culture, seems slow going. And I wonder how many left-wing Black skinheads like me have canceled their Jacobin subscriptions in frustration, run screaming from Democratic Socialists of America meetings, and are still searching for their people.

Interlude: Traditions, Triggers, and Keys

"That's all right, that's OK, you will work for me one day."
I remember gripping my mother while surrounded by belligerent college students chanting that little ditty, sporadically accompanied by ape noises. They were holding out their keys, jangling them in sync toward the players. We were in the arena of the Northwestern University basketball team, watching them play another Big Ten team, the University of Illinois, where my dad was the assistant coach.

I was used to traveling to games, and I was used to hostile environments. Sporting events are very nationalistic. In fact, it's one of the few places where even a global leftist can let their micro-nationalist freak flag fly as you root for your team with bloodthirsty zeal. But I hadn't yet experienced an environment that felt this hostile. I was eleven or twelve years old, old enough to know this wasn't OK but not quite old enough to fully understand what I was witnessing.

"Mama, why are they saying that?" I asked, looking up at her.

She rubbed my back with the gentleness and comfort of a loving mother, but her face was as hard as stone as she stared down the raucous students.

Then, she sighed, briefly looking down at me. "Because they think they own us."

It was the 1990s in the Union stronghold of Illinois, but it might as well have been Mississippi in the 1960s.

On a basketball court that was dominated by almost entirely Black players, I was old enough to know who she meant by "us." My racial analysis, by life circumstances, had come a lot faster than my class analysis. By that time, I had already been called a nigger at least once and had experienced the subtler microaggressions that communicated racial positioning.

"But why do they think that? No one owns anyone."

"Because that's how people like this think. But you're right, they don't own us, baby. Don't you ever, *ever* let anyone tell you otherwise."

Northwestern is a private university in an NCAA "power conference" with a Black undergraduate population of less than 6 percent. The median family income of a student from Northwestern University is around $171,200, and 66 percent come from the top 20 percent of wealth in the country. It has one of the best (white) journalism schools in the country, although the value of journalism schools in general is both relative and highly subjective.

They say for journalists, you want to tell stories, but you never want to *be* the story. Unfortunately, Northwestern is frequently in the news because every few months or so, photos will circulate from a blackface party thrown on campus, or there'll be racist or anti-Semitic graffiti scrawled somewhere, or Black cheerleaders will be told they can't stand next to each other or wear braids because then that part of the cheer line will look too ethnic. Or some other shit like this. Actor Tom Hanks's son Chet went there, too. Chet Hanks is perhaps best known for routinely cosplaying as a Jamaican Rastafarian rapper and for promoting "White Boy Summer." I have no idea what that is, but it's a fan favorite among the 4chan Neo-Nazi incel set. For the record, there's no evidence or reason to believe that Chet himself is any of those things.

This tells you most of what you need to know about Northwestern. I would not feel safe walking around the area at night.

Years later, I would remember some of its troubling history when I was with David at a football game between Northwestern and the University of Illinois. The teams were playing in the Chicago Cubs baseball stadium, and David and I had gone to witness the cool spectacle that seemed like a throwback to the days when fields had to be multipurpose.

I went into the game less committed to its outcome since my dad had long left his position at the University of Illinois in Champaign-Urbana. Plus, by high school, the Chief Illiniwek halftime dancers and Native

American mimicry that back then were part of U of I's brand identity weren't really doing it for me either. In any event, I had graduated from the University of Wisconsin law school and had developed more of a personal attachment to the Badgers as a Big Ten team.

But then, partway through the game, the nice man sitting next to us—a Northwestern fan we had been talking to before the game kicked off—pulled out those fucking car keys and started jangling them. By that time, the story behind its meaning had shifted. Now, it was just an empty ritual in the fans' minds, a coordinated sound effect meant to rile up their team. Some who sought to attach a deeper meaning to it would say it was meant to signal to the other team "warm up your car, you're going home." But I knew exactly what those keys had once meant: *"Go get the car, boy. Remember your place."*

People have a way of softening history. There's a reason why history is written by the victors and those in power. To preserve an ideal of who we are and where we come from, stories get rewritten and hard truths get buried and finessed so we never have to confront our trail of inhumanity. This is how the sound of jangling keys, like school songs that once had slurs in them, becomes a tradition that offers all the comforts of nostalgia, not a class- or race-based symbol of ultimate superiority. Not a reminder that when the game ends, win or lose, the spectators will still own the house and the car, and you will just be their laborer and source of entertainment.

But I hadn't forgotten that feeling of burying my face in my mom's orange-and-blue sweater amid the sounds of drunken frat-boy ape noises. That feeling of shame that wasn't mine to own yet was left draped over my sloped shoulders.

They think they own us.

Fuck that noise.

In an instant, I became the most rabid and intense University of Illinois football fan you had ever seen. David was caught off guard as my Illinois nationalism and orange-and-blue loyalties made a latent surge.

"RIP THOSE MOTHERFUCKERS' HEADS OFF!" I screamed. Most of the players on the field—on both teams—were people of color, but I didn't let that get in the way of my hostility. It wasn't about them; it was about their shitty-ass alumni and donors.

"Wow . . . no wonder your family got banned from being courtside during games when your dad was a coach," David said, looking at me bemused and possibly a little frightened after I yelled expletives at a referee I thought had gotten a call wrong. He was shocked that his calm, neutral (then) girlfriend had gone from *"I don't care who wins,"* to *"Body that bitch! Finish that quarterback right. the. fuck. Now!"*

It was those damn keys.

When I hear jangling keys at sporting events, it's hard not to be instinctively transported back to the visceral feeling of being surrounded by thousands of (white) college students, alumni, and locals shaking their car keys while smugly chanting "That's all right, that's OK, you will work for me one day." Their singsongy ditty directed toward a basketball court overwhelmingly composed of Black, working-class student athletes. It would grow to hold even deeper meaning for me after Coach Byrdsong's shocking assassination at the hands of a white nationalist.

Ricky Byrdsong was Northwestern's first Black head basketball coach. On July 2, 1999, Coach Byrdsong was out for a jog near his home in Skokie, Illinois, with two of his young children, Sabrina and Ricky, Jr. The family outing would end in tragedy. His children watched helplessly as their father was gunned down, the victim of a Neo-Nazi on a murderous rampage targeting Jewish, Asian, and Black communities. Ten other people were left wounded. Won-Joon Yoon, a twenty-six-year-old graduate student at the University of Indiana, was also killed.

When you distill someone's life down to their final minutes, it does a disservice to their humanity and how they lived. Though I didn't know Won-Joon Yoon, I'd met Coach Byrdsong—one of the few Black men's basketball head coaches in the NCAA—through my father, who is also part of this small fraternity. As head coaches in Illinois in the late 1990s, their names were inevitably linked to one another. They occasionally played one another's teams. Beyond his passion for basketball, Coach Byrdsong's love of God and his commitment to community and family shone bright.

As news of Coach Byrdsong's murder spread, the community gathered on the street where he was known to jog, and congregations of mourners walked around the neighborhood as he once had. A charity 5K and 10K race in his honor, The Race Against Hate, still takes place in that community. His son, Ricky, Jr., would tell me later Coach Byrdsong had been stalked by his killer, targeted for not belonging in the idyllic white community. His death would be a lesson—*you don't belong here; you will never belong here.*

Byrdsong's killer, Benjamin Nathaniel Smith, had grown up a few miles away from Northwestern University. That same toxic energy I had seen on display in the early 1990s at Northwestern games had spawned a local son who would be groomed to kill just a few years afterward. It's hard for me not to draw parallels. When you think you own someone or something, it's easy to develop a sense of entitlement over their (or its) destiny. Their property is yours to do with as you see fit. Their property is yours to take care of, shine up, show off, lose, or even destroy. And if you think people are or should be your property, will their life ever matter unless they are operating in service to you? How will you react when you see they are not? It's a mentality that can take a range of forms—from misguided paternalism to an absence of care to even unmitigated violence.

Do I think that any of this was top of mind for the Northwestern fan sitting next to me jangling his keys, just trying to enjoy a football game? No, definitely not. I'm sure he had Black friends and all that (maybe). But that's the problem with decontextualized traditions: they can become so deeply ingrained that it becomes harder to remember the history and power dynamics they represent. We ignore all the little ways in which people are told their place. We mindlessly accept what is, and we lose the way toward what should be.

It didn't matter what that man's intentions were. Those keys triggered a flashback to ape noises and classist chants, to feeling shame and isolation as I held on to my mom. Except I was a grown-ass woman now, and my shame had transformed to indignation.

At that moment, he became my enemy, and I had to shut him down.

The nice Northwestern fan and I dueled back and forth, each trying to hype up our respective teams. Finally, he sat down, out of breath. A small victory. His little team lost, too. Good. I never made eye contact after our friendly conversation before the game. Nor did he. Screw that nice man and the Mercedes horse he rode in on.

Shit was cool until the keys came out.

12

The Stories We Live With
Reflections on Black Pain and Gothic Healing

I feel things pretty deeply, but I've gotten pretty good at hiding it. Except, apparently, from my family. I don't remember ever feeling particularly unhappy, but I think I came into this world with an axe to grind. I'm a product of nurture to be sure. But also, there's just certain personality quirks about me that I can't fully explain. I don't know if I would call myself goth, but, according to my mom, I was always kind of a dark kid.

My mom always jokes that until she met me, she had never met a kid who demanded their room be painted black. When I was five or six, she'd try to tell me scary stories, and I'd stare at her blandly and say, "You don't really believe that, do you?" Halloween is still my favorite holiday, and until I outgrew it, my favorite outfit was a dark navy Victorian-style dress with off-white lace that I first got for my grandmother's funeral.

My mom would see me playing by myself and ask me what I was doing. I'd inform her I was "playing funeral." She also says I was the only thirteen-year-old she knew who listened to music like Mozart's *Requiem* to relax. That sounds really creepy to me in hindsight. She chalked it up to the number of deaths I'd experienced at an impressionable age. And it's true. I had lost my maternal grandmother, aunts, and uncles within a few years of each other.

Several of my first real childhood memories revolve around death and funerals.

Sensing a connection between my own gothic tendencies and the death that had been ever-present in my life, I wondered if I were alone in processing this way. I asked my mom about whether she considers herself gothic. And while she said she didn't, she also recalled, "Well, I used to draw coffins as a child, so maybe you are your mother's daughter, my gothic child."

The term *gothic* originated with a fifth-century barbarian tribe—the Goths. Today, we often use it to describe art and cultural products that encompass mystery, horror, and gloom. Many people associate it with fiction and art from the eighteenth and nineteenth centuries.

Gothic is typically associated with whiteness, thanks both to artists like Edgar Allan Poe and to teenage "goth phase" clichés. Toni Morrison, who wrote about the gothic genre in the American literary canon, talks about the genre as embracing and coding white American "fears of being outcast, of failings of powerlessness; their fear of boundarylessness, of Nature unbridled and crouched for attack." The rise of Black presence and power was sure to accompany the "absence of so-called civilization."

Many modern scholars believe Poe, who was writing in the decades leading up to the Civil War, was channeling those white racial anxieties into his writing. His short stories can be read as metaphors warning of the Black monsters in the night, rising up to disrupt white purity. Oftentimes, Black and Native American characters, when they appear in Poe's writing, are shown as crude, bloodthirsty savages. If they are not kept in line, his words seem to hint, they will destroy the house of America.

And yet to me, it is not whiteness but Blackness that is extremely gothic—perhaps even more so than whiteness. In Leila Taylor's book, *Darkly,* Taylor explores in compelling detail whether to be Black is to be inherently gothic.

Our joy, pain, and trauma are often hijacked and used for "front page" fodder, and oftentimes, as they say in the newsrooms, "If it bleeds, it leads." Our stories are frequently told without our consent, our voice, or our context. And every day, too many of our communities—Black, Brown, and Indigenous people, poor people, women, LGBTQ+ folks, and others—are let down by media that reflects the biases, paternalism, condescension, and indifference of those who are often charged with telling our stories for us and about us.

As Taylor explains, the perpetual sorrow of the Black gothic stems in part from the foundational trauma of Africans' forced voyage across the Atlantic Ocean, known as the Middle Passage, and those who died during the journey. In addition to the death toll, the lack of an official national memorialization for those who died during the Middle Passage also underpins our suspended state of mourning: the hazy ancestral memory of the unnamed losses of people chained together at the bottom of the Atlantic Ocean.

But Black gothic also comes from the unnamed horrors that met those who made it through the Middle Passage alive. The unspeakable monsters, manifested in the forms of enslavers and their entourage of enablers. People who were invested in the story of our inhumanity. For example, slave patrols—which, by the way, is one of the origins of modern policing in the United States.

These were squadrons of white volunteers that were given legal authority to pursue, locate, and sell back enslaved people who had escaped (and some Black people who had never been enslaved at all), crushing uprisings led by enslaved people and punishing enslaved workers found or believed to have violated plantation rules. Slave patrols could forcibly enter anyone's home, regardless of their race or ethnicity, purely based on suspicions they were sheltering escaped Black people.

Even up North, police officers were charged with controlling what was deemed a dangerous underclass, which was composed of Black, immigrant, and working-class people. They were given permission to engage in brutal acts in the name of social control, a legacy that continues to this day. They were never meant to protect and serve Black people. Not ever. They were meant to instill fear and horror in Black people.

You should know that. If you don't, it's because your media has failed you.

The violent removal of both legally free people and people who had escaped bondage inflicted trauma and an unspoken layer of melancholy over Black communities—a Black gothic rooted in the legacy of this trauma.

My draw to what's called media justice (or political, economic, and cultural fights for media rights, access, and representation) has always been rooted in the belief that media is where the invisible war is constantly waged on Black lives, spirits, and bodies (as covered in the chapter Hood Vampires). Frequently in my work, I would encounter people who would say, "Well, who cares about what the news says? That's not important." But to me, winning media and cultural fights is crucial to dismantling barriers and challenging the hidden set of rules and norms that govern our society.

They're crucial to countering the narratives that tell us in explicit and implicit ways that police officers are infallible and their stories should go unquestioned. The ones that tell us Black people and Black culture are inherently corrupt for breaking the rules of decorum that were never meant to apply to us. The ones that tell us our lives can be distilled down to a criminal record or the circumstances of our deaths instead of the humanizing details of our lives.

In times when our trauma becomes hypervisible, we are draped in a veil of gothic mourning. Our weeping is palatable, our bodies and names memorialized, but our lives and who we are as people too often remain cloaked in the shadows.

The House that Trauma Built

What if I told you none of us is born with a clean slate? That your life doesn't start from birth, or even conception, but several generations in the past? As wild as this may sound, this is what researchers in the field of epigenetics have been studying for years.

Epigenetics, a field established in the 1940s, is the study of heritable phenotype changes that do not involve alterations in the DNA sequence. To account for changing environmental conditions, as humans have evolved over millions of years, we have gotten taller, heavier, and longer lived. But as part of this process, we can also inherit a set of survival mechanisms and responses that are directly linked to the experiences of our ancestors—especially traumatic ones. As Dr. Mark Wolynn describes it, "Even if the person who suffered the original trauma has died, even if his or her story lies submerged in years of silence, fragments of life experience, memory, and body sensation can live on, as if reaching out from the past to find resolution in the minds and bodies of those living in the present." In other words, we can pass trauma and mental disorders down from family member to family member the same way we do other physical and genetic traits.

Dr. Mark Wolynn, psychologist and author of the award-winning *It*

Didn't Start with You, is one of the world's leading experts in the field of inherited family trauma. Wolynn stumbled upon what would become his life's work while he was treating a patient he calls Sarah, a young woman who was self-harming with suicidal intent. When Wolynn began to ask her more about why she was self-harming, she expressed that she didn't feel she deserved to live.

Wolynn had worked with suicidal and self-harming patients before, but Sarah was different. In his words:

> This cutter, Sarah, cut in such an extreme way that she would nearly bleed to death when she would cut. They weren't superficial cuts. She would cut so deeply into her arms or her legs or her abdomen that she would hit a major vessel and had to be rushed to the hospital by her parents. Then they'd put her in a psych ward for months, thinking she was suicidal.

Wolynn had the idea to hand her a pen and tell her to pretend it was her razor. He asked her to hold it to her arm as though she was going to make a cut and tell him the first feeling, thought, or image that came to mind.

The twenty-four-year-old said, "I don't deserve to live. I don't deserve to live."

What he found so peculiar was that Sarah didn't have any immediate trauma or known history that would lead her to that conclusion. She had grown up in a happy home with two present parents. She was young, and she had a lot to live for, by the world's standards. It didn't make obvious sense to Wolynn why she would do this. So Wolynn decided to drill deeper. He asked her about her grandparents and their respective relationships to her parents. And that was when the story started to emerge.

Sarah shared that on her father's side, her grandmother had been an alcoholic. When Sarah's father was young, there had been a bad car accident. His mother had crashed a car carrying her and her husband, Sarah's grandfather. Sarah's grandmother had lived, but the accident had killed her grandfather. Sarah's father hadn't really talked about it much—it was too hard to talk about Sarah's grandfather and how he had died at her grandmother's hands.

Without Sarah even knowing the full details of the story, that trauma and a set of traumatic responses had somehow transferred to Sarah. All of that angst and guilt from her grandmother, and the range of emotions experienced by her father, had been tattooed onto her, becoming a part of her identity, leading her to feel in her blood that she didn't deserve to live.

Dark shit, right?

To be gothic is to carry a certain melancholy. As Black people, we are filled with violent histories, known and unknown, that shape how we exist, how we feel, and how we are seen. As I began to learn more about epigenetics, I couldn't help but wonder how it applied to me. What are the sets of triggers, survival mechanisms, and anxieties I'd inherited even before I knew the full story of my family?

Eureka, an Essay on the Material and Spiritual Universe

My father's mother, Lorraine, would've been about three years old when the Great Mississippi Flood of 1927 ripped through her hometown, leaving more than 325,000 people—disproportionately Black and poor—displaced. Black men and boys were forced to work for months in the storms and ensuing flood to try to protect white-owned land. Any people caught attempting to find shelter would either be locked in barns and cotton gin houses until they went back to work or driven into the waters at gunpoint. According to contemporary published reports in the *Chicago Defender,* "those who die are cut open, filled with sand, then tossed into the Mississippi River." Their bodies were used as human levees.

My grandmother would've been nine years old when Richard Roscoe, a tenant farmer and deacon at a local Black Baptist church, was hunted down and lynched by a white mob after a disagreement with a wealthy white plantation owner. One of her earliest memories might have been seeing Deacon Roscoe's dead body dragged through the streets of Minter City, tied to the back of the town sheriff's car. It was a warning to all the Black folks not to get too uppity. Dreaming wasn't allowed in those parts.

"Did our family ever own any land?"

I was sitting with my father in the hospital waiting room. He didn't want to be there. He had been there all day, and the hospital had no room to check him in. It was 2020 after all. He had been there for so long that my mom, my oldest sister, and I had to take shifts waiting with him as early morning turned to night.

I was trying to keep him distracted any way I could, so I pushed him for more of our family story.

"No. We never owned anything before my generation."

After his death, I confirmed something surprising: this was not true. In fact, my great-great-grandparents on my father's side had owned one hundred acres of farming land outright in the years following the Civil War in Attala County, Mississippi. On that land, they had built a school and a church. The farm had been successful. In addition to being a farmer, my great-great-grandfather had also been a pastor. For at least two generations, they'd successfully built a way of life—an independent life that was geographically close but worlds away from the plantation where my great-great-grandparents had met.

My father never knew this. My grandmother never knew it, or if she did, she never talked about it. I learned it because the white descendants of the family who owned mine published a book telling our "entwined" (as she would romantically title the book) stories and lineages. Apparently, my cousin Tina, the family historian, had been piecing this story together before she'd unexpectedly died in 2020. She'd been planning to write our family's story.

As I understand it, a descendant of the family that owned mine spoke with Tina. And the descendant took that information and used it to tell our family history through her own distorted lens. Under her narration, relationships were good between the families. She speculated maybe her family had helped mine, the unspoken implication being there was no way my family would have been smart, savvy, or hardworking enough to achieve land ownership on their own. Ugh, this book really pissed me off, so much so that I've now bought several copies to send to my family members with a note: *Can you believe this?* Capitalism, man, it's a twisted mistress.

This is the thing about how our narratives are often taken from us and reinterpreted. We are stripped of our voices even when telling the stories of our own lives, families, and histories. We're told we've never had anything, which plays into public pathologies of Black people as having not done enough to improve our own station in life, when the

THE STORIES WE LIVE WITH   203

reality is many of us were actively deprived of property ownership and economic opportunities. But even when your mind doesn't know, your body does. Those memories of fear and struggle live in your body for generations.

Somehow, between 1876, when my great-great-grandparents purchased the land, and when my grandmother was born, something happened. We don't know why, but the land never made it down the direct line of descendants. Somehow, the property ended up in the hands of a local white family who had a business monopoly in the area.

After my dad was gone, I asked my mom if she knew anything about what could have happened. According to her, they didn't know anything about owning any land. But when my grandmother was a baby, her father had gotten into an altercation with a white man. A white man had come onto the land, and her father had shot at the man to get him off it. Her father didn't kill him, but he knew that the man would be back, so he took off.

Since her mother had died—possibly giving birth to her youngest child—her father had been the only parent in the house. Now, without him, the children had nothing, not even milk. They kept the youngest children alive by giving them flour mixed with water. She said she remembered a group of white men had come around looking for her dad one time. The older kids hid her under the stairs, and they told her not to make a sound. Not one peep. The men came in and ransacked the house, looking for her daddy. They said that when they found that "nigger," he was going to hang. She never saw her daddy again, and she never knew what happened to him. Then, when my grandmother was thirteen, she was married off to my grandfather, who was twelve or more years her senior. My grandmother and many of her siblings didn't learn to read until they were adults, so they could have signed over the land, and they wouldn't have known the difference.

My grandmother would always say she didn't like talking about her childhood, that it brought back too many memories. My mom reminded me that when Grandma got older and she developed dementia, she would sit in the house with a blanket over her lap. For a while, she even had a gun under her chair, until it became too risky to leave it with her and my dad took it away.

She would sit very still, staring out the window, looking into the darkness. "Shh, shh, be quiet. The white men are out there. They're coming for us."

When my mom told me that story, my blood went cold. I felt numb. All I could think about were the times when I used to watch my dad sitting in the dark on the couch, looking out the window, watching every car that drove past. He would never say a word. I would tease him that he was being paranoid, and he would look over at me and smile.

"Better to be paranoid than sorry," he'd sometimes say.

Even though he didn't consciously know the history, my dad's body had reminded him of the family story of having to hide in the shadows from the white men driving around the house with guns. My dad lived in an essentially safe, all-Black community with a well-fed family in a house with security cameras, but his genetics remembered what it was like to be denied that. His mom's fear as a little girl hiding under the house had been passed on to him.

I Hurt Myself Today

Every day of our lives, we have experiences that profoundly shape and change who we are and how we move through space and time. Or, as author Octavia Butler put it: "All that you touch you Change. All that you Change Changes you. The only lasting truth is Change. God Is Change." While 2015 was the first year that almost broke me, 2020 was the year I might have finally broken.

In 2014 in Ferguson, Missouri, a community took to the streets to express collective agony, anger, and deep sadness, publicly mourning the killing of Michael Brown. As photos, videos, and commentary flooded Twitter, a twenty-first-century civil rights movement was born, one anchored in the demand for accountability for the many Black lives taken with impunity by those acting under the cover of law. Eyes were open now; surely there would be the change that we as Black people were so desperately seeking. Surely now we would begin to be seen in the fullness of our humanity and dignity.

But as 2014 faded into 2015, the stakes became even higher. By the summer of 2015, I was working at Color Of Change. Internally, we had different departments, each charged with running different "campaigns" or initiatives calling for accountability and systemic changes in service of Black life, dignity, and humanity. My department at that time focused on media, technology, economic, and health justice.

The transition into the summer of 2015 had been a brutal killing season, and as an organization, we were left reeling. In April 2015, Walter Scott, a forklift operator who had been studying massage therapy, was hunted down like a dog in North Charleston, South Carolina, and shot five times in the back by a police officer.

Less than two weeks later in Baltimore, Freddie Gray was taken on a "rough ride" by police officers, leading to his death. He was described as an athlete, who—despite being a small and thin boy—had been a wide receiver for a local football league. His friends said sports were a refuge for him. He was also described by his friends and family as a joker who was also generous, respectful, and easygoing.

The hits kept coming. At a pool party in McKinney, Texas, a group of teenagers and kids probably were scarred for life when police officers descended on their party because white residents had decided Black kids didn't belong there. Video footage showed a young girl, unarmed, still wearing her bikini, being thrown to the ground and physically and verbally assaulted by grown men with guns. For being at a fucking pool party.

Then, back in South Carolina, June 17, 2015. A man, whose white supremacist ramblings were reprinted in many news publications and can still be found online, walked into Emanuel African Methodist Episcopal Church. Though he was a stranger, congregants welcomed him through their doors.

He sat and prayed with:

Clementa C. Pinckney (41)—the church's pastor and a South Carolina state senator.

Sharonda Coleman-Singleton (45)—a pastor. She was also a speech therapist and track coach at Goose Creek High School, and mother of Major League Baseball prospect Chris Singleton.

Cynthia Graham Hurd (54)—a Bible study member and manager for the Charleston County Public Library system. She was a sister of former state senator Malcolm Graham.

Susie Jackson (87)—a member of the board of trustees and of the

Women's Missionary Society. She sang in the choir and was a fixture of the weekly Bible study.

Ethel Lee Lance (70)—the church's sexton. She had worked at the church for more than three decades.

DePayne Middleton-Doctor (49)—a pastor who was also employed as a school administrator and admissions coordinator at Southern Wesleyan University.

Tywanza Sanders (26)—a graduate of Allen University. He was Susie Jackson's grandnephew.

Daniel L. Simmons (74)—a pastor who also served at Greater Zion AME Church in Awendaw, South Carolina.

Myra Thompson (59)—a Bible study teacher.

And he murdered them.

He said, "I have to do it. You rape our women, and you're taking over our country. And you have to go."

He said, "Y'all want something to pray about? I'll give you something to pray about."

He reloaded his gun five times.

Tywanza Sanders's mother and his five-year-old niece only survived by pretending to be dead on the floor.

That one took me out, but the horrors didn't stop there. In the following week, there were fires at no fewer than six predominantly African American churches.

At the time, I managed a small team, and I saw the sadness and anger on their faces. Entering our Oakland, California, office, where most of the criminal justice team worked, I felt like I could feel their sorrow before I even walked through the door. Some of my team slept in the office, working late into the night and early morning in service of justice.

"We aren't fucking safe anywhere," I heard one of my colleagues say, the anguish and rage clear in her voice. "We can't walk down the street, we can't drive in our car, we can't go to a pool party, we can't pray in our church. We're never safe." As a director, I knew my team wanted me to have answers, but I had none. What would we say to our one million members? What could we campaign for that would make one bit of difference? What could we do?

Our organization called us all together for a meeting. The managers tried to open up the floor for us to grieve together, mourn together, and be resilient together. But what can you really say? You can't say "this too shall pass" when it has been four seasons of mourning. You can't say "it will get better" when it feels like shit is getting worse. I think about this moment often whenever I read data about the COVID-era spikes in Black suicides and deaths of despair. It's tied to alienation, a loss of community, and a crisis of imagination for what a Black future can look like when we are forced to constantly watch and process replayed videos of Black death and trauma.

I kept telling myself, *Figure this shit out, bitch. You have to lead right now. They're waiting. Your team is waiting. Your bosses are waiting. Our Color Of Change members are waiting. People out there are waiting. They need something to do, something to hold on to.*

I learned I would be going with some of the criminal justice team members to Columbia, South Carolina. Color Of Change had partnered with another organization that had collected signatures from across the country demanding the Confederate flag that the Emmanuel 9 murderer so proudly waved in his pictures be removed from the South Carolina State House grounds. We would march those petitions to the door of then-governor Nikki Haley, and I would have to give a speech.

I went home, went into the bathroom, and locked the door. My husband wasn't home from work yet, but I didn't want him to come home and see me like this. I dropped my bag on the floor, not caring my fancy laptop made what would normally be an alarming clunk. With all my clothes on, I climbed into the tub and sat with my head up against the rim. I cried until the cries turned into gasps, until I frantically gulped the air, just trying to breathe. I felt like I could physically feel my heart breaking inside of my chest. Then I went numb.

I reached for my shaver on the side of the tub. I had nicked myself with it doing a rush shave job that morning. I stared at it for a while. I didn't want to kill myself, but at that point, my body had gotten so numb that I'd almost started to panic. I wanted to see if I could feel anything other than my heart breaking. But I put the razor down. I washed my hands and my face. I got out of the tub, booked my flight, and started to write my speech. The show must go on.

Later, I stood on the steps of the South Carolina State House, staring out at a small group of white men and their families waving Confederate flags and holding signs that said all sorts of fucked up—but pithy—shit. The guns at their waists were very visible, threatening but perfectly legal. Around me, our partner organization had staged the perfect visual, a group of people clustered together holding our own signs.

The lineup of speakers included a member from each of our organizations that had started petitions and amassed more than 600,000 signatures from people calling for the Confederate flag's removal. I had worn a black, 1950s-style dress, with my flat-ironed hair half pulled up. I wanted to mirror the aesthetics of one of those old civil rights photos. We were surrounded by boxes that acted as a visible representation of all the signatures. But inside each box was just a thumb drive with all of the electronic signatures and addresses for confirmation because nobody was trying to carry 600,000 pieces of paper up all those stairs at the State House. Everything is framing.

I stood on the steps in front of the mic, shaking, sweating out my press. In my speech, I told the story of my grandmother and my great-grandfather, the sharecropper in Mississippi who disappeared after a disagreement with a white man. I said the Confederate flag that waved over my grandmother's head when she carried her youngest baby boy—my father—out of town for a better life was the same one that had been waved around by a psychopath whose manifesto continues to fester online.

I said it's not an accident the Confederate flag didn't start flying at the South Carolina State House until 1961, a century after the Civil War began. That it was hung up there specifically to inspire the racial animus and hostility toward Black lives that we saw displayed by the man who murdered nine people in a Black South Carolina church. That if Nikki Haley gave a damn about the Black people in her state or in this country, then that flag needed to come down.

We marched up to Nikki Haley's offices, where security waited to accept the staged boxes and quickly usher us away before we could meet with her. As I passed, keeping my distance from the "counterprotesters," I felt a shiver up my spine. While walking through the airport on the way back home, I couldn't help but wonder how many white people would just as soon see my dead body hit the floor even if they were too polite (or scared) to say it to my face.

Gothic Healing

> Beloved, there is something about the night. The night calls us, and yet it has been neglected, and [it] drew by us in the West— the Western tradition in particular has made assumptions about the dark and the night. We have a simplified, binary view of light and dark when a nonbinary definition of the sacred is necessitated. We use a language that demonizes all things dark, and we relish the stories of the unknown that lurks in the night. . . . I submit to you today, I want, for what it is worth, to offer redemption of the dark and put forth that we should never seek a night-less existence where our goal is to live a life without the night.
> —REVEREND OTIS MOSS III, PASTOR OF CHICAGO'S TRINITY UNITED CHURCH OF CHRIST

When my father died in 2020, I began to think more about spirituality and mental health than I really had in the past. I also began to get super gothic in various ways, including listening to more drill music. Something about the music's violence helped channel my dangerous roller coaster of emotions. I found myself taking comfort in the rituals of the dead, almost like I was playing funeral all over again. I learned to find comfort in the darkness, even as I sought out the light. One of my lights is my dark-souled sister Kelechi Ubozoh. She's a gothic girl after my own heart, and our friendship was built on our love of vampires (shout out to Aaliyah in *Queen of the Damned,* even if they lowkey did her dirty in the movie's editing), Trent Reznor, the color black, and the beauty of a good mimosa.

Kelechi has worked in the California mental health system in the areas of research and advocacy, community engagement, stigma reduction, and peer support. She began her career as an investigative reporter in New York City and was the first student-reporter ever published in the *New York Times.*

After witnessing the impact of trauma and mental health issues on the people she was writing about, Kelechi decided to change her focus to providing direct mental health support. This is something she herself has dealt with as a suicide-attempt survivor. She later coedited the book *We've Been Too Patient: Voices from Radical Mental Health*.

She talks a lot about facilitating healing-centered spaces for Black employees internationally to respond to the ongoing violence toward the Black community. My question to her was: How do we move past all of the trauma we live with and start healing? It feels like a constant struggle for me and the people I work with in movement spaces. This was her response to me:

I think about the way that we carry things that our ancestors have carried, things that we're not supposed to carry anymore. And I think that's the big reckoning beyond BLM. We do not need to suffer or push through, we need to release that pain. When we think about what Afrofuturism could look like, some people think about what it would have been like if we hadn't been colonized. But in terms of the question of what is the world we want to create, I actually would love for us to get more comfortable with understanding that it's OK to have a reaction to all of these horrible things that have happened. We can have that darkness and still connect to joy and work on releasing that because it's stored in our bodies. If we don't release it, we're just passing it down to the next generation. And this is not to shame past generations. This is what they did to survive.

But what if we were to say: OK, that's what my grandmother did, and that's what my mother did, but I'm going to do something different. How do we shift intergenerational trauma to intergenerational wisdom? Because we can transform this. We are so powerful. We have gone through so much. And I don't think we need to pass down this pain. But there is wisdom about what we've learned. What do we want to do with that wisdom? In the spirit of Afrofuturism, what if we asked: What do my ancestors dream for me? And I do think that's the transformative healing and liberation that we as Black folks need to sit with now.

This is what I think we need to get to: the real work of healing ourselves even in the midst of pushing back against all the systems that seek to destroy us. And there are many systems seeking to destroy us. But how do we get the twenty-second century in our vision while also accounting for the fights that envelop us right now? How do we find safety even though we live in a world where we're never truly safe? How do we find safety if even our bodies remember generations of instilled horror?

I've been asked more than once what it's like to be in an interracial relationship and how that impacts how I process things. So here's what it's like for me.

It's like finding someone who makes you laugh, who gets your dark humor, who shares your values, and who knows you better than anyone else on the planet. Someone who will go to every shitty and amazing Black movie that comes out on opening weekend and won't ask too many *Do Black people really do that?* questions. Someone who will do their absolute best not to get annoyed when everyone in the theater is talking back at the movie or someone arrives really late and has to climb over you with all their snacks to get to the last or best seat in the theater.

It's like writing a book from sunup past sundown and having food, water, coffee, and wine magically appear in your hand without even asking for it, with a polite reminder that it's been a couple (few) days since your last shower. It's like at the drop of a hat, in the middle of a global pandemic, having someone pack up the car, load up your cat, and drive with only gas, bathroom, and food stops halfway across the country, and then staying on an air mattress in a basement, so you can be by your father's side in his final days.

And it's like feeling a weight off your shoulders when you casually probe their family history and learn that his family were furniture makers in the North who never enslaved people. It's like holding your breath during election season and letting it out when there's only two Trump voters in his massive family tribe who you can strategically avoid having political conversations with. It's like seeing the slightly panicked look come over your in-laws' faces when his grandma starts to get into some potentially dicey race territory, and the relief when she doesn't go full on Paula Deen because she's a very lovely ninety-year-old lady with no secret Klan past.

It's like knowing you have someone by your side who will fight all the little and big fires beside you, and around you, but can never really be your fire blanket.

Because at the same time, there's only so much they can ever do to quell the fire in your chest or make you feel safe. Because even if they can feel in their heart and understand in their mind the process of mourning the loss of Black life, they will never truly feel it in their blood. His epigenetics aren't filled with the same stress and survival signals as mine.

He will never sit in a bathtub with a dull shaver, trying to remind himself he's human, too, because someone he never met and only knew existed in death was murdered just for being Black and therefore deemed less than human. He won't sit in the park by your parents' house having a panic attack not just because his father died before you had a child, but also because now even if you do, that child will never grow up seeing the Black love of your parents or feeling the love of a Black grandfather. And in a world that constantly strips us of our humanity, the disruption of that link is devastating.

It's not going to be like that for everyone in an interracial relationship. But it's like that for me. It doesn't feel that way all the time—the joy and the laughter far outweigh the pain. But then there are those moments when I'm alone, and I feel like the Black gothic girl with no nation.

It's in those quiet moments the Black skinhead emerges.

Conclusion: Maggot Brain

I decided to go on the journey into the Black skinhead's mind when I saw Kanye being interviewed around the release of his album *Jesus Is King*. In one interview, he said he had been "canceled before cancel culture," that he wasn't for the culture, and that "we" (presumably Black people) are culture-less. It broke my heart. Also, I don't believe it. Black culture is something that various actors over the years have sought to commodify, break down, and even destroy. But if there's one thing I've learned over the course of this journey, it's that, in fact, culture is the only thing we have left to design a future beyond economic caste, beyond party polarization, and even beyond all of the ways in which tech can work against us.

But it gets hard not to feel alone when we're facing such an uncertain future. When I first started writing this book, I felt certain of the community around me. But as we all moved further into our COVID isolation bubbles, I left my job and watched my dad and other members of my family die in ways that didn't make sense to me. I started to feel so incredibly alone. I understood more than ever that feeling of becoming a Black skinhead. I found myself becoming preoccupied with all the ways that we were fucked as a society.

Sometimes, when I want to feel closer to my dad or when I'm feeling at my most disillusioned or just lost in the world, I put on *Maggot Brain* by Funkadelic.

It was one of his favorite recordings. It feels chaotic, crazy, dark, sometimes hopeful, but more than anything it feels urgent. The album is many things, but underneath it all, it is also a testament to Black culture's vitality. When I listen to it, I can see in my head all the ways in which road trips with my dad allowed me to bear witness to all the ways that we are asked to *rise above it all*, live through one thing or another, or risk drowning not just in our own shit but everyone else's that has been dumped there.

Where we last left my dad, he was dead. I want to resurrect him one more time to help me conclude this book. Let's take one more road trip down memory lane.

Road trips with Dad were a summer tradition growing up. But summer vacations for me often overlapped with work for him. He was an assistant basketball coach at the University of Illinois at Urbana-Champaign, where I spent most of my childhood. He was known as the recruiting specialist. He was really good at not just identifying talent but getting kids to leave home and move to a town most of them had never been to before. Wherever the talent was, he went looking for it. He could get a kid from just about anywhere if he could talk to him. He just needed to get there.

He would pack up his Pontiac Bonneville and hit the road. Whenever I could, I would go with him. We would drive though places in Chicago; Gary, Indiana; St. Louis, Missouri; and other mostly Black areas and communities in search of basketball players. Most of them were working-class urban areas. Around us were all the signs of urban decay—you could see the ways that people were fighting to build community, even as they were being left behind due to economic segregation. Some of the places we went to could almost be mistaken for places you'd see in photos of obliterated European towns after World War II.

We didn't move through those places in fear—we didn't have to. Yes, it probably helped that my dad was a licensed gun carrier and former probation officer. It helped that so many of these places resembled Syracuse, so in some ways felt like home for him, and distant epigenetic-driven memories of home for me. But more than a weapon or sense of home, he brought with him an opportunity. Everyone who knew his name and face welcomed him in like he was basketball's version of Santa Claus, even if they didn't know for sure, the multiple championship rings on his fingers let them know. He held the gift of a different future in his hands. The athletes had to do much of the work, but the opportunity was there.

During one road trip we took, I remember vividly sitting in the bleachers watching him do his thing. Every now and again he would look over to make sure I was doing OK, throw me a wink, and get back to doing a full-court press on the family. He was really good at recruiting. My mom said he could sell sand at the beach. And he could.

Getting to the pros was a long shot, but as was the case for my dad, a lot of his recruits had nothing to lose and everything to gain. Most of the kids my dad recruited didn't have any other way to get to college, besides that basketball scholarship he could offer. Access to college could be their ticket to a better life. And everyone in their family knew it.

But they also wanted to make sure that wherever they sent their kid, that kid would be safe. There are no guarantees, especially not in sports. Anything can happen on the road to the NBA. Anything can happen when you get to the NBA. Not everyone could be Michael Jordan. No matter what happened, life had to go on.

He understood all of those things. As a player, he understood hunger, the will to succeed, the determination to make something better for yourself and your family. As a former player, he understood the bitterness and disappointment that can settle in when things don't break your way. And, as a parent, my dad understood the desire to make sure that your kid was safe, that you were putting them into the hands of someone who would not just guard them but guide them on their journey into adulthood. Someone who wouldn't abandon them on the side of the road if things didn't work out. And when I looked around some of the places we drove through, it was clear that some kids had already been let down by society more than others.

In a rental car on the way back to the motel we were staying at, he handed me a CD to unwrap and pop in. It was a rediscovered classic: *Maggot Brain* by Funkadelic. I stared at the CD cover: a Black woman with a curly Afro, beautiful teeth, and long eyelashes—model Barbara Cheeseborough, I would later learn—is buried up to her neck in the dirt of the earth. Her face is frozen in a silent scream, but it also looks like she could be laughing with maniacal joy. I suppose it depends on your perspective. On the back, where the woman's head had been, there was just a skull, as though she had rapidly decomposed to just a skeleton.

Funkadelic bandleader George Clinton would later say that they initially had the idea to have a picture of a vampire with pearl fangs and a glass of blood that came from squeezed-out tampons. Apparently that was too extreme, so they went more subtle. Looking at the cover, it was scary. It was intriguing. I put it in, expecting to hear funk sounds that were in the vein of later classics like *One Nation Under a Groove*. But this was not that. This was a total mindfuck.

I was with my dad as we drove through a lightning storm, and I remember staring out of the window into what seemed like infinite darkness. The title track wastes no time making things weird, opening up with a spoken word piece.

> *Mother Earth is pregnant for the third time*
> *For y'all have knocked her up*
>
> —"MAGGOT BRAIN," FUNKADELIC

These words are accompanied by the mournful crying of Eddie Hazel's legendary guitar solo. Clinton would later explain that he told Hazel to play the guitar as if his mother had died. To picture that day—what he would feel and how he would make sense of his life. The result is eerie.

Clinton has said that for him, the whole concept behind the song and the album was about "going places that Black groups hadn't gone, into questions about whether America was still on the right path or whether the promise of the late sixties had completely evaporated."

According to urban legend, the name of the song and the album comes from Clinton finding his brother in a Chicago apartment. Supposedly Clinton found him days after he had died of a drug overdose, with his skull cracked and maggots coming out of his head. A literal maggot brain.

For his part, Clinton says the origins are not nearly so ghoulish. He's talking in the abstract, about inner-city rot, the shortsightedness of consumerism, and the need for people to free their mind. The song and album were about expanding beyond the physical barriers that work to keep us confined. Lyrics throughout the album stripped away romantic notions of a distant future that could be dreamed into reality. They were urging people to wake up, take in the urban decay around them, get up and fight for social progress. He recorded the album in the early '70s, but twenty years later I could see all the failures of the promise of social progress as I looked out the window of my dad's Pontiac, driving through a number of cities that were distinct but that carried hauntingly familiar characteristics.

Clinton talks about Mother Earth being "knocked up," for the third time—one interpretation is that this refers to the ways the world had shifted from an agricultural society to an industrial one and was moving rapidly at the time of the song's recording toward a post-industrial society. Moreover, the song is speaking to myriad ecological consequences of continued racism. He didn't have to look any further than Detroit, where the song was recorded. Detroit was a city that once had more than 1.8 million people, but at the time of the recording people were leaving in droves; today it has less than 700,000. From 1940 to 2000, Black people went from representing less than 10 percent of the Motor City's population to more than 80 percent.

Think about how much natural land and untouched forests were lost as people fled farther from the city into sprawling suburbs. Think of all the added miles that need to be driven and the vehicle emissions that result. As climate change worsens, we're going to need more density, but in America it's more important to ensure that the upper class—mostly white people—don't have to be near the communities that they deem undesirable, specifically Black, working-class communities. This is the story of many cities in America, and I see it every day when I walk around my adopted city of Baltimore. That was the warning that George Clinton and Funkadelic were issuing in "Maggot Brain."

When Funkadelic recorded "Maggot Brain," Clinton vividly recalled thinking about the initial lure of the Motown sound and record label that had brought him and his doo-wop group, The Parliaments, out to what was then optimistically called the City of the Future. But in the time between when The Parliaments had arrived and Funkadelic was recording *Maggot Brain,* the city was starting to feel more dystopian than utopian.

Detroit, like many US cities, had rushed to become the city of the future without an inclusive vision that reflected its ethnic and cultural demographics. It was hard to see where working-class Black people would fit into a future that was never meant to include them. In cities like Detroit, Chicago, Oakland, and Baltimore, where I live today, those in power had gone out of their way to exclude so many of them.

What emanates from the *Maggot Brain* album and songs like "Wars of Armageddon" are the types of sounds generated amid rapidly disappearing or disappeared spaces. In the skeletal remains of lost businesses and abandoned warehouses. In the shadows of gorgeous foreclosed homes that remind you of a time when Black people were building wealth in the City of the Future. The noises and lyrics warn of imminent collapse and a type of Afropessimism that speaks to the ongoing effects of racism and colonialism, as well as contemporary and historical systems of enslavement.

> *For I knew I had to rise above it all*
> *Or drown in my own shit.*
>
> —"MAGGOT BRAIN," FUNKADELIC

In 1970s and '80s Detroit, though businesses were disappearing, the music and culture remained. Even in those hard times, Black culture endured, and it would continue to create the future. It would find a way to rise and create yet another sound that, like Motown Records before it, would influence the world.

Over the following decades, a post-Motown sound would emerge in Detroit, directly influenced by the music of George Clinton and Parliament Funkadelic, and ultimately leading to the founding of techno. Techno music—founded by The Belleville Three—was a way to humanize and harness technology, but it was also iconoclastic, lonely, and even unhinged. The sounds seek to find comfort amid an uncertain future. For example, Drexciya, a Detroit techno duo, created a whole mythology around their music, influenced by Paul Gilroy's *The Black Atlantic*. The mythical world that shapes the music is populated by the unborn children of pregnant African women tossed off slave ships during the Middle Passage. Drexciya imagines a world where Black people in America can feel untethered from the weight of centuries of enslavement.

There are two cultural frames I see clashing in Black politics. The first is the type of demoralizing Democrat realism that suggests to Black voters there is no alternative to the capitalist conservative nucleus of the

Democratic Party. In fact, there is no future without the party. There's a failure to imagine our power to reshape or leave the party. This is where I live sometimes.

On the other hand, there's full-on Black libertarianism as politics continue to move further to the Right because of government failures throughout history. I see us giving in to the idea that extreme capital and shrinking government is the only thing that can save us, a type of corporatized Afrofuturism. A *fuck it, I'll do it myself* type of amnesia that ignores how race was constructed through economic caste and how autonomous Black communities have been snuffed out throughout history.

There has to be something out there better than either of those two options, right?

I talked about this with a former colleague, Bernard, who wrote his master thesis about race, technology, and data access. He offered this:

> We have to upend the systems because they are built on racism and the fungibility of Blackness. But you don't just upend the systems then leave; you have to imagine what comes next. We have to really [and] radically rethink how we live in this world on all fronts so that we can create a better future, have a freer world. I'm an Afropessimist because we can't understand technology without understanding how the system was built. But to me, that's an aspirational theory that's necessary to not just imagine but [also] design a Black future.

Ultimately, I believe in institutions. I believe in government. I really do. I understand the problem of institutions. I understand the problem of government. I understand why we feel let down by them sometimes. But sometimes I fear we are all too willing to ignore the role of institutions in building a Black politique that has not always been about serving the Democratic Party or the status quo. We ignore the role of institutions in building a Black culture.

I fear on the Left that the underlined mistrust and absence of faith in the abilities of institutions will lead us to abandon a power source that has been crucial to important historical fights and wins. This is why fights like antitrust, landownership, and reparations matter—because our ability to own and control capital and resources is crucial to being able to shape our own destiny.

The question to me is this: What would it look like to truly manifest an intergenerational, interclass movement committed to the unresolved economic and political issues that lie before us?

Whether we're talking about media, business, or religion, we need institutions that are concerned with issues of Black justice first and foremost. We need institutions with a liberation philosophy embedded within them and a vision for independent power that is the north star. We need institutions that are not beholden to corporate interests and gatekeepers. We need institutions that are built to last past their high-profile leadership and function to support—not block—emerging leadership. Institutions that support the people who are the future.

Too often, we get scared of upstart Black leaders, the type who likes to rock the boat. I totally get it. I don't relish those moments when someone gets *All About Eve* on me and tries to come for my neck. But part of what we see playing out over and over again is a stagnation of leadership. Increasingly, those who are the content creators, narrators, makers, and gatekeepers of Black culture occupy a certain class status. Like me, I know. I acknowledge my privilege and also have and will commit to fighting for space for all of us.

Right-wing institutions have sought to develop dark mirror versions of liberal institutions. There are several reasons why they can do that, and I'm certainly not naïve to that. But we cannot sustain a vision of power, racial progress, and equity without looking at holistic strategies that are about building Black institutions, pushing for leaders who will work in our interests, and pushing to reform the corporations that hold an overwhelming amount of power over our everyday lives.

We also have to be clear that charity does not secure rights. Institutions will tell you that, corporations will tell you that. Billionaires looking for tax breaks and loopholes will tell you that. But they don't. Only the government can ensure societal rights. Every time the government abdicates its fundamental obligation and responsibility to uphold the people's rights, corporations will always be there to tell you they can save us. They will tell us they can give us Wakanda. But they can't. Corporatization will not be our salvation. Our salvation can never live in the hands of people who are operating to consolidate power and build capital off of the backs of our labor.

For decades, US jobs have been increasingly un-unionized, gig based, and tech dependent. We have become resigned to the role of extreme capitalism and corporate control over our day-to-day lives, so much so that we can't imagine a world without it. As Mark Fisher puts it, it's easier to imagine the end of the world than the end of capitalism. But unchecked capitalism did not save our places of Black sanctuary, and it will not save us.

Lately, I've been having nightmares that inevitably we will live in President Mark Zuckerberg's America. A place where essential government services are turned over to Silicon Valley whiz kids and managed by a consultant class charged with delivering basic needs. The idea of "society" and all that it entails is a charming little relic of the past, lost to "inefficiencies," "opportunity costs," "core competencies," and other jargon on a boardroom slide deck. What passes for a "community" is acted out on weekends in a remote coastal outpost, like a ghoulish mash-up of *Citizen Kane* meets *The Fountainhead* meets *The Great Gatsby*. But then, I wake up and realize we still have time. We still have us. Black culture was not built overnight, and it cannot be broken overnight.

I was reminded of that when, toward the end of writing this book, I reconnected with my older brother, Kenny. Up until I saw him at my dad's funeral, we hadn't really talked in years. It was one of those things where you fight with someone and then time passes and you forget what you fought about, but you have also forgotten what it means to have that person in your life.

He had been my hero when we were growing up. We would watch Prince's movie *Purple Rain* over and over again while doing the dance moves to all the songs. We would ride around on his bike with me in the basket like ET. He would draw stuff for me. I love my sisters, too, don't get me wrong, but Kenny and I were creative and imaginative together in a different way.

We barely talked at my dad's funeral. It was the height of COVID, and everyone was wearing masks and trying to maintain the proper amount of distance even while trying to mourn together as a community.

But we didn't fully reconnect until months later in the spring at my uncle Early's funeral. We weren't wearing masks anymore. Kenny looked too much like my dad for me to stay mad. Next thing I know, the family was all drunk at Uncle Early's house, drinking his expensive liquor, laughing together, sharing memories of him and my dad. It was like no time had passed.

Kenny signed up for the army after dropping out of college. He thought it was a good way to get money, and besides, there hadn't been a war or military conflict in years. The week he graduated from boot camp, Operation Desert Storm kicked off, and he was deployed. My mom cried; my dad offered to drive him to the US border. But he felt like he had to go—not for his nation, but for us. He wanted to make his family and his community proud. He was good at his job. The memories of how good still haunt him.

The last time we had been in contact, he was an army recruiter. He was very good at that as well. I know that because one time, he butt dialed me while recruiting a kid at a McDonald's drive-through.

He said he knows it's not for everyone, but it is for someone. There are kids who don't have better alternatives, don't have a way to pay for college, and live where gangs are circling. Sometimes, a job in the military is the best option a kid has, especially as a vehicle to the middle class.

He said he can tell if they have something better for them or if they won't make it in the military. He didn't recruit those kids just to hit numbers. He felt responsible for anyone who chose to join the army, and he cared about whether he was going to fuck someone up or over. Today, he's retired from the military and working at a veteran support and mental health facility.

As we caught up on the years we'd been apart, I started telling him about the book. Once I told him the theme, he cut in to tell me a story.

OK, so let me go back for a second to my recruiting stint at South Holland [Army] Recruiting Station. I put in a kid named Ralph. He was a smart kid—he was a street kid, but he was smart. I met him at Thornwood High School. I tried to recruit him, but he was noncommittal. He said, "I may do it, but, you know, I got better stuff to do. You know, I'm doing music stuff, but I understand I got to get something to fall back on. My mother told me I gotta have something to fall back on because it might not work out."

Kenny told him to come to the office to get tested for the military. He came in with two guys. Kenny thought, *Oh good, maybe I'll get three.* Ralph took the test, one of his other friends did, too. The third one was not convinced.

He was like, "Nah, I'm good." I was like, "OK, what are you going to do?" Man is like, "Be a rapper." And I was like, "Do you know how many people come in here and say they're going to be a rapper? They're right back here later." And he's like, "Yeah, but I'm gonna make it. I'm making my own music, and we're making some money." So I said, "OK, man, you do you." Ralph said to me, "No, you don't understand; he's good. He's gonna make it. He doesn't need this."

Ralph's friend handed Kenny a purple CD, a demo, which afterward he threw away and forgot about. Ralph passed the test, the other one didn't. Ralph ended up going into the military, and he and Kenny stayed in contact. One day, he phoned Kenny up.

KENNY: And he's like, "You remember my friend? That dude you were trying to get to join?" And I was like, "Yeah man. Yeah." He told me, "My friend just got signed to Def Jam." It was either Def Jam or Roc-A-Fella, something like that.

ME: No fucking way! Don't tell me what I think you're going to tell me.

KENNY: That's right, Brandi-wine—it was your guy Kanye. I should've kept that damn purple CD. You know how much that shit would be worth right now?

ME: OK, that's definitely going into the book.

They say that in Black Chicago, people are only one or two degrees separated from each other. Maybe there's something to that. Talking to Kenny was a full-circle moment. It was a healing moment. Talking to him reminded me of what we both had lost when we stopped being in community and what we gained by finding each other again.

The link we had to each other and the love we have for each other was still there even after all this time. It had been forgotten, but it hadn't been broken. And even though our entire family was heartbroken over all those we had lost, talking to him made me envision a time when things could be OK. It's not always perfect, but it's healing to have a community that doesn't just hold you down but one that you can also create and imagine a future with, even after loss. Especially after loss.

We have to talk about the terror and the pain of the past. All of it. Not just the specific glimpses that make it into the mainstream media, but all the things that don't. Scars are a sign of survival and resilience. They are a part of healing.

We can't forget the dope stuff either, though—the sugar, not just the vinegar. There is beauty in the boundlessness of the imagination, and there is also beauty to be found in the concreteness of the naked truth.

Earlier, I said it is hard to see where Black people fit into a future that was never meant to include us. In cities like Detroit, Chicago, Oakland, and Baltimore, where I live today, so many have gone out of their way to exclude us. But in each of those cities, the culture is still there; dreams of our future are still present. You can see it, you can feel it. The link is not totally gone. Power can look a lot of ways.

The Black skinhead is the monster in the dark, hiding in the folds of the untold story. But if we turn on the light, the Black skinhead can also be our guide or at least a warning. The story of the Black skinhead is a story about disillusionment. But also, it's about hope. It's about change. Not just the marketing and signifying of hope and change, but the fight to make it so and the unfinished work that lies ahead. One day, it may be too late for us, but we haven't gotten there yet. So, while there's time, we have to figure out the way to rise above it all. Otherwise, we'll drown in our own shit.

Afterword

May 2023

> Ye and Nick are on info right now and ye just said "I love hitler" b4 they went to commercial break . . .

> Well . . . Fuck . . .

In fall 2022, I had just released *Black Skinhead*. My colleague Brian Friedberg had also just released a book he had cowritten called *Meme Wars: The Untold Story of the Online Battles Upending Democracy in America*, a book about the resurgence online of white identity politics. Together we had spent years in the trenches of the research, looking at figures like Kanye West and Candace Owens, who I've discussed in this book, and Nick Fuentes and Milo Yiannopoulos, key figures in American far-right postmodern identitarianism, who are discussed in depth in *Meme Wars*. Though *we* saw the clear connection between these various figures and the direct link between books that we had produced, it wasn't immediately obvious to people who hadn't spent time in some of the more bizarre and disconcerting corners of the political web. But soon those overlapping worlds would be exposed to the public eye in a major way.

First came the 2022 Paris Fashion Week. Kanye West—who, after most of the writing of this book, legally changed his name to Ye—made headlines when he showed up with right-wing political commentator Candace Owens wearing matching WHITE LIVES MATTER T-shirts. It was yet another example (as discussed in the chapter "An Abomination of

Obamanation") of how "Conservative Inc." uses celebrity access to launder white nationalist rhetoric while ignoring a burgeoning Black conservative grassroots movement.

In the book, I refer to the relationship between Ye and Owens as a symbiotic one similar to that which exists between a polar bear (Ye) that makes the kill and the arctic fox (Owens) that follows behind in winter feeding off the scraps. This episode was no different. After attempting to offload her husband's junk asset Parler onto Ye, and extracting increased attention for her mockumentary on Black Lives Matter, Owens faded back into her niche corner of the internet as Ye took center stage and dominated the news cycle for weeks.

Ye unleashed a series of interviews, social media posts, and various sound bites that trafficked in anti-Semitism, misogyny, and anti-Blackness. As the news cycle struggled to keep track, we learned that none of this was new territory. Editorial discretion of interviews dating back as far as his infamous "Slavery is a choice" interview covered in the chapter "Kanye Was Right-ish," had been generously edited to remove his anti-historical comments about the Holocaust. What came sharply into focus in late 2022 is that Ye's political agenda is increasingly less about Black economic power and autonomy at scale and more about centering himself as a Christ-like figure for a disaffected generation swimming the shark-infested waters of the dark web.

When I wrote my last sentence for this book in early 2022, I saw Kanye as a late-stage Black skinhead with no community. I set out to warn us of the implications of that. But still, I held out hope that he—and others disillusioned by failed systems—could eventually find their way home. I'm admittedly more cynical about those prospects today.

Ye has proclaimed himself as someone who stands for peace and love. He also brings together people who do not engage with the pretense of democracy, people more concerned with shattering the idea that peace or a "more perfect union" could ever exist in the multicultural experiment we call America. Ye has emerged as a gateway to the constantly evolving fringes of the web, the spaces that have become flourishing post-Gamergate, incel communities. These are, in part, men and boys who want to feel justified in their anger, misogyny, and bigotry, who feel like they have been stripped of their freedoms in a modern society, but who grew up with hip-hop and don't gravitate toward the Dylan Roof or Richard Spencer side of the internet.

Ye speaks in an anti-Semitic, new-age-Christian-values frame meshed with gender essentialism, body and cultural policing. He laces his rhetoric with references to things like trade agreements and economic autonomy to appeal to people with a class analysis. And though in late 2022 he found time to talk about Donald Trump, Ye was clear that another presidential run in 2024 was in the cards for him regardless of whether or not Trump was eligible and inclined to run. In 2020 many dismissed Ye's ill-fated campaign as an attempt to draw votes away from the Democratic party—to the benefit of Trump, I think there was, and continues to be, something more at play.

The public reintroduction of key Gamergate figure Milo Yiannopoulos and January 6 insurrection leader Nick Fuentes as Ye's presidential campaign advisors fully unmasked what our research team had long observed. Ye was not just (or even primarily) drawing his influence from Black agenda–setting factions and influencers online. The bizarre and specific conspiracies he espoused—which I won't repeat here—are not ones proven to have wide-scale acceptance in Black American communities, despite public discourse to the contrary. Instead, Ye's scorched earth campaign in fall 2022 became the rants that launched a thousand (plus) "alt-right" memes. Memes that refashioned the visual of "Ye" into a symbol that looked like a swastika. Memes that said charming things like:

> Never thought I'd die fighting side by side with a Nigger.
> What about side by side with an anti-Semite?
> Aye, I could do that.

Many white supremacists (or identitarians) say it's more important to be anti-Semitic than pro-white, as waking people up to so-called Jewish influences is necessary to throw off the globalization mechanisms that force multiculturalism and valorize nontraditional identities. For them, Ye is a useful tool, and an onramp for their message. In that sense, the Republican Party was never meant to be a permanent political home, there is no interest in even a remote pretense of traditional partisan politics. It's a temporary pit stop on the way to the type of fascism promoted by the likes of Fuentes and Yiannopoulos, a type of fascism that has to be more reflective of the demographics of America (versus, say . . . pre–World War II Germany) and engage fellow disillusioned travelers from outside of identitarian spaces in order to work. This piece is crucial to understanding why simply summing it up as white nationalism or just the Republican Party misses how these movements can continue to evolve and find allies even amid shifting demographics and anti-party politics.

All of this stands to collide with the growing number of Black conservatives, who are younger than Black Democrats as well as white Republicans and are more likely than white Republicans to be working class, according to a 2022 study released by the Pew Research Center. In 2022 a historic number of Black Republican candidates (more than eighty) ran for Congress in 2022 (many more for state and local offices). Around thirty of them were on the ballot in November. Many of them lost, for various reasons. Most of them did not have the full funding support of the Republican/GOP apparatus throughout the entire election cycle, with a small chosen few getting more funding in the final months leading up to the election. Some (many) were longshots to begin with, either because they were in a dark-blue district or they were extremely unserious from the word go.

It's noteworthy that Ye didn't appear to use any of his social capital to support Black Republican candidates. Based on my research, he didn't use his celebrity to turn a spotlight on the short list of lesser known Black Republicans that were running on the principles of Black conservatism that Ye purports to embrace: independent Black businesses and more support for trade agreements that incentivize job growth in the United States, the right to protect Black families through gun ownership, and support for US veterans.

Instead Ye turned the spectacle on himself, at this point a well-oiled machine when it comes to using music, fashion, Jesus Christ, and social media as vehicles to reinforce the cultlike qualities of his persona. More and more, his whole vibe displays a type of faux Black conservatism that subverts respectability politics and embraces identitarianism, playing into the false idea that Black culture is fundamentally corrupt and irredeemable and he is the liberator speaking truth to power, who is willing and able to create a new culture.

Even in the name change from Kanye to Ye there is meaning. While the name *Kanye* means in Yoruba, "next in line to the chieftaincy," and in Igbo, "let's give (God praise)," *Ye* means "you" in second-person plural, or as the artist himself says, "So I'm you, I'm us, it's us" . . . which is not *not* cult like. *Ye* as a male name of Chinese origin, can also mean light. Or as written in the King James Version of the bible, "Ye are the light of the world. A city that is set on a hill cannot be hid." More than ever it's clear: Ye is not "*for* the culture" because Ye wants to *be* the culture, the light, maybe even the demise. Whether he can continue his impressive run of staying just enough ahead of the curve to remain relevant is anyone's guess.

But whether it's Ye or the next one, let us all be aware of false idols.

Acknowledgments

What a long, strange, beautiful, and daunting trip writing this book has been. There are so many people who helped make this possible that I want to thank. Thank you to the Celadon team, especially Ryan Doherty, for your encouragement and Cecily van Buren-Freedman, for your patience and energy and for pouring over every word and pages of changing content. Thank you to my agent, Michael Signorelli at Aevitas Creative Management, for believing in me and working hard on my behalf to get *Black Skinhead* out into the world. Thank you to Adam Moss, for recognizing my potential as a book writer.

I want to shout out the Shorenstein Team at Harvard. Brian and Yulan, 100 percent I could not have done this without your genius, research, insight, and dark humor. Thank you to Eesha Ramanujam for helping me with updates for the paperback edition. Brooklyne and Marya, thank you for your support, for helping me further refine my Black feminist lens and for your inspirational research. Appreciation to Setti Warren, Nancy Gibbs, and Laura Manley for your ongoing support of the team's race and technology research.

When I announced that I was going to write this book, I was blown away by the people who reached out to support me on this journey. Deep gratitude goes to Chance and Lori for research capacity support. Special thanks and appreciation to Steven Renderos and the team at Media Justice, for capacity support—DJ Ren, you will always be one of my favorite people, and your friendship has meant more than words can convey. Too many people to thank—but Team Media Justice past and present, thank you for being my first and most consistent political home. Deep respect and gratitude to my friend and inspiration, Joseph Torres, the Media2070, as well as the FreePress team. Thank you and appreciation to Briahnna Brown, Claire de Leon, and Jen Carnig at Spitfire Strategies. Your enthusiasm and coaching have been clutch. Huge thank-you to Ayana M., for transcribing something like eighty hours' worth of interviews. I also want to thank my grief counselor, Dr. Nyasha Grayman, for helping me go to the places I needed to in order to finish the book.

My Color Of Change Dream Team, you all continue to have a special place in my heart. Specifically, Jade Ogunnaike, Johnny Mathias, Evan Feeney, and Amanda Jackson, but to all of you, please know that I've learned so much from each of you and will continue to root for you from afar. Thanks and gratitude also goes to Kwesi Chappin, a good friend and amazing interview, and my confidant and early-morning-call buddy, Jenni Edwards. I also can't forget my loves Hope and Peggy WoodMoore— thank you for your big brains and always bringing in the glass-half-full perspective when I'm feeling empty.

Thank you to my antitrust people, who have been so deeply supportive, and from whom I've learned a great deal. Special thanks to Matt Stoller, for reading my initial proposal, putting me in touch with key sources, and being a well of historical information. Thanks also to the team at American Economic Liberties Project and the Action Center on Race and the Economy, for also being amazing resources and other political homes for me. Special acknowledgment to all the people I've strongarmed into reading various chapters and drafts, including Linda Lu, Chris Glasser, Alexei Abrams, Nima Shokat, Zoe Schmitz, and Nima Shirazi.

If I started talking about all the Black families who have had a hand in raising me, that would be a whole other book. But there's a few folks that I want to especially give thanks to. Thank you to Mrs. Linda Page, for reading several versions of *Black Skinhead,* and thanks to Mr. Joe, Courtney, and Kim for all the love and support. Thank you to the Harris family, Dr. Zelema Harris, and my bestie, Jay, as well as Cynthia Bond and Blackbird Collective, you have been such a source of strength and inspiration, more than you know. Thank you to my God family, the Rogers. And beautiful flowers and thanks to Dr. Barbara Henley and Diane Williams.

I don't even know what to say about or to my family, but all of you are one of a kind, and I'm incredibly grateful for you. Thank you to my in-laws, the Dexter-Miller family, you all have welcomed me in with such warmth and energy, and I'm so grateful. Thanks especially to Martha, Pat, Catherine, and Max, and a special hug for Marjie, Carolyn (RIP beautiful, tiny lady), Martha V., and Nancy.

Mom, you are so amazing and brilliant. While writing this book, I got to see so much of you, and I thank you for letting me see all the parts of a parent's humanity that sometimes you miss when you're a kid. Thank you to my second mom, Erica: you fight for me, love me, and make me laugh like no other—you are truly one of a kind! Thank you to my siblings, Semaj and Kenny, and the extended family—life would be less colorful without you. Thank you to the extended Collins family—I hope I did the family justice. Kisses and hugs to the Lynch, Kellum, and Ledford families; there is so much of our story left to tell, and I hope I get the chance to tell it. Thank you, Dad, for looking down on me and guiding me through this process when I didn't think I could make it—I hope I made you proud.

Last, but not least, thanks to David. You let me tell our story even when you didn't love how I told it. You read pages and pages of the book, and you were right about mostly everything, even when I didn't listen. You're my anchor and my light. Thank you for validating my feelings, and bless you for telling me when I'm being off the wall. Love you.

A Note on Additional Sources

This book is a work of nonfiction and anthropological documentation based on events unfolding in real time during the research and writing of the book. Since 2019, I've spent a great deal of time researching and studying Black, US-based social movements on- and offline at the Technology and Social Change Project (TaSC) housed within the Shorenstein Center on Media, Politics and Public Policy at the Harvard Kennedy School. The primary lead researchers working with me on sourcing and documentation were Yulan Grant, a multidisciplinary artist, DJ, and research fellow at Shorenstein, and Brian Friedberg, the senior researcher at TaSC. Methodologies used for background research and documentation include metadata scraping, live tracking of major political events that took place between 2019 and 2021, fieldwork, investigative digital ethnography, and raw Black voter data sets. Their tireless work and receipt gathering was indispensable to this book's writing. Any errors are mine.

Dr. Brooklyne Gipson, distinguished postdoctoral fellow in the digital humanities at the University of Illinois Urbana-Champaign, helped with additional sourcing on communications, subcultures, nationalism, and hip-hop history. Dr. Joan Donovan, research director of the Shorenstein Center, provided guidance and sourcing on populism and online communities.

Confirmation and documentation of statements of fact about my personal family history were compiled through detailed interviews with relatives, newspaper archives, the Red Squad Collection at the Chicago

History Museum, and an Ancestry.com-commissioned research report. Additional compiled documents include government surveillance documents, birth certificates, military records and draft cards, census records, death and marriage certificates, land deeds, and authentication of ancestry via DNA testing and genealogy mapping. I have not cited all those records with specificity in the notes to prevent unnecessary intrusiveness.

Much of the thought, insight, and perspectives that populate the book come from many interviews and correspondence with a wide range of people whom I'm incredibly grateful to for taking the time to connect with me both on and off the record. I want to give special thanks to Yulan Grant, Katara Patton, James Harris, and Matt Stoller, who helped broker interviews with many people who informed the book, those who are named here and those who aren't:

ON RECORD ISSUE, SUBJECT AND KNOWLEDGE
EXPERTS (AND VOTERS)

Amanda Jackson	Kevin Connelly	Peggy Moore
Arisha Hatch	Kwesi Chappin	Rashad Robinson
Brian Dolinar	Jade Ogunnaike	Reverend Eric Wallace
DeForrest Brown, Jr.	Jimmy Collins	Ricardo Levins Morales
Diane Williams	Lotus Lain	Setti Warren
Hettie Collins	Marlon Marshall	Shireen Mitchell
Kamilah Mathias	Mary Muse and Mrs. Juanita	
Katara Patton	Mitchell	

POTENTIAL VOTERS (AND EXPERTS IN THEIR OWN RIGHT)

April	Katina	Mrs. Mitchell
Bernard	Keith	Querrida
Charles	Lisa	Randy
Chelsea	Louis	Reign
Clifford	Mary	Tariq
Dr. Karmen	Maya	Vic
Eric	Malcolm	
Jay	Mrs. Richardson	

Notes

PROLOGUE: THE STORIES WE DIE WITH

xiv *Sweet Valley High*: Erin McCarthy, "12 of the Sweet Valley High Books' Most Ridiculous Plotlines," Mental Floss, April 2, 2017, https://archive.ph/ATliT.

xiv *Vampire Diaries*: Jessica Sherman, "Have You Felt the Magic?," L. J. Smith official website, accessed January 19, 2022, https://archive.ph/DfCVx.

xv *A League of Their Own*: Bill Francis, "A Quarter Century of 'A League of Their Own,'" National Baseball Hall of Fame and Museum, accessed January 19, 2022, https://archive.ph /IGmD4.

xv **Roy Hamilton:** Vincent L. Stephens, "Learning to Listen (LTL) Excerpt 11: Roy Hamilton: Star, Pioneer, and Misfit," *Riffs, Beats & Codas*, December 31, 2015, https://archive.ph/fbP5P.

xv **"The Impossible Dream (The Quest)":** Roy Hamilton, "The Impossible Dream," Discogs.com, accessed January 19, 2022, https://archive.is/sZDm0. Text of the lyrics can be found here (original composer was Mitch Leigh): Joe Darion, "The Impossible Dream (The Quest)," STLyrics.com, accessed January 19, 2022, https://archive.ph/j9Bth.

xv **New Mexico Sports Hall of Fame:** Rick Wright, "'20 NM Sports Hall of Fame Inductees to Finally Have Their Day," *Albuquerque Journal,* updated July 25, 2021, https:// archive.ph/mxZ6S.

xvi **he had been inducted:** Chris Carlson, "Jimmy Collins, Final Four Basketball Player and One of Best in CNY History, Dies at 74," Syracuse.com, December 13, 2020, https:// archive.ph/crSxo.

xvi **ceremony promised:** Wright, "'20 NM Sports Hall of Fame."

xix *documented* **lynchings:** "Mississippi Lawmaker Denounced for Lynching Remark Following Confederate Monument Removal in New Orleans," Equal Justice Initiative, May 22, 2017, https://archive.ph/qP63x.

xix **Chicago boy by the name of Emmett Till:** Gabriela Szymanowska, "'Hard to Understand': Emmett Till Marker Broken Days after 66th Anniversary of His Death," *Mississippi Clarion Ledger,* September 3, 2021, https://archive.fo/RCrwr.

xx **in his high school yearbook:** Thomas J. Corcoran High School, *The Glen Echo— Class of 1966* (Syracuse, New York: 1966).

xxi **40 percent of Black residents:** Geoff Herbert, "Syracuse Named One of the 'Worst Cities for Black Americans' to Live," Syracuse.com, updated January 4, 2019, https://archive .ph/dV9rz.

xxi **oft-studied 15th Ward in Syracuse:** Alana Semuels, "How to Decimate a City," *The Atlantic,* November 20, 2015, https://archive.ph/Wk34R.

xxi **"refuge from discrimination,":** "The Destruction of Syracuse's 15th Ward," Onondaga Historical Association, accessed January 19, 2022, https://archive.fo/x3rI6.

xxii **He even named his autobiography:** Lou Henson and Skip Myslenski, *Lou: Winning at Illinois* (Champaign, IL: Sports Publishing LLC, 1989).

xxii **One of the origins of policing in the US was patrols:** Connie Hassett-Walker, "How You Start Is How You Finish? The Slave Patrol and Jim Crow Origins of Policing," American Bar Association, January 11, 2021, https://archive.is/5TFRc.

xviii **law enforcement and white nationalism:** FBI Counterterrorism Division, "White Supremacist Infiltration of Law Enforcement," Federal Bureau of Investigation Intelligence Assessment, October 17, 2006, https://tinyurl.com/ybmx8b8k.

xxiii **voted the best high school player ever in Central New York:** Nolan Weidner, "Top 75 Basketball Players: No. 1 Jimmy Collins Remembers Good (and Bad) from High School Days," Syracuse.com, updated August 27, 2019, https://archive.ph/SBzAW.

xxiv **Innocent Black people are twelve times more likely than white people to be falsely convicted of crimes:** Samuel R. Gross, Maurice Possley, and Klara Stephens, *Race and Wrongful Convictions in the United States* (Irvine, CA: National Registry of Exonerations, 2017), https://tinyurl.com/3nr69dcr.

xxvi **"But that wasn't my experience in New Mexico":** James Collins, interview by author, Chicago, IL, September 2, 2020.

xxvii **Black poverty in the United States:** Nadra Kareem Nittle, "Why Black American Athletes Raised Their Fists at the 1968 Olympics," History.com, May 25, 2021, https://tinyurl.com/2xv2smk4.

xxvii **"disciplined when playing the game":** Collins, interview.

xxvii **All-American honors:** "James 'Jimmy' Earl Collins," New Mexico Sports Hall of Fame, https://archive.fo/xX9jO.

xxvii *Sports Illustrated* **in 1970:** *SI* Staff, "Cover Description—Four for the Championship," *Sports Illustrated,* March 16, 1970, https://tinyurl.com/2p9y47hc.

xxviii **"Can somebody please go get him!":** "1970 Final Four—NMState Highlight," uploaded on October 24, 2017, by Nicole Sack, YouTube video, 3:00, https://www.youtube.com/watch?v=JE0mRxO6OAw.

xxviii **"tired of talk":** Lamberta Voget, "The Nature of Prejudice," *Focus on Youth,* July 1968, 4–5.

INTRODUCTION: WHERE ARE WE GOING?

1 **"a house that was built by slaves":** Michelle Obama, "Watch First Lady Michelle Obama's Full Speech at the 2016 Democratic National Convention," filmed July 25, 2016, uploaded by *PBS NewsHour,* YouTube video, 14:45, https://www.youtube.com/watch?v=4ZNWYqDU948. A transcript of the speech can also be found here: *Washington Post* Staff, "Transcript: Read Michelle Obama's Full Speech from the 2016 DNC," *Washington Post,* July 26, 2016, https://archive.ph/kBTDR.

4 **highest rated in seven years:** Kate Stanhope, "Ratings: Record-Breaking 11.4 Million Viewers Watch 2010 MTV VMAs," *TV Guide,* September 13, 2010, https://tinyurl.com/2p8vc54d.

4 **critically acclaimed work:** Shawn Grant, "Billboard Names Kanye West's 'My Beautiful Dark Twisted Fantasy' the Greatest Album of the Decade," *Source,* November 19, 2019, https://tinyurl.com/8muepbau.

4 **undergoing several cosmetic surgery procedures:** Luke Morgan Britton, "Kanye West Claims Mother Would 'Still Be Alive If I Had Never Moved to Los Angeles,'" NME, July 1, 2015, https://tinyurl.com/2p8r97b4.

4 **immediately canceled:** *Rolling Stone,* "Lady Gaga, Kanye West Cancel 'Fame Kills' Tour," *Rolling Stone,* October 29, 2009, https://tinyurl.com/yeyv4fke.

4 **blackballed out of the industry:** "Joe Jackson Wants to 'Blackball' Kanye," TMZ, September 14, 2009, https://tinyurl.com/y5pjb44h.

4 **laughing media people:** "A Brief History of Kanye's Fraught Relationship with Barack Obama," Outline, accessed January 21, 2022, https://tinyurl.com/2p8fdhky.

5 *ignite the people like Obama*: Peter Hamby, "Barack Obama Gets Name-Dropped in Hip-Hop," CNN, August 17, 2007, https://archive.ph/NwZZv.

5 **exile in Hawaii:** Shea Serrano and Brandon Jenkins, "Kanye West: 'My Beautiful Dark Twisted Fantasy,'" Ringer, November 11, 2021, https://archive.fo/eltdb.

6 **He had become disillusioned:** Cole Cuchna, "S2E15—Lost in the World by Kanye West," May 2018, in *Dissect,* produced by Spotify Studios, podcast, 38:25, https://tinyurl.com/r9yjxwf4.

6 **two years on the Billboard charts:** Will Lavin, "All That Power: Celebrating the Genius of Kanye West's 'My Beautiful Dark Twisted Fantasy,' a Tumultuous Decade On," NME, November 22, 2020, https://archive.ph/AsM6O.

6 **wouldn't give him a long-term contract:** Cole Cuchna, "S8E1—Kanye West: YEEZUS," March 2021, in *Dissect,* produced by Spotify Studios, podcast, 45:52, https://tinyurl.com/ym44m7te.

7 **$53 million by 2016:** Emily Jane Fox, "Kanye West's $53 Million Debt, Explained," *Vanity Fair,* February 17, 2016, https://archive.ph/evR67.

7 **like a fuck-you:** Cuchna, "S8E1."

8 **toward economic libertarianism and a type of social conservatism:** Will Welch, "Inside Kanye West's Vision for the Future," GQ, April 16, 2020, https://archive.ph/UVmYJ.

8 **He no longer needed Nike:** Jake Woolf, "Adidas Just Made Kanye West Their Michael Jordan," GQ, June 29, 2016, https://archive.fo/iMJjm.

8 **industrial jobs and manual labor:** Greg Foley and Andrew Luecke, *Cool: Style, Sound, and Subversion* (New York: Rizzoli, 2017), 74–75.

9 **inherently political:** Stuart Hall and Tony Jefferson, *Resistance Through Rituals: Youth Subcultures in Post-War Britain* (London: Hutchinson, 1976), 9–17.

10 **unseasonably warm:** "Baltimore, MD, Weather History for Saturday, November 7, 2020," Weather Underground, https://tinyurl.com/44m68x4x.

11 **new records for voter turnout:** Jacob Fabina, "Despite Pandemic Challenges, 2020 Election Had Largest Increase in Voting Between Presidential Elections on Record," United States Census Bureau, April 29, 2021, https://archive.ph/5CYKO.

11 **youth turnout skyrocketed:** Erin Duffin, "Youth Voter Turnout in Presidential Elections in the United States from 1972 to 2020," Statista, March 19, 2021, https://archive.ph/NbOml.

11 **ongoing budget cuts:** Philip Montgomery and Vauhini Vara, "Millions of Votes Are in Postal Workers' Hands. Here Is Their Story," *New York Times Magazine,* November 2, 2020, https://tinyurl.com/y3z8j9jb.

11 **had worked extra shifts:** Jacob Bogage, "Postal Service Workers Quietly Resist DeJoy's Changes with Eye on Election," *Washington Post,* September 29, 2020, https://archive.fo/Qq88A.

11 **The loser of the 2020 election:** Natalie Colarossi, "Donald Trump's 73.6 Million Popular Votes Is Over 7 Million More Than Any Sitting President in History," *Newsweek,* November 19, 2020, https://archive.fo/tKU4X.

11 **"They called it. Georgia.":** Tamar Hallerman, Mark Niesse, Greg Bluestein, and David Wickert, "UPDATE: Atlantans React to Biden Win as He Leads Trump by Nearly 10,200 in Ga," *Atlanta Journal-Constitution,* updated November 8, 2020, https://archive.fo/uiQht.

12 **I've long talked about the battle:** Molly Finnegan, "Read Joe Biden's Full Victory Speech after Winning the Presidential Election," *PBS NewsHour,* November 7, 2020, https://archive.fo/UF6Da.

13 **while wearing Yeezys:** Saul Loeb, *Supporters of US President Donald Trump, Including Jake Angeli (C), a QAnon Supporter,* January 6, 2021, photograph, Getty Images, https://archive.fo/0J3Xv.

13 **while blasting Kanye songs on his internet show:** Nick Fuentes, "Follow God (Lo-Fi Remix)—America First Lobby Music 2021," Genius, January 1, 2021, https://archive.fo/cxPCA.

1: BLACK PEOPLE LOVE ME, AND OTHER THINGS YOU SHOULD NOT ASSUME ABOUT BLACK VOTERS

15 **"I really appreciate it.":** "Joe Biden 'You Ain't Black' Interview Transcript on Radio Show with Charlamagne tha God," Rev.com, May 22, 2020, https://archive.ph/Q7NGs.

16 **eight million listeners each month:** Stephen Battaglio, "'The Breakfast Club' Is a Radio Forum for the Nation's Racial Reckoning," *Los Angeles Times,* July 15, 2020, https://archive.ph/mx9hz.

16 **Their YouTube channel:** Breakfast Club Power 105.1 FM, *The Breakfast Club,* YouTube channel, accessed February 5, 2022, https://www.youtube.com/c/BreakfastClubPower1051FM.

16 **found himself in hot water:** Christina Santi, "Sen. Bernie Sanders Says He's Not 'Dodging' Reparations Question," March 4, 2019, https://tinyurl.com/2bwv2rf7.

16 **a devastating impact on the Black community:** "The War on Drugs and Mass Incarceration," Howard University School of Law Library, accessed February 5, 2022, https://archive.fo/rpcku.

17 **"I won a larger share of the Black vote than anybody has":** "'You Ain't Black.'"

18 **it's not called that ironically:** Shamira Ibrahim, "'The Breakfast Club' Calls Itself 'The World's Most Dangerous Morning Show'—Maybe It's Time We Listen." Okayplayer, June 16, 2020, https://archive.fo/Wd4kd.

18 **The Breakfast Club is a syndicated radio show:** Maxwell Tani and Gideon Resnick, "How Hip-Hop Talk Show 'The Breakfast Club' Became a Must-Stop Spot for 2020 Democratic Candidates," Daily Beast, March 11, 2019, https://archive.fo/QF000.

19 **which is . . . charming:** "Charlamagne tha God Interview (Part 1)—Talks About Kelly Rowland, Chief Keef, and Being Attacked," uploaded on April 8, 2013, by Mansa Media, YouTube video, 14:56, https://www.youtube.com/watch?v=jsNebjOGq5c.

19 **In the book:** Juan González and Joseph Torres, *News for All the People: The Epic Story of Race and the American Media* (London: Verso, 2011).

19 **Black radio station WERD:** Ibid., 287.

19 **readership is only 4 percent:** Milos Djordjevic, "25 *New York Times* Readership Statistics [The 2021 Edition]," Letter.ly, March 14, 2021, https://archive.ph/TL78f.

20 **Media 2070:** Joseph Torres et al., "Media 2070: An Invitation to Dream Up Media Reparations," Media 2070, accessed February 5, 2022, https://tinyurl.com/2p8s4f75.

20 **released a report called:** Ibid., 40–41.

21 **even superiority:** Mark Ellis, "J. Edgar Hoover and the 'Red Summer' of 1919," *Journal of American Studies* 28, no. 1 (1994): 39–59, https://www.jstor.org/stable/27555783.

21 **sold to Viacom in 2001:** *L.A. Times* Archives, "Viacom Completes BET Acquisition," *Los Angeles Times,* January 24, 2001, https://archive.fo/b5p9G.

21 **Black-centric news and public affairs:** Paulette Brown-Hinds and Artelia C. Covington, "BET Cancels Ed Gordon's Show, 'Lead Story,' and 'Teen Summit,'" Black Voice News, December 22, 2002, https://archive.fo/1uyL1.

22 **technology as both inevitable and a space:** Charlton McIlwain, *Black Software: The Internet and Racial Justice, from the AfroNet to Black Lives Matter* (New York: Oxford University Press, 2020), 175.

23 **2004 Democratic National Convention:** González and Joseph Torres, *News for All the People,* 344.

23 **ColorOfChange.org:** Wesley Lowery, "How Civil Rights Groups Are Using the Election Create Black Political Power," *Washington Post,* November 8, 2016, https://archive.fo/HEd5K.

23 *Black Software:* McIlwain, *Black Software,* 5.

23 **Black people of all ages over-index:** "Nielsen Examines the Digital Habits and Impact of Black Consumers," Nielsen, September 13, 2018, https://archive.fo/ZiaSf.

24 **Radio reaches 93 percent of all Black Americans weekly:** Court Stroud, "Everything You Need to Know About Urban Radio," *Forbes,* May 23, 2018, https://archive.fo/0Wh1E.

24 **fewer than 250:** RBR-TVBR, "Black Media Owners to America: 'Actions, More Than Words,'" *Radio and Television Business Report,* June 15, 2020, https://archive.fo/swsEL.

25 **9.2 million views monthly:** Cheryl Brownlee, "Roland Martin Makes Strides with Digital Newscast," Black News Channel, December 18, 2020, https://archive.fo/IXQHH.

2: ARE YOU BEING SERVED?

27 **rhetorically tied to the 1920s-era Ku Klux Klan:** Sarah Churchwell, *Behold, America: The Entangled History of "America First" and "The American Dream"* (New York: Basic Books, 2018), 148.

28 **the most important summation:** Michael C. Dawson, *Black Visions: The Roots of Contemporary African-American Political Ideologies* (Chicago: University of Chicago Press, 2001).

31 **Black Americans weren't always so tied:** Leah Wright Rigueur, *The Loneliness of the Black Republican: Pragmatic Politics and the Pursuit of Power* (Princeton, NJ: Princeton University Press, 2015).

31 **in 1936:** Brooks Jackson, "Blacks and the Democratic Party," FactCheck.org, April 18, 2008, https://archive.fo/JaZiy.

31 **a migration of Black voters to the Democratic Party:** "When African-American Voters Shifted Away From the GOP," NPR, August 25, 2016, https://archive.fo/7fGJE.

32 **linked fate:** Michael C. Dawson, *Behind the Mule: Race and Class in African-American Politics* (Princeton, NJ: Princeton University Press, 1994).

32 **Black people who don't believe in abortion:** Nate Cohn, "Some Voters Are at Odds with Their Party on Abortion," *New York Times,* December 11, 2021, https://archive.fo/rXGwO.

32 **benefit the working class:** Theodore R. Johnson, "Why Are African Americans Such Loyal Democrats When They Are So Ideologically Diverse?," *Washington Post,* September 28, 2016, https://archive.fo/DjPoW.

33 **will not serve the community's needs:** Maurice Mangum, "Psychological Involvement and Black Voter Turnout," *Political Research Quarterly* 56, no. 1 (March 2003): 41–48, https://doi.org/10.1177/106591290305600104.

33 **"voter depression":** Leah Wright Rigueur (@LeahRigueur), "What's wild is that people have been pointing out the alarming trends of the Cambridge Analytica-Facebook-Trump data mining & voter depression strategies," Twitter, April 5, 2018, 4:22 PM, https://archive.fo/X1rAq.

33 **socialize with one another:** Donna R. Braden, "Black Entrepreneurs During the Jim Crow Era," *The Henry Ford,* February 21, 2018, https://tinyurl.com/3xj899jr.

33 **Black political power:** Ismail K. White and Chryl N. Laird, "The Roots of Black Political Unity," in *Steadfast Democrats: How Social Forces Shape Black Political Behavior* (Princeton, NJ: Princeton University Press, February 27, 2020), https://archive.fo/WeQDo.

3: WHO WILL SURVIVE IN AMERICA?

37 **"as you might think":** Lisa, interview with author via Zoom, October 11, 2020.

37 **who once lived there:** Hayley Grgurich, "Explore Chicago's Historic Pullman Neighborhood," Choose Chicago, updated September 3, 2019, https://archive.fo/fFp6K.

37 **look that up later:** Richard Schneirov, "The Pullman Strike," Northern Illinois University Digital Library, accessed February 6, 2022, https://archive.fo/ahRMy.

37 **Black people in the country:** Beth Tompkins Bates, *Pullman Porters and the Rise of Protest Politics in Black America, 1925–1945* (Chapel Hill: University of North Carolina Press, 2001).

38 **Pullman leaders having a fingerprint:** William Hamilton Harris, *Keeping the Faith: A. Philip Randolph, Milton P. Webster, and the Brotherhood of Sleeping Car Porters, 1925–37* (Champaign: University of Illinois Press, 1977).

39 **building power and influence:** Ivan Phifer, "Hidden History Reveals Pullman Porters' Link to Black Press," *Minnesota Spokesman-Recorder,* June 13, 2017, https://archive.fo/uxDRI.

39 **were now falling apart:** Laurent Belsie, "One Neighborhood Reaches for Resilience: A Letter from Chicago," *Christian Science Monitor,* December 23, 2021, https://archive.fo/RjWQf.

40 **"That's what we need":** Lisa, interview.

40 **economist Alan Greenspan:** Zach Carter, "A Master of Disaster," *Nation,* December 16, 2009, https://archive.fo/VD832.

40 **building independent wealth:** Brian S. Feldman, "The Decline of Black Business," *Washington Monthly,* March 19, 2017, https://archive.ph/jrZz5.

41 **"sound like a carpetbagger":** Querrida, interview with author via Zoom video, October 1, 2020.

42 **Black farmers organized:** William F. Holmes, "The Demise of the Colored Farmers' Alliance," *Journal of Southern History* 41, no. 2 (1975): 187–200, https://doi.org/10.2307/2206013.

42 **out of their baby daughter:** William F. Holmes, "The Leflore County Massacre and the Demise of the Colored Farmers' Alliance," *Phylon (1960–)* 34, no. 3 (1973): 267–74, https://doi.org/10.2307/274185.

43 **Mississippi for good:** Vann R. Newkirk II, "The Great Land Robbery," *Atlantic,* updated September 29, 2019, https://tinyurl.com/2p9h2vns.

43 **levels of child poverty:** Staci Bell and Sara Robinson, "Small Area Income and

Poverty Estimates: 2019," United States Census Bureau, December 8, 2020, https://archive
.ph/1XD4o. Refer to the tables for more information.

43 **$16 trillion:** David Brancaccio, Nova Safo, and Alex Schroeder, "U.S. Suffered $16
trillion Loss over 20 Years Due to Racism New Citigroup Study Finds," Marketplace.org,
September 23, 2020, https://archive.fo/KvmtR.

43 **"I'm so Greenwood":** "I'm SoGreenwood 2017," uploaded on May 30, 2017,
by Sidney Stevenson, Jr., YouTube video, 10:44, https://www.youtube.com/watch?v
=fcz4mkwa1aE.

43 *Blacks in and out of the Left*: Michael C. Dawson, *Blacks in and out of the Left* (Cambridge, MA: Harvard University Press, 2013).

44 **race cannot be severed from class:** T. H. Breen, "A Changing Labor Force and
Race Relations in Virginia 1660–1710," *Journal of Social History* 7, no. 1 (Autumn 1973):
3–25, https://www.jstor.org/stable/3786495.

44 **Pan-African bent:** Malcolm, interview with author via Zoom video, November 17,
2020.

45 **Kwame Ture (Stokely Carmichael):** "Honoring Kwame Ture, Pan-Africanist," All-
African People's Revolutionary Party, accessed February 6, 2022, https://archive.fo/KyxSc.

45 **"crumbs off of the table":** Malcolm, interview.

45 **at the memorial services:** Peniel E. Joseph, "What Bill Clinton Got 'Exactly Wrong'
About Stokely Carmichael's Role in the Black Freedom Struggle," *Washington Post,* August
4, 2020, https://archive.fo/hSbic.

46 **"you gotta be radical":** Chelsea, interview with author via Zoom video, November 19, 2020.

46 **"Trump only paid $750 in taxes":** Kemberley Washington and Korrena Bailie,
"The $750 Question: How Trump's Taxes Reveal the Deep Unfairness of the U.S. Tax
Code," October 2, 2020, https://archive.fo/cuCX0.

46 **nothing in federal income taxes:** Jesse Eisinger, Jeff Ernsthausen, and Paul Kiel,
"The Secret IRS Files: Trove of Never-Before-Seen Records Reveal How the Wealthiest
Avoid Income Tax," ProPublica, June 8, 2021, https://archive.fo/vRSPt.

46 **"pays the most money in taxes":** Eric Bronson, "Why Black Women Are Paying
More in Taxes Than Washington's Billionaires," YWCAWorks.org, March 3, 2020, https://
archive.ph/RSASi.

46 **"the most educated demographic in the country":** Rachaell Davis, "New
Study Shows Black Women Are Among the Most Educated Group in the United States,"
Essence, updated October 27, 2020, https://archive.fo/veLHo.

47 **"IRS calling them":** Dorothy A. Brown, "The IRS Is Targeting the Poorest Americans," *Atlantic,* July 27, 2021, https://archive.ph/UdmFh.

47 **Medicare for All:** Sahil Kapur, "The Coronavirus Crisis Hasn't Changed Joe Biden's
Mind on 'Medicare for All,'" NBC News, March 30, 2020, https://archive.fo/Q8EVX.

48 **kente cloth hats in solidarity:** Chip Somodevilla, *House and Senate Democrats Unveil
Policing Reform and Equal Justice Legislation,* June 8, 2020, photograph, Getty Images, https://
archive.fo/qHRD4.

48 **silenced calls for legislation:** Aaron Ross Coleman, "Republicans Claim Democrats Want to Defund the Police. Biden's Plan Calls for More Police," Vox, August 25, 2020,
https://archive.ph/JxiMK.

48 **increase funding to police departments:** Kiara Alfonseca, "More Than a Year

After George Floyd's Killing, Congress Can't Agree on Police Reform," ABC News, September 23, 2021, https://archive.ph/MmyKt.

48 **people across the political spectrum agree:** Chris Kahn, "Exclusive: Most Americans, Including Republicans, Support Sweeping Democratic Police Reform Proposals— Reuters/Ipsos Poll," Reuters, June 11, 2020, https://archive.ph/hHmZI.

48 **"Black people have achieved equity.":** Rashad Robinson, interview with author via Zoom video, February 11, 2021.

49 **A 2016 survey:** Rachel Tillman, "Nearly 40 Percent of Americans Report Tension with Family or Friends over Election," ABC News, October 16, 2016, https://archive.fo /yDIkJ.

INTERLUDE: FEMINISM FOR BLACK GIRLS WHO HAVE STOPPED CARING ABOUT WHAT YOU THINK

51 **#BlackRingMafia:** "Agnes Scott College," Colleges That Change Lives, accessed February 6, 2022, https://tinyurl.com/29u95rh4.

51 *For Colored Girls:* Ntozake Shange, *For Colored Girls Who Have Considered Suicide/ When the Rainbow Is Enuf* (San Lorenzo, CA: Shameless Hussy Press, 1976).

52 **Black women are more likely to experience:** Susan Green, "Violence Against Black Women—Many Types, Far-Reaching Effects," Institute for Women's Policy Research, July 13, 2017, https://archive.fo/Wo9nL.

52 **more likely to be disbelieved:** Allante Adams, "Why Are Black Women Less Likely to Report Rape?," *Baltimore Sun,* June 9, 2015, https://archive.ph/stZpY.

52 **perceived as more sexual:** Rebecca Epstein, Jamilia J. Blake, and Thalia González, *Girlhood Interrupted: The Erasure of Black Girls' Childhood,* Georgetown Center on Poverty and Inequality, accessed February 8, 2022, https://tinyurl.com/4h6rc5n8.

53 **had recently been coined:** Joan Morgan, *When Chickenheads Come Home to Roost: A Hip-Hop Feminist Breaks It Down* (New York: Simon and Schuster Paperbacks, 1999).

54 **"but I still feel like":** William Reed, "Respect: As You Celebrate 'Empire' Remember C. Delores Tucker," Black Star News, April 1, 2015, https://archive.ph/0R3jL.

54 **including mainstream feminism:** Marian Jones, "'If Black Women Were Free': An Oral History of the Combahee River Collective," *Nation,* October 29, 2021, https://archive .ph/M0I6o.

54 **Above all else, our politics:** Keeanga-Yamahtta Taylor, *How We Get Free: Black Feminism and the Combahee River Collective* (Chicago: Haymarket Books, 2017), 18.

55 **"always and forever":** Chelsea, interview with author via Zoom video, November 19, 2020.

55 **deify Black women:** Ishena Robinson, "Stacey Abrams Is Not Your Superhero, Mule or God. She Is a Black Woman with a Vision You Can Honor by Showing Up for Black Women, Too," The Root, January 6, 2021, https://archive.fo/9lPcW.

55 **want them to say:** Cassie Da Costa, "MSNBC Contributor's Misogynistic Smear of Bernie Staffers: 'Island of Misfit Black Girls,'" Daily Beast, February 21, 2020, https://archive .ph/XGxlu.

55 **working across the aisle:** Zachary Warmbrodt, "Why Republicans Actually Like Maxine Waters," POLITICO, October 29, 2018, https://archive.ph/HHKlS.

56 **civility is not seen:** Crystal Marie Fleming, "Maxine Waters and the Trope of the 'Angry Black Woman,'" Vox, June 29, 2018, https://archive.fo/rCZBf.

4: OBAMA FOR AMERICA

59 **"And it was something I've never, ever experienced before":** Jay, interview with author via Zoom video, September 2, 2020.

61 **Clinton had the upper hand:** Joseph Carroll, "Clinton Maintains Large Lead over Obama Nationally," Gallup, December 18, 2007, https://archive.ph/j97fF.

61 **I spoke about this with Marlon Marshall:** Marlon Marshall, interview with author via Zoom video, December 4, 2020.

62 **which was what spoke to Kwesi Chappin:** Kwesi Chappin, interview with author via Zoom video, September 2020.

62 **Retail politics means:** Roger Dow, "Presidential Hopefuls Still Bank on Retail Politics," *The Hill*, August 25, 2016, https://archive.fo/O9ev7.

64 **email and outreach list of 2.2 million:** Elizabeth McKenna and Hahrie Han, *Groundbreakers: How Obama's 2.2 Million Volunteers Transformed Campaigning in America* (New York: Oxford University Press, 2014).

64 **When Oprah arrived in South Carolina:** Halley Nani, "Oprah to Speak at Obama Rally at U. South Carolina," CBS News, December 7, 2007, https://archive.ph/VQpsg.

65 **Obama across the country:** "New Orleans House Party for Barack Obama's Nomination," uploaded on September 4, 2008, by BarackObamadotcom, YouTube video, 2:39, https://www.youtube.com/watch?v=6PNxL85f3bk.

66 **Obama for America '08 barber and beauty shop program:** Helen Kennedy, "Obama's Beauty Parlor Strategy for S.C.," (New York) *Daily News,* January 21, 2008, https://archive.ph/rVkHW.

66 **refers to as the "virtual barbershop":** Catherine Knight Steele, "The Virtual Beauty Shop: Crafting a Digital Black Feminism in the Blogosphere," Academia.edu, accessed February 10, 2022, https://archive.fo/yVeIr.

67 **the freedom to have discussions:** Melissa Victoria Harris-Lacewell, *Barbershops, Bibles, and BET: Everyday Talk and Black Political Thought* (Princeton, NJ: Princeton University Press, 2010), 4.

67 **it was a modification:** McKenna and Han, *Groundbreakers.*

67 **Community Organizing 101:** "Community Organizers Discuss Obama's Role as an Activist," *Nation,* August 13, 2008, https://archive.fo/NEYFM.

68 **talking about race:** "How South Carolina Shifted Obama's Election Strategy," Video. *CNN,* February 14, 2020, https://tinyurl.com/2p8pun75.

69 **"live what we preach":** Chappin, interview.

69 **"Organizing for America":** Mikolaj Jan Piskorski, Laura Winig, and Aaron Smith, "Barack Obama: Organizing for America 2.0," Harvard Business School, revised April 2013, https://archive.fo/oiBRG.

69 **level of resourcing:** Shireen Mitchell, interviews with author via Zoom video, September and October 2020.

70 **top-down approach to the structure:** Edward-Isaac Dovere, "How Clinton Lost Michigan—and Blew the Election," POLITICO, December 14, 2016, https://archive.fo/RiCaj.

71 **"immediately see and feel":** Arisha Hatch, interview with author via Zoom video, November 2020.

71 **Color Of Change's community organizing program:** Eillie Anzilotti, "How Color of Change Is Moving from Activism to Electing DAs," *Fast Company,* August 6, 2018, https://archive.fo/fgzd8.

71 **change that is driven and led**: Jacqui Germain, "How Brunch Helped Defeat a 7-Term Incumbent," *Nation,* August 24, 2018, https://archive.ph/iw13Q.

72 **wealth Black people lost**: Linda Qiu, "Sanders: African-Americans Lost Half Their Wealth Because of Wall Street Collapse," Politifact, February 11, 2016, https://archive.ph/TkUwt.

72 **overreliance on computers**: *All Watched Over by Machines of Loving Grace,* episode 1, "Love and Power," directed by Adam Curtis, aired May 23, 2011, on BBC, https://watchdocumentaries.com/all-watched-over-by-machines-of-loving-grace/.

72 **concentrated economic power**: "The Courage to Learn: A Retrospective on Antitrust and Competition Policy During the Obama Administration and Framework for a New Structuralist Approach," American Economic Liberties Project, January 12, 2021, https://archive.fo/Udkgr.

72 **cast a ballot without voting**: Philip Bump, "1.7 Million People in 33 States and D.C. Cast a Ballot without Voting in the Presidential Race," *Washington Post,* December 14, 2016, https://archive.fo/xTH9U.

73 **creating a playbook**: Joy Cushman, "Republicans Are Studying Obama's Campaign Playbook," *New York Times,* August 26, 2019, https://archive.fo/qcX7K.

5: KANYE WAS RIGHT-ISH

75 **"NO MORE POLITICS OR APOLOGIES"**: Jake Woolf, "The 5 Kanye West Rants That Make Us Miss His Blog," *GQ,* June 8, 2017, https://archive.fo/0hhAM.

75 **Safer Foundation**: Raymond "Bernie" Curran and Gus Wilhelmy, "Bernie & Gus Their Vision," uploaded on May 14, 2015, by Safer Foundation, YouTube video, 2:36, https://youtu.be/cHJ016RnYVU.

76 **"I'mma let you finish"**: Gil Kaufman, "2009 VMAs Oral History: What You Didn't See When Kanye West Rushed the Stage on Taylor Swift," *Billboard,* August 21, 2019, https://archive.fo/a86zH.

77 **Kanye West on *TMZ Live* in May 2018**: Kanye West, "Kanye West's Rant In TMZ Office (Extended Cut)," uploaded on May 2, 2018, by TMZ, YouTube video, 12:14, https://www.youtube.com/watch?v=IeA7lvC1ego.

78 **Black people on their roofs in Louisiana**: Courte C. W. Voorhees, John Vick, and Douglas D. Perkins, "'Came Hell and High Water': The Intersection of Hurricane Katrina, the News Media, Race and Poverty," *Journal of Community & Applied Social Psychology* 17, no. 6 (November/December 2007): 415–29, https://doi.org/10.1002/casp.945.

78 **police chief blatantly lied**: A. C. Thompson, "Post-Katrina, White Vigilantes Shot African-Americans with Impunity," ProPublica, December 19, 2008, https://archive.fo/rfGtv.

78 **"I hate the way they portray us in the media"**: Kanye West, "Kanye West Hurricane Katrina," uploaded on March 4, 2006, by aquaSlime, YouTube video, 1:51, https://www.youtube.com/watch?v=9pVTrnxCZaQ.

79 **un- or underreported in the immediate days**: Anna Karrer, "In the Eye of the Storm: Hurricane Katrina and Its Local News Coverage," Center Austria Research, Paper 1, (2015), https://archive.ph/IYTI7.

80 **"free will"**: Kanye West, "Kanye West's Slavery Was a Choice Controversy," Know Your Meme, accessed February 10, 2022, https://archive.fo/iJ7a3.

80 **Psychological warfare**: Daudi Ajani ya Azibo, "The Psycho-Cultural Case for Reparations for Descendents of Enslaved Africans in the United States," *Race, Gender & Class* 18, no. 1/2 (2011): 7–36, http://www.jstor.org/stable/23884865.

80 **Charlamagne tha God**: Sam Valorose, "Kanye West's Interview with Charlamagne tha God: Read The Full Transcript," iHeartRadio, May 3, 2018, https://tinyurl.com/2p8ffkku.

81 **mental health effects from frequent exposure**: Greg Johnson, "Police Killings and Black Mental Health," *Penn Today*, June 23, 2020, https://archive.ph/zHEXp.

81 **numb to the pain and suffering**: Jamil Smith, "Videos of Police Killings Are Numbing Us to the Spectacle of Black Death," *New Republic,* April 13, 2015, https://tinyurl.com/mryb7y3w.

81 **"constant onslaught of images"**: Laurel Wamsley and Vanessa Romo, "Defense Presents Closing Arguments in Derek Chauvin Trial," NPR, April 19, 2021, https://archive.fo/JIt7B .

83 **"Follow God"**: Kanye West, "Kanye West—Follow God," uploaded on November 8, 2019, YouTube video, 2:27, https://www.youtube.com/watch?v=ivCY3Ec4iaU.

84 **Cody, Wyoming**: Will Welch, "Inside Kanye West's Vision for the Future," *GQ,* April 16, 2020, https://archive.ph/UVmYJ.

84 **forty acres**: Henry Louis Gates, Jr., "The Truth Behind '40 Acres and a Mule,'" PBS, accessed February 10, 2022, https://archive.fo/DrafU.

84 **"protosocialist"**: Ibid.

84 **massive wealth inequalities**: Matt Stoller, *Goliath: The 100-Year War Between Monopoly Power and Democracy* (New York: Simon & Schuster Paperbacks, 2020).

84 **all-Black towns**: Tara Aveilhe, "Oklahoma: Home to More Historically All-Black Towns than Any Other U.S. State," University of Tulsa, March 16, 2018, https://archive.fo/0t098.

84 **"Black Wall Street"**: Shomari Wills, *Black Fortunes: The Story of the First Six African Americans Who Survived Slavery and Became Millionaires* (New York: Amistad, 2018).

84 **burned to the ground**: *"Tulsa Star,"* Oklahoma Historical Society, accessed February 10, 2022, https://archive.ph/QC5IO.

85 **finding success**: Mark Beaumont, *Kanye West: God and Monster* (London: Omnibus Press, 2015).

85 **Katz Drug Store lunch counter**: Portwood Williams, "Civil Rights Leader Portwood Williams (Now 98) Speaking Strong at 95," uploaded on July 27, 2013, by Maggie Abel, YouTube video, 11:57, https://www.youtube.com/watch?v=dvMM59_4NF8.

85 **commitment to civil rights**: Donda West and Karen Hunter, *Raising Kanye: Life Lessons from the Mother of a Hip-Hop Superstar* (New York: Pocket Books, 2007).

85 **"Atlanta Compromise"**: Booker T. Washington, "Booker T. Washington's 'Atlanta Compromise' Speech," Library of Congress, accessed February 10, 2022, https://tinyurl.com/nf8cbzjw.

85 **surprising online spaces**: ★trigger warning for language usage★ "How Does/pol/ Feel About Thomas Sowell?," 4chan, accessed February 10, 2022, https://archive.fo/iHi4o.

86 **Sowell sees the combination**: Thomas Sowell, *Black Rednecks and White Liberals* (San Francisco: Encounter Books, 2009).

86 **Nick Fuentes**: Nick Fuentes, "Nick Fuentes: Thomas Sowell," uploaded on July 3, 2020, by Liberum Arbitrium, BitChute video, 3:50, https://www.bitchute.com/video/4BFR3WqGj4Eu/.

86 **you guessed it**: Rush Limbaugh, "Kanye West Quotes Dr. Sowell!," The Rush Limbaugh Show, May 1, 2018, https://archive.fo/LeQiU.

86 **modern alternative Black conservative thought:** Jon Levine, "Trump's Support Among Black Men Doubles After Kanye West Endorsement, Reuters Poll Says," *The Wrap*, May 3, 2018, https://archive.fo/oqqLX.

86 **political identity:** Corey D. Fields, "The G.O.P. Prizes Black Republicans—as Long as They Don't Alienate White Members," *America: The Jesuit Review of Faith & Culture*, February 26, 2021, https://archive.ph/1sr8V.

87 **MTV Vanguard Award:** Rolling Stone, "Read Kanye West's Blunt, Poignant VMA Video Vanguard Award Speech," *Rolling Stone*, August 31, 2015, https://archive.fo/Tn7ED.

6: HARD TIMES

90 **23 percent of WWE fans are Black:** Martenzie Johnson, "It's a New Day at the WWE," The Undefeated, August 18, 2016, https://archive.ph/fquGP.

90 **WWE fans are more left leaning:** Walt Hickey, "Your Politics Are Indicative of Which Sports You Like," Business Insider, March 19, 2013, https://archive.ph/7GEJZ.

90 **problematic as hell ten-year deal:** Justin Barrasso, "WWE's Return to Saudi Arabia Reignites Questions About Controversial Partnership," *Sports Illustrated*, October 30, 2019, https://archive.ph/anqT5.

91 **As Thomas Frank documents:** Thomas Frank, *The People, No: A Brief History of Anti-Populism* (New York: Metropolitan Books, 2020).

91 **in his seminal work:** Ernesto Laclau, *On Populist Reason* (London: Verso, 2018).

92 **a turbocharged version:** Daniel Glenday, "Professional Wrestling as Culturally Embedded Spectacles in Five core countries: the USA, Canada, Great Britain, Mexico and Japan," (2013), https://archive.ph/4NRP4.

92 **Cody and Dustin Rhodes:** AEW Staff, "Dustin Rhodes Signs Multi-Year Wrestling Deal with AEW," *All Elite Wrestling* (blog), August 29, 2019, https://tinyurl.com/2p83mfk5.

93 **"The Common Man":** Ashish, "Jim Ross on If Dusty Rhodes Polka-Dot 'Common Man' WWE Gimmick Was a Rib by Vince McMahon Designed to Humiliate Him, Why Dusty Agreed to Do It," 411MANIA," June 23, 2019, https://archive.fo/A8nbz.

93 **"Hard Times" promo:** Dusty Rhodes, "Dusty Rhodes Talks About 'Hard Times': Mid-Atlantic Wrestling, Oct. 29, 1985," uploaded on April 9, 2013, by WWE, YouTube video, 3:31, https://www.youtube.com/watch?v=9py4aMK3aIU.

95 **Ric Flair:** 21Savage, "21 Savage, Offset, Metro Boomin—Ric Flair Drip (Official Music Video)," uploaded on March 1, 2018, YouTube video, 3:08, https://www.youtube.com/watch?v=LPTlvQ1Zet0.

95 **this wasn't just kayfabe:** Dusty Rhodes and Howard Brody, *Dusty: Reflections of an American Dream* (Champaign, IL: Sports Publishing LLC, 2005).

96 **Automation:** US Congress, Office of Technology Assessment, *Automation of America Offices* (Washington, DC: US Government Printing Office, OTA-CIT-287, December 1985), https://tinyurl.com/4ufrbm28.

96 **auto workers were being hit:** Doron P. Levin, "Grim Outlook of Early 1980's Is Back for U.S. Auto Makers," *New York Times*, December 7, 1989, https://archive.fo/V9QGa.

96 **honoring their plight:** Rhodes and Brody, *Dusty*.

99 **younger voting base was more excited:** William A. Galston and Clara Hendrickson, "How Millennials Voted This Election," Brookings, November 21, 2016, https://archive.ph/gfnuB.

100 **more left wing:** Marie Solis, "Why Gen Z Is Turning to Socialism," Vice, May 4, 2020, https://archive.fo/c4U47.

100 **saddled with student loan debt:** Melanie Hanson, "Student Loan Debt by Generation," Education Data Initiative, October 12, 2021, https://archive.fo/8tL4F.

100 *The Cosby Show*: Leslie B. Inniss and Joe R. Feagin, "*The Cosby Show*: The View from the Black Middle Class," *Journal of Black Studies* 25, no. 6 (July 1995): 692–711, https://doi.org/10.1177/002193479502500604.

100 **racial wealth gap:** Signe-Mary McKernan et al., "Nine Charts About Wealth Inequality in America (Updated)," The Urban Institute, October 5, 2017, https://archive.ph/Yil5T.

101 **concentrated resources:** Bertrand Cooper, "Inequality Is High Within the Black Community," People's Policy Project, September 10, 2020, https://archive.fo/lHU1f.

101 **Linda McMahon:** Alfred Konuwa, "Linda McMahon's Trump Ties Under Scrutiny as WWE Is Deemed Essential in Florida," *Forbes*, April 15, 2020, https://archive.fo/xABcK.

101 **abusive behavior:** Javier Ojst, "Wrestling Union—Failed Attempts and a History of Blackballing by WWE," Pro Wrestling Stories, accessed February 10, 2022, https://archive.fo/wY832.

102 **Reclaim America:** "Patriot Front," Southern Poverty Law Center, accessed February 10, 2022, https://archive.ph/ahYzl.

INTERLUDE: BECAUSE WE ARE NOT WHO THEY SAY WE ARE . . .

103 **"This morning at 4:30":** "WBBM Criminalizes 4-Year Old," uploaded on July 27, 2011, by Bob Butler, YouTube video, 1:42, https://www.youtube.com/watch?v=mu_LK_iEFE8.

103 **they often get it wrong:** Juan González and Joseph Torres, *News for All the People: The Epic Story of Race and the American Media* (London: Verso, 2011).

104 **Gen Z journalism student:** Maya, interview with author via Zoom video, October 7, 2020.

108 **trusted information coming from the local news:** Sara Atske, Michael Barthel, Galen Stocking, and Christine Tamir, "7 Facts About Black Americans and the News Media," Pew Research Center, August 7, 2019, https://archive.ph/4uNdR.

109 **scrambled to issue an apology:** NewsOne Staff, "Chicago TV Station Apologizes for Making 4-Year-Old Sound Violent," NewsOne, July 31, 2011, https://tinyurl.com/3cs4jy2v.

110 **white people don't have any nonwhite friends:** Christopher Ingraham, "Three Quarters of Whites Don't Have Any Non-White Friends," *Washington Post*, August 25, 2014, https://archive.ph/VfjVf.

7: HOOD VAMPIRES

111 **"Hood Vampires":** K.T. Filmz, "Hood Vampires Part 1," uploaded on January 8, 2013, YouTube video, 18:06, https://www.youtube.com/watch?v=JcyLRF15fjQ.

112 **"Black America's CNN":** Alex Eichler, "Rap Isn't 'Black America's CNN,'" *Atlantic*, October 12, 2010, https://archive.ph/pW72A.

113 **An extension of the African diaspora:** Murs, "From Jay Z to the Migos, What Does 'For The Culture' Really Mean?," uploaded on May 26, 2018, by HipHopDX, YouTube video, 15:28, https://www.youtube.com/watch?v=NzTNn9VXWIw.

113 **South Bronx in the 1970s:** Murray Forman and Mark Anthony Neal, *That's the Joint!: The Hip-Hop Studies Reader* (New York: Routledge, 2004).

113 **crucial form of resistance:** Nkemka Anyiwo, Daphne C. Watkins, and Stephanie J. Rowley, "'They Can't Take Away the Light': Hip-Hop Culture and Black Youth's Racial Resistance," *Youth & Society* (March 17, 2021), https://doi.org/10.1177/0044118x211001096.

114 **"an age-old image":** David Samuels, "The Rap on Rap," *New Republic,* November 11, 1991, https://tinyurl.com/bd8fky8b.

115 **these four elements:** Black Dot, *Hip-Hop Decoded: From Its Ancient Origin to Its Modern Day Matrix* (Bronx: MOME, 2021).

116 **"noise pollution":** "Noise Control Act of 1972," Ballotpedia, accessed February 10, 2022, https://archive.ph/Zg8Cx.

116 **break up public gatherings:** Emily Davis, "Sounding the Alarm: Petal Samuel on the Criminalization of Noise," UNC Global, June 11, 2020, https://archive.ph/kq5UL.

116 **"broken windows theory":** "Broken Windows Policing," Center for Evidence-Based Crime Policy, accessed February 10, 2022, https://archive.ph/uRH1H.

117 **"the bitterness is still there":** James Collins, interview with author via Zoom video, August 2020.

117 **three or more people:** "What Is a Gang? Definitions," National Institute of Justice, October 27, 2011, https://archive.ph/jcqaf.

118 **"What the hell is that?":** Hettie Collins, interview with author via Zoom video, September 2, 2020.

118 **violence leveraged on Black communities:** "Hip-Hop and the FBI: A Little-Known History," *Esquire,* June 4, 2013, https://archive.ph/xbgwP.

119 **it's often censored:** Dan Hancox, "The War Against Rap: Censoring Drill May Seem Radical but It's Not New," The Guardian, June 22, 2018, https://archive.ph/Humuy.

119 **nebulous ways:** Sam Biddle, "Police Surveilled George Floyd Protests With Help From Twitter-Affiliated Startup Dataminr," The Intercept, July 9, 2020, https://archive.ph/8wrS0.

119 **horrific thuggery:** Andy Greene, "Karl Rove Calls Common a 'Thug' Over Poetry Event," *Rolling Stone,* May 12, 2011, https://archive.ph/59YKE.

120 **operated under surveillance:** Simone Browne, *Dark Matters: On the Surveillance of Blackness* (Durham: Duke University Press, 2015).

120 **It is not an accident:** Andre Gee, "How Drill Music Took Over Chicago—and Was Almost Forced Out," Complex, June 10, 2021, https://archive.ph/Wtiz3.

120 **new lives for their families:** Dempsey J. Travis, *An Autobiography of Black Chicago* (Chicago: Urban Research Institute, 1981).

120 **Homeownership was crucial:** Natalie Y. Moore, *The South Side: A Portrait of Chicago and American Segregation* (New York: Picador, 2016).

120 **lost their homes:** Kim Janssen, "Seven Years After the Great Recession, Some Chicago Suburbs May Never Recover," *Chicago Tribune,* March 26, 2016, https://archive.ph/MMCps.

120 **fifty Chicago public schools:** Valerie Strauss, "Chicago Promised That Closing Nearly 50 Schools Would Help Kids in 2013. A New Report Says It Didn't," *Washington Post,* May 24, 2018, https://archive.ph/TUa9z.

120 **reverse Great Migration:** Tanasia Kenney, "'Reverse Migration' to Blame for the Sudden Drop in Chicago's Black Population, Residents Head for Suburban South," Atlanta Black Star, June 29, 2016, https://archive.ph/GiR8n.

121 **blow up New Jersey:** "Faneto," YouTube Music, track 4 on Chief Keef, *Back from the Dead 2,* RBC Records, 2014.

122 **the true illusion:** Stuart Wolpert, "The American Dream Is More Attainable for TV Characters Than Americans," Phys.org, November 9, 2021, https://archive.ph/tpf4g.

122 **prospects for upward mobility:** Shai Davidai, "Why Do Americans Believe in Economic Mobility? Economic Inequality, External Attributions of Wealth and Poverty, and the Belief in Economic Mobility," *Journal of Experimental Social Psychology* 79 (November 2018): 138–48, https://doi.org/10.1016/j.jesp.2018.07.012.

122 **consistently declined:** "Most Americans Say There Is Too Much Economic Inequality in the U.S., but Fewer Than Half Call It a Top Priority," Pew Research Center, January 9, 2020. https://archive.ph/HKbM5.

122 **top 20 percent held 77 percent:** Isabel V. Sawhill and Christopher Pulliam, "Six Facts About Wealth in the United States," Brookings, June 25, 2019, https://archive.fo /rmoBG.

122 **correlate directly to race:** "Economic Mobility: Measuring the American Dream," HUD User, accessed February 10, 2022, https://archive.ph/KgOXK.

8: THE BAY AREA HUSTLERS

126 **a son of Oakland:** Taylor Crumpton, "An Oaklander's Q&A With Ryan Coogler: Black Panther, Revolution, and the Town," YR Media, September 30, 2018, https://archive.ph/84bzO.

126 **The Huey P. Newton–inspired poster:** Ashley Pickens, "The 'Black Panther' Promotional Poster Believed to Be Inspired by Huey P. Newton," *VIBE*, June 12, 2017, https://archive.ph/96QAv.

127 **do yourself a favor:** "Black Panther | Teaser Trailer—Reactions Mashup," uploaded on June 25, 2017, by Elijah, YouTube video, 3:23, https://www.youtube.com/watch?v =wNTiP3iSzq0.

127 **revolves around T'Challa:.** "Black Panther," Marvel Cinematic Universe Wiki, accessed February 10, 2022, https://archive.ph/p3uPg.

127 **opinion of the movie:** Jade Ogunnaike, interview with author via Zoom video, December 4, 2020.

128 **Panthers were heavily surveilled:** Stanley Nelson, "The Black Panthers: Vanguard of the Revolution," IMDb, accessed February 10, 2022, https://archive.ph/8vUPr.

128 **Too $hort have talked about:** Too $hort, "Cusswords," Genius, accessed February 10, 2022, https://archive.ph/aBeQP.

128 **reporter Gary Webb:** Greg Grandin, "'The New York Times' Wants Gary Webb to Stay Dead," *Nation,* October 10, 2014, https://archive.ph/OjP4v.

129 **tweeting about it:** Diana Bradley, "The Story Behind the CIA's Oscar Night 'Black Panther' Tweets," PR Week, February 27, 2019, https://tinyurl.com/2tjjdjn5.

129 **deft navigation of this fine line:** Kaitlyn Booth, "Political Themes and Crafting the Sympathetic Villain of Black Panther," Bleeding Cool, February 15, 2018, https://archive.ph /XU3rM.

129 **make the world right:** Joseph Campbell, *The Hero with a Thousand Faces* (Novato, CA: New World Library, 2008).

129 **it's OK to let other Black people struggle:** Shannon Liao, "Chadwick Boseman Says T'Challa Is the Enemy in Black Panther," The Verge, February 28, 2018, https://archive .ph/0IxWp.

129 **cooperative economics:** Jessica Gordon Nembhard, *Collective Courage: A History of African American Cooperative Economic Thought and Practice* (University Park: The Pennsylvania State University, 2014).

130 *"cocoon* **is the only word":** Kamilah, interview with author via Zoom video, September 2020.

130 **"hyphy":** Steven J. Horowitz, "An Oral History of Hyphy," Complex, June 13, 2016, https://tinyurl.com/2p9dsmb3.

131 **RICH + RIOT:** "My Story," RICH + RIOT, accessed February 10, 2022, https://tinyurl.com/yndcdjjw.

131 **less than 6 percent Black:** Lauren Hepler, "The Hidden Toll of California's Black Exodus," CalMatters, July 15, 2020, https://archive.ph/4xk8H.

131 **nearly 50 percent Black:** David DeBolt, "Oakland's Population Grew by 50,000 over the Past Decade, 2020 Census Data Shows," The Oaklandside, August 18, 2021, https://archive.ph/ZZRmJ.

131 **Droves of Black people:** Angela Rowen, "Black Oakland's Story," A Changing Oakland—Documentary Series, accessed February 10, 2022, https://archive.ph/9zZLn.

131 **more regimented:** Donna Murch, "Watts, Lowndes County, Oakland: The Founding of the Black Panther Party for Self Defense," *VersoBooks.Com* (blog), October 15, 2016, https://archive.ph/FtieT.

131 **Black multimedia artists:** Jerry Thompson, and Duane Deterville, *Black Artists in Oakland* (Charleston, SC: Arcadia Publishing, 2007).

131 **and business owners:** Bryan Wiley, *A Changing Oakland,* A Changing Oakland—Documentary Series, accessed February 10, 2022, https://tinyurl.com/54tnckh3.

131 **Merritt College:** "Huey P. Newton Lounge," accessed February 10, 2022, https://tinyurl.com/yfr8f5us.

132 **"Survival Programs":** "Black Panther Community Survival Programs, 1967–1982," Black Panther Party Alumni Legacy Network, accessed February 10, 2022, https://archive.ph/YxVvJ.

132 **feeling safe:** Mrs. Richardson, interview with author via Zoom video, September 2020.

132 *"We march all day, dog":* "Power to the Youth," AYPAL: Building API Community Power, accessed February 10, 2022, https://archive.ph/0Dfw7.

132 **hubs of streetwear fashion:** Keezy TV, "Streetwear HISTORY (2000–2015) BAY AREA," uploaded on April 4, 2020, YouTube video, 28:00, https://www.youtube.com/watch?v=cYlV6IeFpbQ.

133 **founder of the Feelmore Adult Gallery in Oakland:** Flora Tsapovsky, "Oakland's Feelmore Social Club Wants to Make Space for Black and Queer Bargoers," Berkeleyside.org, October 18, 2021, https://archive.ph/3Lezc.

134 **selling sex toys and vidoes out of the trunk:** DjKw3si, "In Other Words with Nenna Feelmore ft Brandi Collins-Dexter," in *Don't Die Before the Podcast,* produced by Don't Die Before the Podcast Productions, podcast, 53:21, https://tinyurl.com/yckpcvy9.

134 **on the same weekend:** Kai Wright, "Why Alton Sterling and Philando Castile Are Dead," *Nation,* July 7, 2016, https://archive.ph/O7Rox.

135 *For the Culture:* Hoda Emam, "For the Culture Market Spotlights Black Women-Owned Businesses This Holiday Season," Local News Matters, November 25, 2020, https://tinyurl.com/2p8t9x6n.

135 **upward mobility for generations:** Brian S. Feldman, "The Decline of Black Business," *Washington Monthly,* March 19, 2017, https://archive.ph/jrZz5.

135 **keep tax dollars within:** Andre M. Perry and Carl Romer, "To Expand the Economy, Invest in Black Businesses," Brookings, December 31, 2020, https://archive.ph/OiC2U.

135 **Black financial institutions:** Charles Gerena, "Opening the Vault," *Region Focus: The Federal Reserve Bank of Richmond* 11, no. 2 (Spring 2007): 46–49, https://tinyurl.com/2p9d5dxw.

135 **support for civil rights movements:** Louis Ferleger and Matthew Lavallee, "Lending a Hand: How Small Black Businesses Supported the Civil Rights Movement," *Institute for New Economic Thinking Working Paper Series* no. 67 (December 1, 2018), https://doi.org /10.2139/ssrn.3125212.

135 **home of alternative economies:** "The Other Occupy Oakland: Lessons from Depression-Era Mutual Aid," It's Going Down, accessed February 10, 2022, https://archive.ph /y5UKu.

135 **reimagine the Oakland pimp:** Alex McLevy, "*The Mack* Remains One of Blaxploitation's Most Artistically Ambitious Films," The A.V. Club, June 12, 2018, https://archive.ph /ruyBh.

136 **The Mack, 1973:** Michael Campus, "The Mack," IMDb, accessed February 10, 2022, https://archive.ph/UfR2I.

136 **Al Capone once (allegedly) said:** Martin Parker, *Alternative Business: Outlaws, Crime and Culture* (New York: Routledge, 2012).

137 **Black employers declined:** Feldman, "Decline."

137 **one in five for Black businesses:** Color Of Change, "First COVID-19 Survey of Black and Latino Small-Business Owners Reveals Dire Economic Future," May 18, 2020, https://archive.ph/lFNo6.

137 **1,382 times wealthier:** Bertrand Cooper, "Inequality Is High Within the Black Community," People's Policy Project, September 10, 2020, https://archive.fo/lHU1f.

137 **Oakland's Changing Landscape:** Boots Riley, "*Sorry to Bother You* Director Boots Riley Takes a Ride Through Oakland's Changing Landscape," *Vanity Fair,* July 2, 2018, https://archive.fo/hHuAa.

138 **dropped to 28 percent:** Sam Levin, "'We're Being Pushed Out': The Displacement of Black Oakland," The Guardian, June 1, 2018, https://archive.ph/hajg1.

138 **sacred and safe spaces for Black culture:** Alaina Demopoulos, "The Rich History of Black Roller Skating Rinks—and Their Civil Rights Legacy," Daily Beast, February 4, 2021, https://archive.ph/YSfJR.

138 **1,200 roller rinks:** Tiffany Fisher-Love, interview with author, 2021. Interview included unpublished raw data on closed roller rinks in the United States, which was used for Dyana Winkler. Tina Brown and Dyana Winkler, "United Skates," IMDb, accessed February 10, 2022, https://archive.ph/sWjs0.

139 **growing divide:** Patrick Sharkey, "Spatial Segmentation and the Black Middle Class," *American Journal of Sociology* 119, no. 4 (January 2014): 903–54, https://doi.org/10.1086 /674561.

139 **central to their identity:** Amanda Barroso, "Most Black Adults Say Race Is Central to Their Identity and Feel Connected to a Broader Black Community," Pew Research Center, February 5, 2020, https://archive.ph/urrYA.

140 **top 1 percent:** Cooper, "Inequality."

140 **Black people could be underprepared:** Pippa Stevens, "Digital Racial Gap Could 'Render the Country's Minorities into an Unemployment Abyss,' Says Deutsche Bank," CNBC, September 2, 2020, https://archive.ph/pWOey.

9: BASEMENT POLITICS

142 **radical politics of Chicago:** Steven Watts, *Mr. Playboy: Hugh Hefner and the American Dream* (Hoboken, NJ: Wiley, 2009).

142 **"socialized capitalism":** Ibid.

143 **Chicago mayor Harold Washington:** Walter Lowe, Jr., "20 Questions: Harold Washington," Official Playboy Archive, February 1988, https://www.iplayboy.com/issue /19880201.

143 **right-wing thinkers:** Peter Carlson, "The Unexpurgated Story at Reader's Digest," *Washington Post,* February 12, 2002, https://archive.ph/ycNUO.

143 **financially supported Mayor Washington:** Mitchell Locin, "Mayor Spends an L.A. Kind of Day at the Playboy Mansion," *Chicago Tribune,* March 3, 1987, https://archive.ph /k5pDM.

143 *Playboy* **was a venue:** "Hugh Hefner's Little-Known History as Civil Rights Activist," *EBONY Media Operations,* September 28, 2017, *Ebony,* https://archive.ph/0FohT.

143 **in the** *Playboy* **archives:** Official Playboy Archive, accessed February 10, 2022, https:// www.iplayboy.com/.

144 **references to Karl Marx:** James McKinley, "Playboy's History of Assassination in America," Official Playboy Archive, February 1976, https://www.iplayboy.com/issue /19760201.

144 **never shown women:** Nalina Eggert, "Hugh Hefner Death: Was the Playboy Revolution Good for Women?," BBC News, September 28, 2017, https://archive.ph /wyGLp.

144 **emotionally abusive:** Molly Redden, "Effusive Hugh Hefner Tributes Ignore Playboy Founder's Dark Side," The Guardian, September 29, 2017, https://archive.ph/rjCeQ.

144 **empowered sexual agents:** Mireille Miller-Young, *A Taste for Brown Sugar: Black Women in Pornography* (Durham, NC: Duke University Press Books, 2014).

144 **"contrast both her skin color and afro":** Morgan Jerkins, "What Happened to *Playboy*'s First Black Cover Girl?," ZORA, February 10, 2020, https://archive.ph/z3y2f.

145 **"a Nazi manual":** Carrie Pitzulo, *Bachelors and Bunnies: The Sexual Politics of Playboy* (Chicago: University of Chicago Press, 2011).

145 **going fully digital:** Kayla Kibbe, "What Will an All-Digital Playboy Look Like?" Inside-Hook, April 24, 2020, https://tinyurl.com/2e7kn4an.

145 **Ezra Miller:** Ryan Gajewski, "The Magic of Ezra Miller," Playboy.com, November 15, 2018, https://archive.ph/wlhQa.

145 **creative director in residence:** Tara C. Mahadevan, "Cardi B Officially Launches New Platform Centerfold with Playboy as Creative Director," Complex, December 25, 2021, https://archive.ph/7hD6q.

145 **culturally diverse array:** Shivani Kumaresan, "Playboy Unveils CENTERFOLD with Cardi B as Platform's Founding Creative Director," Markets Insider, December 21, 2021, https://archive.ph/CiwPY.

145 **"respect these strippers":** Brittney McNamara, "Cardi B Won't Let You Disrespect Her Because She Used to Be a Stripper," *Teen Vogue,* February 28, 2018, https://archive.ph /6eY5J.

146 **reproductive justice fights:** "Black Women's Maternal Health: A Multifaceted Approach to Addressing Persistent and Dire Health Disparities," National Partnership for Women & Families, April 2018, https://archive.ph/saDNo.

146 **still earn significantly less:** Sonia Thompson, "Despite Being the Most Educated, Black Women Earn Less Money at Work, in Entrepreneurship, and in Venture Capital. Here Are 3 Ways to Fix It," *Inc.*, August 22, 2019, https://archive.ph/GUnKJ.

146 **White-Slave Traffic Act:** Erin Blakemore, "The 'White Slavery' Law That Brought Down Jack Johnson Is Still in Effect," History, updated February 25, 2019, https://archive.fo/SFfX2.

147 **40 percent were Black:** Samantha Davey, "Snapshot on the State of Black Women and Girls: Sex Trafficking in the US," Congressional Black Caucus Foundation, accessed February 8, 2022, https://tinyurl.com/5xn58uu4.

147 **pleasures and joys of sex:** Jennifer C. Nash, *The Black Body in Ecstasy: Reading Race, Reading Pornography* (Durham, NC: Duke University Press, 2014).

147 **vulnerable because of a lack of legal protections:** Juno Mac and Molly Smith, *Revolting Prostitutes: The Fight for Sex Workers' Rights* (London: Verso, 2020).

147 **including consensual sex work:** Aja Romano, "A New Law Intended to Curb Sex Trafficking Threatens the Future of the Internet As We Know It," Vox, updated July 2, 2018, https://archive.ph/OJGp9.

148 **nonconsensual interactions:** Natasha Lennard, "Law Claiming to Fight Sex Trafficking Is Doing the Opposite—By Cracking Down on Sex Work Advocacy and Organizing," The Intercept, June 13, 2018, https://archive.ph/cSC5G.

148 **Black sex workers:** Anju Jindal-Talib, "SESTA-FOSTA's Impact on Black, LGBTQ+ Sex Workers' Use of the Internet and Digital Support Tools" (thesis, University of Michigan at Ann Arbor, 2021), https://tinyurl.com/5damv4r5.

148 **moral policing of Black bodies:** Miller-Young, *Brown Sugar.*

148 **criminalization of marijuana:** Richard J. Bonnie and Charles H. Whitebread, *The Marijuana Conviction: A History of Marijuana Prohibition in the United States* (Bookworld Services, 1999).

148 **legitimate marriage:** Deenesh Sohoni, "Unsuitable Suitors: Anti-Miscegenation Laws, Naturalization Laws, and the Construction of Asian Identities," *Law & Society Review* 41, no. 3 (September 2007): 587–618, http://www.jstor.org/stable/4623396.

148 **have low-wage workers:** Michelle Alexander, "Tipping Is a Legacy of Slavery," *New York Times,* February 5, 2021, https://archive.ph/nIlRg.

149 **informal economies:** LaShawn Harris, *Sex Workers, Psychics, and Numbers Runners: Black Women in New York City's Underground Economy* (Urbana: University of Illinois Press, 2016).

149 **an additional $20 billion:** "Arguments for and Against Legalising Prostitution," Debating Europe, accessed February 11, 2022, https://archive.ph/UGpyO.

149 **"Well, I was modeling for *Playboy*":** Hettie Collins, interview with author via Zoom video, September 2, 2020.

151 **"Doing union work":** Hettie Collins, "*Washington Journal:* Airline Operations," C-SPAN, December 24, 2004, https://tinyurl.com/3f4evp6m.

151 **weight requirement:** Carol Kleiman and Jobs writer, "Flight Attendants Win Fight over Weight Rules," *Chicago Tribune,* March 13, 1991, https://archive.ph/Feu8e.

152 *too* **Afrocentric BLACK:** E. R. Shipp, "Braided Hair Style at Issue in Protests over Dress Codes," *New York Times,* September 23, 1987, https://archive.fo/JQl2Z.

152 **creator-led, digital platform:** Ngozi Nwanji, "Playboy's Centerfold Set to Rival OnlyFans in the Metaverse with Creative Direction from Cardi B," AfroTech, December 17, 2021, https://archive.ph/oY7O7.

INTERLUDE: AWKWARD ADVENTURES ON ONLYFANS

153 **Lotus Lain:** Holly Randall and Lotus Lain, "Lotus Lain," uploaded on May 22, 2019, by Holly Randall Unfiltered, YouTube video, 58:23, https://www.youtube.com/watch?v=p3Tg4 -ffPKw.

153 **industry relations advocate:** Free Speech Coalition, accessed February 11, 2022, https://www.freespeechcoalition.com/.

154 **interested in the articles:** Matt Giles, "The Genius of the Playboy Interview," *Longreads* (blog), September 29, 2017, https://archive.ph/cwm48.

154 **10 Questions with Lotus Lain:** Lotus Lain, interview with author via Zoom video, April 2021.

155 **"'Old bitches' category":** Lynsey G., "Does Mainstream Porn Have an Age Problem?," *Glamour,* August 16, 2017, https://archive.fo/L7lgl.

155 **"I found my best friend":** Hallie Lieberman, "Black Performers Make Millions for Porn Sites—While Being Underpaid, Verbally Abused, and Subjected to Racism," *Cosmopolitan,* December 8, 2020, https://archive.ph/jNgMD.

156 **"supposedly a health risk":** Gregory Krieg, "Ted Cruz and Porn: A Brief History," CNN, September 12, 2017, https://archive.ph/yIZn3.

156 **"fanned the flames of the insurrection":** Bret Jaspers, "Sen. Ted Cruz Faces Backlash for His Role in Capitol Violence," NPR, January 10, 2021, https://archive.ph /mbhMD.

156 **"feces":** Devon Link, "Fact Check: Photo Shows U.S. Capitol Cleanup After Rioters Left American Flag Among Debris," *USA TODAY,* updated February 14, 2021, https:// archive.ph/LvS7D.

157 **"White supremacy is the public health crisis":** "Racism and Health," Centers for Disease Control and Prevention, last reviewed November 24, 2021, https://archive.ph /2vcm5.

159 **"Mike Adriano Productions":** "Mike Adriano," Wikipedia, last edited February 1, 2022, https://archive.ph/0fC4Y.

10: AN ABOMINATION OF OBAMANATION

162 **Jordan 1 sneakers:** Justin Sayles, "The Once and Future Sneaker King," *Ringer* (blog), May 4, 2020, https://archive.ph/ifPR1.

162 **inaugural Young Black Leadership Summit:** Alex Thompson, "Trump Jr. Praises Black Conservatives at D.C. Gathering," POLITICO, October 25, 2018, https://archive.ph /HTahn.

163 **So here's the deal:** "Who Is Charlie Kirk? Narrated By Shakina Nayfack | NowThis," uploaded on May 13, 2020, by NowThisNews, YouTube video, 8:26, https://www.youtube .com/watch?v=cfrdPcR28Pk.

163 **he wrote a piece:** Charlie Kirk, "Liberal Bias Starts in Economic Textbooks," *Breitbart* (blog), April 27, 2012, https://archive.ph/uQtAg.

163 **Bill Montgomery:** John Keilman, "Before Trump and Kanye Became Fans, Charlie Kirk Battled 'Marxist' High School Teachers in Chicago's Suburbs," *Chicago Tribune,* October 22, 2018, https://archive.ph/jZPLw.

163 **MoveOn.org:** "This Boy Wonder Is Building a Conservative MoveOn.Org in a Lemont Garage," Crain's Chicago Business, May 7, 2015, https://archive.ph/t8yox.

163 **pioneer of email-based petitions:** Theodore Hamm, *The New Blue Media: How Michael Moore, MoveOn.Org, Jon Stewart and Company Are Transforming Progressive Politics* (New York: The New Press, 2008).

163 **voices for President Obama's:** Jeff Zeleny and Patrick Healy, "Obama Wins Endorsement of MoveOn.Org," *New York Times,* February 2, 2008, https://archive.ph/xjng6.

163 **and 2012:** Sam Stein, "Obama 2012 Campaign Helped by MoveOn.Org, AFL-CIO Super PAC Alliance," HuffPost, August 21, 2012, https://archive.ph/Nf1v.

164 **Phil Agre:** "Philip E. Agre's Home Page," UCLA, accessed February 11, 2022, https://tinyurl.com/adk9e4nj.

164 **over decades:** Phil Agre, "While the Left Sleeps," *WIRED,* August 1, 1995, https://archive.ph/tIZOZ.

164 **American Legislative Exchange Council:** Patrick Guerriero and Susan Wolf Ditkoff, "When Philanthropy Meets Advocacy," *Stanford Social Innovation Review* 16, no. 3 (2018): 49–54, https://doi.org/10.48558/9H3S-N247.

165 **didn't really like Trump:** Zachary Petrizzo, "Students for Trump Chair Charlie Kirk Once Destroyed Trump on Fox: 'Self Destructing in Front of Us,'" Mediaite, March 2, 2020, https://archive.ph/DgCgU.

165 **Donald Trump, Jr.:** Amanda Carpenter, "Charlie Kirk, Trump's Pied Piper," The Bulwark, July 7, 2020, https://archive.ph/tzV6j.

165 **Charlottesville happened:** *Frontline* and ProPublica, "Documenting Hate: Charlottesville (Full Film) | FRONTLINE," uploaded on August 12, 2019, by Frontline PBS, YouTube video, 54:15, https://www.youtube.com/watch?v=jPLvWO_SOgM.

165 **thought they were white nationalists:** Brendan Joel Kelley, "Turning Point USA's Blooming Romance with the Alt-Right," Southern Poverty Law Center, February 16, 2018, https://archive.ph/FtQpa.

165 **"End of story":** Kali Holloway, "She Said 'I HATE BLACK PEOPLE'—Now She's a Rising GOP Star," Daily Beast, October 7, 2021, https://archive.ph/q27LQ.

165 **But now they had a brand problem:** Ashley Feinberg, "Turning Point USA Keeps Accidentally Hiring Racists," HuffPost, April 25, 2018, https://archive.ph/tzAys.

166 **she didn't stay canceled:** NewsOne Staff, "Every Receipt Proving Candace Owens Is a Con Artist Who Is Following the Money," NewsOne, October 22, 2021. https://archive.ph/j6GAM.

166 **very small:** Joseph Bernstein, "The Newest Star of the Trump Movement Ran a Trump-Bashing Publication—Less Than Two Years Ago," BuzzFeed News, May 15, 2018, https://archive.ph/JJ0Z8.

166 **Red Pill Black Girl:** Tree Of Logic, "Candace Owens: Leader of the Conservative Plantation," uploaded on May 15, 2018, YouTube video, 22:58, https://youtu.be/4UhGj3odFkg.

166 **"I can make you a celebrity overnight":** "Candace Owens Confronts Black Lives Matter Protesters," Yahoo Finance, April 22, 2018, https://tinyurl.com/298v3nu3.

167 **Candace got even bigger:** Brandy Zadrozny, "YouTube Tested, Trump Approved: How Candace Owens Suddenly Became the Loudest Voice on the Far Right," NBC News, June 23, 2018, https://archive.ph/KUb85.

167 **Diamond and Silk:** Ben Schreckinger, "Donald Trump's Sizzling Sister Act," *POLITICO Magazine,* February 2016, https://archive.ph/1ZLtc.

167 **to help counter:** Savannah Behrmann, "DHS Contradicts Candace Owens on Same Day She Testifies Before Congress About White Nationalism," *USA TODAY,* September 20, 2019, https://archive.ph/TlKji.

167 **polar bears and arctic foxes:** National Geographic, "Arctic Fox Raids Polar Bear Kill | National Geographic," uploaded on September 10, 2013, YouTube video, 2:32, https://www.youtube.com/watch?v=FMAO4ESe4eQ.

168 **#Blexit:** "Blexit," Know Your Meme, accessed February 11, 2022, https://archive.ph /NwDzg.

168 **#Blexit was already being used:** NewOne Staff, "'I Was Shocked:' Founder of Original Blexit Threatens Candace Owens with Legal Action," NewsOne, November 1, 2018, https://tinyurl.com/4vyn8bs6.

168 **"so counter":** Morgan Simon, "Will the Real Blexit Please Stand Up?," *Forbes,* November 21, 2018, https://archive.ph/GXWqK.

168 **using stock photos:** Duncan Cooper, "BLEXIT's Website Is Made up of Stolen Photos and Stock Images," *FADER,* October 30, 2018, https://archive.ph/J5VsP.

169 **to fill seating:** Tree Of Logic, "Proof That #BLEXIT Is a Fraud & There's Nothing Black About It!!!," uploaded on November 14, 2019, YouTube video, 19:24, https://www .youtube.com/watch?v=sRYQLiPhFa8.

169 *"concentration camps":* Zadrozny, "YouTube Tested."

169 **fighting with Steve Bannon:** Candace Owens, "The Candace Owens Show: Steve Bannon," uploaded on August 4, 2019, by PragerU, YouTube video, 60:46, https://www .youtube.com/watch?v=qC-r0izU4j0.

169 **turnoff to many:** Tom Boggioni, "Candace Owens Buried by Black Conservative for Lying in an Attempt to Incite More Racism," Raw Story, March 6, 2021, https://archive.ph /pna2A.

169 **very public exit:** Tree Of Logic, "#BLEXIT."

169 **new Black right-wing leaders:** "Solutionary Summit 2021," streamed live on September 4, 2021, by Black Guns Matter, YouTube video, 7:22:03, https://www.youtube.com /watch?v=6u37hw71czA&t=3415s.

170 **spread their gospel:** *Fox & Friends,* "More Young Black Americans Calling Themselves Conservative," uploaded on December 6, 2021, by Fox News, YouTube, 3:49, https:// www.youtube.com/watch?v=17PFvMf_Kfg.

170 **"King teaches his kids":** *Fox News Primetime,* "King Randall Says His Opposition 'Doesn't Know My God,'" uploaded on November 10, 2021, by Fox News, video, 5:29, https://video.foxnews.com/v/6281209153001#sp=show-clips.

170 **coming-out party:** Bradford Traywick, "Race Conscious Conservatism," Empower American Project, February 8, 2020, https://archive.ph/rxrVp.

170 **refused to cater a gay wedding:** Justin Wm. Moyer, "Conservative Commentator Lawrence B. Jones Behind Crowdfunding for Ind. Pizza Shop That Won't Cater Gay Wedding," *Washington Post,* April 6, 2015, https://archive.ph/ONdXy.

171 **skewed older:** Yulan Grant, Brian Friedberg, and author, "Historical Tracking of Black Pundits on Fox News," Metadata scraping, The Technology and Social Change Project (TaSC) at the Harvard Kennedy School, 2022.

171 **Sonnie Johnson:** *Fox News Primetime,* "Sonnie Johnson: Identity Politics Doesn't Work in Black America," uploaded on November 13, 2021, by Fox News, video, 6:19, https:// video.foxnews.com/v/6281722657001#sp=show-clips.

171 **Felecia Killings:** "Lawrence B. Jones FOX Primetime With Hotep Jesus and Felecia Killings," uploaded on November 10, 2021, by Hotep Jesus, YouTube video, 4:51, https:// www.youtube.com/watch?v=2zszTvCiNUU.

171 *Conscious Black Conservative:* Charrise Lane, "What Is Conscious Black Conservatism?," uploaded on July 29, 2021, YouTube video, 6:20, https://www.youtube.com/watch ?v=688-g84qK6E.

171 **Olivia Rondeau:** *Fox News Primetime,* "Clay Travis: This Is Why Voters Are Running

from the Democratic Party," uploaded on November 11, 2021, by Fox News, YouTube video, 4:21, https://www.youtube.com/watch?v=9VfOYIL6QMU.

171 **conspiracy pusher:** "#1318—Hotep Jesus," PodScribe—The Joe Rogan Experience, June 27, 2019, https://archive.ph/r1uDS.

171 **King Randall:** *Fox News Primetime,* "King Randall."

172 **largest platforming:** Grant, Friedberg, and author, "Historical Tracking."

172 **different energy:** Olivia Rondeau, "LIVE #15: Juneteenth & Anarcho-Communism?? w/ Skye Daddy," streamed live on June 20, 2021, YouTube video, 1:13:49, https://www.youtube.com/watch?v=_6KuLbiM6Ec&t=2740s.

172 **for other young people:** "I Came Out on an HBO Talk Show," uploaded on June 1, 2021, by Olivia Rondeau, YouTube video, 16:03, https://www.youtube.com/watch?v=jkgLuumhIyc.

172 **independent conservative voters:** *Fox & Friends,* "Young Black Americans."

172 **primarily composed of:** Grant, Friedberg, and author, "Historical Tracking."

172 **"Black Conservative Inc.":** Todd Neikirk, "African American Conservative Jeff Charles: Candace Owens Is Lying About Black Culture Again," HillReporter.com, March 6, 2021, https://archive.ph/T9Atv.

172 **historic realignment:** Leah Wright Rigueur, *The Loneliness of the Black Republican: Pragmatic Politics and the Pursuit of Power* (Princeton, NJ: Princeton University Press, 2016).

172 **across ideological lines:** *Fox News Primetime,* "King Randall."

172 **opposition to gun control:** "PAUSE with Sam Jay: Racism in Gun Control (Bonus Clip) | HBO," uploaded on June 17, 2021, by HBO, YouTube video, 1:12, https://www.youtube.com/watch?v=fe8Kx-TTgxc.

173 **they don't lie:** Felecia S. Killings, *Conscious Black Conservatism: Building Social, Political, and Economic Empires Based on Kingdom Principles* (Atlanta: Felecia Killings Foundation, 2020), 1–16.

173 **critical race theory:** "Marc Lamont Hill Grills Black Conservative CJ Pearson on Critical Race Theory," uploaded on June 11, 2021, by BNC News, YouTube video, 20:34, https://www.youtube.com/watch?v=ZWLdG_tKqbY.

173 **using streaming services:** DidSheSayThat (Sonnie Johnson), "'The Black Conservative War' . . . How Conservatives Break Things . . . " accessed February 11, 2022, uploaded to Periscope, video, 1:56:06, https://www.pscp.tv/w/1dRKZQMNeqzxB.

173 **Clubhouse:** Talitha McEachlin, "Ask A Black Republican Anything," Clubhouse, accessed February 11, 2022, https://archive.ph/AwGsi.

173 **happened across the ideological spectrum:** Paul Blumenthal, "How a Twitter Fight over Bernie Sanders Revealed a Network of Fake Accounts," HuffPost, March 14, 2018, https://archive.ph/2egvE.

174 **can be exploited:** Elizabeth Culliford, "Facebook, Twitter Remove Russia-Linked Accounts in Ghana Targeting U.S.," Reuters, March 12, 2020. https://archive.ph/bjuxx.

174 **wave of Black conservatism:** Dennis Richmond, Jr., "Why More Young Black Americans Are Calling Themselves 'Conservative,'" *New York Post,* December 4, 2021, https://archive.ph/4qRLE.

174 **Canaan in the West:** Booker T. Washington, *Up from Slavery,* Standard Ebooks, accessed February 11, 2022, https://tinyurl.com/2p92zfws.

174 **Reign:** Black MAGA group, interview with author via Zoom video, October 27, 2020.

174 **an unwillingness to even consider:** Tovia Smith, "'Dude, I'm Done': When Politics Tears Families and Friendships Apart," NPR, October 27, 2020, https://archive.ph/ft8Aj.

174 **place across ideology:** Michael C. Dawson, *Black Visions: The Roots of Contemporary African-American Political Ideologies* (Chicago: University of Chicago Press, 2001).

175 **since the 1920s:** Caroline O'Donovan, "Question Answered: Why Has Chicago Had So Many Democratic Mayors?," *WBEZ Chicago* (blog), October 2, 2012, https://tinyurl.com /59rwe74y.

176 **challenged the very idea:** David Freedlander, "An Unsettling New Theory: There Is No Swing Voter," *POLITICO Magazine,* February 6, 2020, https://archive.ph/31VP4.

176 **Democratic Party loyalists:** Ismail K. White and Chryl N. Laird, *Steadfast Democrats: How Social Forces Shape Black Political Behavior* (Princeton, NJ: Princeton University Press, 2021).

176 **One study by American University:** AU Media, "American University Survey: Young Black Americans Are Key 2020 Swing Voters," American University, July 30, 2020, https://tinyurl.com/2p9x7xw3.

176 **win every time:** Louis Bolce, Gerald De Maio, and Douglas Muzzio, "Blacks and the Republican Party: The 20 Percent Solution," *Political Science Quarterly* 107, no. 1 (1992): 63–79, https://doi.org/10.2307/2152134.

177 **signals:** Donna M. Owens, "EXCLUSIVE: The Republican Party Says It Has a Message for Black Americans," *Essence,* July 29, 2021, https://archive.ph/k7Xp3.

177 **since Reconstruction:** Shawn Steel, "Black Republicans Lead Political Poll Reversal," *Orange County Register,* November 14, 2021, https://archive.ph/9lXd4.

177 **they're not in DC to play:** Versha Sharma, "A Year After the Capitol Riot, Where Is The U.S. Headed?," *Teen Vogue,* January 5, 2022, https://archive.ph/wTXB2.

177 **to embrace socialism:** Cameron Easley, "Black Americans Are Divided over Their Comfort with Socialism," Morning Consult, February 28, 2020, https://archive.ph/qlgtw.

11: MY BEAUTIFUL DARK TWISTED FANTASY

178 **the one person:** Lisa, interview with the author via Zoom, October 11, 2020.

179 **Blacks for Pete:** Michael Harriot, "Pete Buttigieg Is a Lying MF," The Root, November 25, 2019, https://archive.ph/dE44t.

179 **welcomed her group:** Black MAGA group, interview with author via Zoom video, October 27, 2020.

180 **racial egalitarianism:** Leah Wright Rigueur, *The Loneliness of the Black Republican: Pragmatic Politics and the Pursuit of Power* (Princeton, NJ: Princeton University Press, 2016).

180 **by the end of the 1960s:** Ibid., 10.

180 **in Gary, Indiana:** Leonard N. Moore, *The Defeat of Black Power: Civil Rights and the National Black Political Convention of 1972* (Baton Rouge: Louisiana State University Press, 2018).

180 **marks an ideological shift:** Wright Rigueur, *Black Republican,* 317.

181 **often failed them:** Black MAGA group, interview.

181 **used in Florida:** Christopher Bing, Elizabeth Culliford, and Paresh Dave, "Spanish-Language Misinformation Dogged Democrats in U.S. Election," Reuters, November 7, 2020, https://archive.ph/TU7aS.

182 **Mississippi Democratic Freedom Party:** Maegan Parker Brooks, *A Voice That Could Stir an Army: Fannie Lou Hamer and the Rhetoric of the Black Freedom Movement* (Jackson: University Press of Mississippi, 2014).

183 **1980s R&B video:** Oran "Juice" Jones, "Oran 'Juice' Jones—The Rain (Official Video)," uploaded on October 6, 2009, by OranJuiceJonesVevo, YouTube video, 4:22, https://www.youtube.com/watch?v=9dZW1C3neao.

184 **Earlier in the week:** Reverend Eric Wallace, interview with author via Zoom, October 8, 2020.

184 **running for office:** Paula Shelton, "Election 2020: Eric Wallace, Republican Candidate, Illinois State Senate 40th District," *Chicago Defender,* October 28, 2020, https://archive.ph/1ZrFa.

184 **Oklahoma twang:** Colonel Bailey C. Hanes, *Bill Pickett, Bulldogger: The Biography of a Black Cowboy* (Norman: University of Oklahoma Press, 1989).

185 **believe in a divine power:** Besheer Mohamed et al., "Religious Beliefs Among Black Americans," Pew Research Center, February 16, 2021, https://archive.ph/wP47Z.

185 **prayer helps:** Besheer Mohamed et al., "Faith Among Black Americans," Pew Research Center, February 16, 2021, https://archive.ph/C53b9.

185 **Black millennials:** Besheer Mohamed, "10 New Findings About Faith Among Black Americans," Pew Research Center, February 16, 2021, https://archive.ph/7qbnH.

185 **radical religious politics:** Anthea D. Buter, *Women in the Church of God in Christ: Making a Sanctified World* (Chapel Hill: University of North Carolina Press, 2012).

189 **failed to successfully recruit:** Michael C. Dawson, *Blacks in and out of the Left* (Cambridge, MA: Harvard University Press, 2013).

190 **definitely out here:** Teddy Ostrow, "Black Socialists of America Is Putting Anti-Capitalism on the Map," *Nation,* August 28, 2019, https://archive.ph/5RmDA.

190 **They want institutions to work:** Eric Levitz, "America's Most Socialist Generation Is Also Its Most Misanthropic," *New York Magazine,* August 15, 2019, https://archive.ph/poCHE.

INTERLUDE: TRADITIONS, TRIGGERS, AND KEYS

192 **undergraduate population:** Northwestern University, *Diversity and Inclusion Reports for Academic Years 2019–20 and 2020–21* (Evanston, IL: Northwestern University), https://tinyurl.com/mwa84hce.

192 **median family income:** "Economic Diversity and Student Outcomes at Northwestern University," *New York Times,* accessed February 11, 2022, https://tinyurl.com/bdh7kfrs.

192 **"White Boy Summer":** Kenzie Bryant, "The Making and Unmaking of Chet Hanks's 'White Boy Summer,'" *Vanity Fair,* April 15, 2021, https://archive.ph/UYPCJ.

192 **walking around the area at night:** Natalie Frazier, "A Black Ass Nightmare: My Four Years at Northwestern," *Blackboard Magazine,* accessed February 11, 2022, https://archive.ph/Pjgf7.

193 **slurs in them:** Dean Golembeski, "College Fight Songs Stir Up Controversy," August 26, 2021, https://archive.ph/EzzwY.

194 **Coach Byrdsong's:** Brandi Collins-Dexter, "Ricky Byrdsong and the Cost of Speech," *Techdirt* (blog), August 19, 2020, https://archive.ph/UduHn.

195 **His little team lost, too:** Associated Press, "Mikel Leshoure Runs Rampant as Illinois Stomps Northwestern at Wrigley," November 21, 2010, https://archive.ph/KAlsY.

12: THE STORIES WE LIVE WITH

197 **mystery, horror, and gloom:** Leila Taylor, *Darkly: Black History and America's Gothic Soul* (London: Repeater Books, 2019).

197 **"fears of being outcast":** Justine Baillie, *Toni Morrison and Literary Tradition: The Invention of an Aesthetic* (London: Bloomsbury Academic, 2013).

197 **to be Black is to be:** Taylor, *Darkly.*

198 **the origins of modern policing:** Larry H. Spruill, "Slave Patrols, 'Packs of Negro

Dogs' and and Policing Black Communities," *Phylon (1960–)* 53, no. 1 (2016): 42–66. http://www.jstor.org/stable/phylon1960.53.1.42.

198 **dangerous underclass:** Connie Hassett-Walker, "How You Start Is How You Finish? The Slave Patrol and Jim Crow Origins of Policing," January 11, 2021, https://archive.ph/5TFRc.

198 **the invisible war:** Joseph Torres et al., "Media 2070: An Invitation to Dream Up Media Reparations," Media 2070, accessed February 5, 2022, https://tinyurl.com/2p8s4f75.

199 **Epigenetics:** Mark Wolynn, *It Didn't Start with You: How Inherited Family Trauma Shapes Who We Are and How to End the Cycle* (New York: Penguin, 2017).

200 **he calls Sarah:** Tami Simon, "Mark Wolynn: Becoming Aware of Inherited Family Trauma," Sounds True, accessed February 11, 2022, https://archive.ph/av3oP.

201 **human levees:** Marian Moser Jones, *The American Red Cross from Clara Barton to the New Deal* (Baltimore: Johns Hopkins University Press, 2012).

201 **her earliest memories:** Terence Finnegan, *A Deed So Accursed: Lynching in Mississippi and South Carolina, 1881–1940* (Charlottesville: University of Virginia Press, 2013).

202 **Under her narration:** Judith Smith Cassidy, *Entwined Vanarsdale Families* (Independently published: 2020).

202 **public pathologies:** Jelani Cobb and Matthew Guariglia, *The Essential Kerner Commission Report* (New York: Liveright, 2021).

204 **"All that you Change Changes you.":** Octavia E. Butler, *Parable of the Sower* (New York: Open Road Media, 2012).

204 **2015 was the first year:** Carl Root, "Yet Another Ferguson Effect: An Exploratory Content Analysis of News Stories on Police Brutality and Deadly Force Before and After the Killing of Michael Brown," *Graduate Theses and Dissertations* (2018), https://digitalcommons.usf.edu/etd/7360/.

205 **back in South Carolina:** Jennifer Berry Hawes, *Grace Will Lead Us Home: The Charleston Church Massacre and the Hard, Inspiring Journey to Forgiveness* (New York: St. Martin's Press, 2019).

207 **spikes in Black suicide:** Karen Blum, "Suicides Rise in Black Population During COVID-19 Pandemic," John Hopkins Medicine, April 20, 2021, https://archive.ph/ld8oR.

208 **started petitions:** Joe Garofoli, "How Social Media, Not Politicians or Business, Drove Flag Removal," *San Francisco Chronicle,* July 7, 2015, https://archive.ph/upztr.

208 **1961:** Anna Bruzgulis, "Confederate Flag Wasn't Flown at South Carolina Statehouse until 1961, Pundit Claims," June 22, 2015, https://archive.ph/AmOtf.

209 **Kelechi:** L. D. Green and Kelechi Ubozoh, *We've Been Too Patient: Voices from Radical Mental Health—Stories and Research Challenging the Biomedical Model* (Berkeley, CA: North Atlantic Books, 2019).

210 **response to me:** Kelechi, interview with author via Zoom video, April 2021.

CONCLUSION: MAGGOT BRAIN

213 **"canceled before cancel culture":** Kanye West, "Kanye West Says 'I've Been Cancelled Before They Had Cancel Culture,'" uploaded on October 31, 2019, by BigBoyTV, YouTube video, 0:23, https://www.youtube.com/watch?v=2F4yJ9yUVyY.

218 **City of the Future:** Jerome Cavanagh, "Detroit Olympics Bid 1965," uploaded on July 20, 2014, by King Rose Archives, YouTube video, 18:12, https://www.youtube.com/watch?v=7nyuDwaI3fl.

218 **imminent collapse:** Frank B. Wilderson III, *Afropessimism* (New York: Liveright, 2020).

218 **founding of techno**: "Dweller: 'Who Does Techno Belong To? Panel Discussion," streamed live on February 5, 2020, by Hecha NYC, YouTube video, 1:42:25, https://www.youtube.com/watch?v=VI9Pd0EnL8Y.

218 **uncertain future**: Dan Sicko, "The Roots of Techno," *WIRED*, July 1, 1994, https://archive.ph/gnZZl.

218 **Drexciya**: "Afrofuturism and the Myth of Drexciya," uploaded January 28, 2019, by Ivar, Vimeo video, 15:10, https://vimeo.com/313823024.

219 **"He offered this"**: Bernard, interview with the author via Zoom video, September 12, 2020.

219 **"design a Black future"**: Ruha Benjamin, *Race After Technology: Abolitionist Tools for the New Jim Code* (Cambridge, UK: Polity, 2019).

220 *All About Eve*: Sam Staggs, *All About "All About Eve": The Complete Behind-the-Scenes Story of the Bitchiest Film Ever Made* (New York: St. Martin's Griffin, 2000).

220 **dark mirror**: Phil Agre, "While the Left Sleeps," *WIRED*, August 1, 1995, https://archive.ph/tIZOZ.

221 **gig based**: Alana Semuels, "The Online Gig Economy's 'Race to the Bottom,'" *Atlantic*, August 31, 2018, https://archive.ph/NRSF4.

221 **the end of capitalism**: Mark Fisher, *Capitalist Realism: Is There No Alternative?* (Winchester, UK: Zero Books, 2009)

AFTERWORD

225 **matching WHITE LIVES MATTER t-shirts**: Jess Cartner-Morley, "Kanye West Stirs Controversy in 'White Lives Matter' T-Shirt at Paris Fashion Week," *The Guardian*, October 4, 2022, https://www.theguardian.com/music/2022/oct/04/kanye-west-white-lives-matter-t-shirt-paris-fashion-week.

226 **After attempting to offload**: Nitish Pahwa, "Kanye West's Business Empire Isn't Doing so G.O.O.D.," *Slate*, October 17, 2022, https://slate.com/technology/2022/10/kanye-west-parler-ye-yeezy-candace-owens.html.

226 **"Slavery is a choice" interview**: Chloe Melas, "Exclusive: Kanye West has a disturbing history of admiring Hitler, sources tell CNN," CNN, October 27, 2022, https://www.cnn.com/2022/10/27/entertainment/kanye-west-hitler-album/index.html.

226 **Ye has emerged as a gateway**: Emma Grey Ellis, "How Red-Pill Culture Jumped the Fence and Got to Kanye West," Wired, April 27, 2018, https://www.wired.com/story/kanye-west-red-pill/.

227 **The public reintroduction**: Tim Dickinson, "'It's like F-Cking Mean Girls': Yiannopoulos Return Roils Kanye's 2024 Campaign," *Rolling Stone*, May 5, 2023. https://www.rollingstone.com/politics/politics-features/kanye-west-2024-campaign-milo-yiannopoulos-nick-fuentes-1234730624/.

227 **The bizarre and specific conspiracies**: John Blake, "Despite recent anti-Semitic comments, Jews and Black people have long been allies," CNN, July 18, 2020, https://www.cnn.com/2020/07/18/us/anti-semitic-comments-blacks-jews-blake/index.html.

227 **Instead, Ye's scorched earth campaign**: Tess Owen, "Kanye West Is Buying Parler as the Far-Right Scrambles to Co-Opt Him," *Vice*, October 17, 2022. https://www.vice.com/en/article/akeyw8/kanye-west-buys-parler.

227 **Many white supremacists**: Emma Rosenberg, "Taking the 'Race' out of Master Race: The Evolving Role of the Jew in White Supremacist Discourse," *Nationalities Papers*, 2023 (pp. 1–25), https://doi.org/10.1017/nps.2022.111.

228 **All of this stands to collide:** Kiana Cox, Besheer Mohamed, and Justin Nortey. n.d. "10 facts about Black Republicans," Pew Research Center, November 7, 2022, https://www .pewresearch.org/short-reads/2022/11/07/10-facts-about-black-republicans/.

228 **In 2022 a historic number:** Nicole Ellis, "A record number of Black candidates are running on GOP tickets this midterm season. Here's why that matters," *PBS NewsHour*, November 2, 2022, https://www.pbs.org/newshour/politics/a-record-number-of-black-candidates -are-running-on-gop-tickets-this-midterm-season-heres-why-that-matters.

Suggested Further Content

Jack L. Cooper—The first known Black radio announcer in the United States (and another Chicago legend). In 1929, he became the host, producer, and announcer of *The All-Negro Hour*, a variety show devoted specifically to Black performers.

Herb Kent, the Cool Gent—The "longest-running DJ in the history of radio" at the time of his death, Kent emceed Martin Luther King, Jr.'s 1966 Freedom Summer rally at Soldier Field in Chicago.

Petey Greene—An original shock jock from the Washington, DC, area, DJ Petey Greene was a pivotal voice against social injustices and poverty and an advocate for racial pride and prison reform in the 1960s and '70s.

Melvin Lindsey—Another Washington, DC, icon and DJ, Lindsey originated the "Quiet Storm" late-night music programming format that showcased smooth R&B jams by artists like Teddy Pendergrass, Angela Bofill, Teena Marie, Luther Vandross, and others.

Lu Palmer—Veteran journalist, activist, and radio host Lu Palmer was the media backbone, speaker box, and consciousness of Black Chicago politics. He is known for the tagline, "It's enough to make a Negro turn Black!"

Dyana Williams—"The Godmother of Black Music Month" and a broadcaster out of the storied Philadelphia music scene, Williams has been an ambassador of Black music and a critical voice for its preservation.

Honorable Mentions:

Mr. Magic
Kool DJ Red Alert
Tom Joyner
The Electrifying Mojo
Davey D
Wendy Williams

CHAPTER 2: ARE YOU BEING SERVED?

THE "KEEP ON PUSHIN'" MIXTAPE

"Move On Up," Curtis Mayfield

"Who We Be," DMX

"Everybody Loves the Sunshine," Roy Ayers Ubiquity

"Cult of Personality," Living Colour

"List of Demands (Reparations)," Saul Williams

"Banned in DC," Bad Brains

"Disparate Youth," Santigold

"American Terrorist," Lupe Fiasco (feat. Matthew Santos)

"Higher Ground," Stevie Wonder

"Freedom," Beyoncé (feat. Kendrick Lamar)

CHAPTER 3: WHO WILL SURVIVE IN AMERICA?

A SMATTERING OF BLACK AMERICANA EXPERIENCES

Bill Pickett Invitational Rodeo—See Black cowboys and cowgirls put on a great show in this traveling rodeo that pays tribute to those before them who helped shape the West. There's also usually good food, music, and colorful Western attire to scope out.

Central Intercollegiate Athletic Association (CIAA) Men's and Women's Basketball Tournament—Founded in 1912, the CIAA is the oldest African American athletic conference in the United States and features historically Black colleges and universities. The tournament was one of my dad's favorites as the energy, related events, and celebrations are truly Black joy in full effect.

Bud Billiken Parade—An annual "back to school" parade held since 1929 in Chicago, it's essentially the Black Macy's Thanksgiving Day Parade, but in the summer. If you can find and drive the original route it takes you on a Black history tour that passes by the original *Chicago Defender* offices, Ida B. Wells's home and other various Black Chicago history landmarks.

June 27 in Houston—June 27 pays homage to the name and day of the most famous rap freestyle and mixtape in the city's history. It also celebrates legendary producer DJ Screw who pioneered chopped and screwed music. On this day, you'll hear the music blasting out of old-school cars. Check out the Mogul Podcast season three on DJ Screw to learn more about his life, his impact on the musical landscape, and how it connects to George Floyd.

Labor Day Family Reunion Cookout (various locations)—Don't crash a Black family cookout unless you've been invited. But if you have been, definitely check one out.

Any Chicago Steppers Set—Chicago stepping is a social dance that evolved from swing and bop. It rose to prominence in the 1970s, and if you want to see some grown and sexiness, then check out at any local steppers set on the South Side of Chicago.

Black Bike Week—Black Bike Week is an annual motorcycle rally held over Memorial Day weekend in Myrtle Beach, South Carolina. Called a "one-of-a-kind event" and "an exhibitionist's paradise," it is also the largest Black motorcycle rally in the US. Attendance reaches as high as 400,000 people.

Black Thanksgiving, aka NBA All-Star Weekend—Seeing it on TV doesn't do the NBA's All-Star Weekend justice. I promise you.

INTERLUDE: FEMINISM FOR BLACK GIRLS WHO HAVE STOPPED CARING

THE BURGEONING BLACK FEMINIST PLAYLIST (LATE 1990S–MID 2000S)

"Oops (Oh My)," Tweet (feat. Missy Elliott)

"Caught Out There," Kelis

"Superwoman," Lil' Mo

"Got What You Need," Eve

"B R Right," Trina (feat. Ludacris)

"Addictive," Truth Hurts

"A Rose Is Still a Rose," Aretha Franklin (produced by Lauryn Hill)

"Hot Night," Meshell Ndegeocello

"B. K. Anthem," Foxy Brown

"Lighters Up," Lil' Kim

CHAPTER 4: OBAMA FOR AMERICA

PLACES TO CHECK OUT ON YOUR NEXT ROAD TRIP THROUGH AMERICA

Oakland Museum of California (Oakland, CA)

National Steinbeck Center (Salinas, CA)

Meow Wolf (Santa Fe, NM)

Neon Museum (Las Vegas, NV)

National Museum of Funeral History (Houston, TX)

Whitney Plantation (Edgard, LA)

First African Baptist Church (Savannah, GA)

The Legacy Museum: From Enslavement to Mass Incarceration; The National Memorial for Peace and Justice (Montgomery, AL)

Nearest Green Distillery (Shelbyville, TN)

National Civil Rights Museum (Memphis, TN)

National Great Blacks in Wax Museum (Baltimore, MD)

Harpers Ferry, WV

Muhammad Ali Center (Louisville, KY)

Negro Leagues Baseball Museum; American Jazz Museum (Kansas City, MO)

Chicago History Museum (Chicago, IL)

CHAPTER 5: KANYE WAS RIGHT-ISH

A LIST OF MOVIES THAT AREN'T ABOUT HARRIET TUBMAN (RESPECTFULLY)

Zora Neale Hurston Fieldwork Footage (1928)

I Am Somebody (1970)

Ganja & Hess (1973)

The Wiz (1978)

House Party (1990)

Blade (1998)

Akeelah and the Bee (2006)

Dope (2015)

Sorry to Bother You (2018)

Spider-Man: Into the Spider-Verse (2018)

CHAPTER 6: HARD TIMES

MORE WRESTLING PROMOS

"Why Is There Racism Here in the World Wrestling Federation?" Nation of Domination (1997)

"I Am an Addict," Eddie Guerrero (2004)
"This Is MY Moment," Mark Henry (2011)
"I'm Tired of Making Stars," Eddie Kingston (2020)
"Photograph," MJF (2022)

INTERLUDE: BECAUSE WE ARE NOT WHO THEY SAY WE ARE . . .

GREAT BOOKS BY AND/OR ABOUT BLACK JOURNALISTS (WITH MAJOR CHICAGO BIAS AT PLAY)
The Defender: How the Legendary Black Newspaper Changed America by Ethan Michaeli
A Foot in Each World: Essays and Articles by Leanita McClain edited by Clarence Page
The Light of Truth: Writings of an Anti-Lynching Crusader by Ida B. Wells
Missing Pages—Black Journalists of Modern America: An Oral History by Wallace Terry
Diversity, Inc.: The Fight for Racial Equality in the Workplace and Within the Veil: Black Journalists, White Media by Pamela Newkirk

CHAPTER 7: HOOD VAMPIRES

CINEMA CLASSICS TO SEE BEFORE YOU DIE
Cooley High (1975)
I Like It Like That (1994)
Set It Off (1996)
Attack the Block (2011)
Moonlight (2016)

CHAPTER 8: THE BAY AREA HUSTLERS

THE "EAST BAY LEGENDS" MIXTAPE
"Somethin' to Ride To (Fonky Expedition)," The Conscious Daughters
"I Got 5 On It," Luniz
"Oakland Blackouts," Hieroglyphics
"Feelin Myself," Mac Dre
"Tell Me When to Go," E-40 (feat. Keak da Sneak)
"Let's Get Down," Tony! Toni! Toné!
"The Playaz Club," Rappin' 4-Tay
"The Life," Mystic
"CussWords," Too $hort
"I Get Around," 2Pac (feat. Digital Underground)

CHAPTER 9: BASEMENT POLITICS

SOME OF MY FAVORITE PLAYBOY ARTICLES (AVAILABLE ON THE IPLAYBOY ONLINE ARCHIVES)
"The Evidence of Things Not Seen" by James Baldwin (December 1981)
"20 Questions with Harold Washington" by Walter Lowe, Jr. (February 1988)
"Alex Haley Interviews George Lincoln Rockwell" (April 1966)
"The Bog Man" by Margaret Atwood (January 1991)
"The Handsomest Drowned Man in the World" by Gabriel García Márquez (November 1971)

INTERLUDE: AWKWARD ADVENTURES ON ONLYFANS

WHERE YOU CAN FIND MORE LOTUS LAIN

The Not Safe for Work List

Chemistry Eases the Pain, PinkLabel.TV

Filthy Fashion Models, Filly Films

Whipped Ass Series, Kink.com

Between the Headlines: A Lesbian Porn Parody, Filly Films

The Should Be Safe for Work List

2022 Black History Month HotMovies Instagram Live Interview Series with
Lotus Lain

Interview, Holly Randall Unfiltered podcast (May 15, 2019)

Interview, The Pornhub Podcast with Asia Akira (June 16, 2020)

The Untitled Body Project, Level Ground (2018)

CHAPTER 10: AN ABOMINATION OF OBAMANATION

"KANYE SAMPLES" MIXTAPE (ORIGINAL SONGS KANYE SAMPLED)

"Home Is Where the Hatred Is," Gil Scott-Heron ("My Way Home")

"Memories Fade," Tears for Fears ("Coldest Winter")

"Kid Charlemagne," Steely Dan ("Champion")

"Are Zindagi Hai Khel," Asha Bhosle and Manna Dey ("I Am a God")

"Can You Lose by Following God," Whole Truth ("Follow God")

CHAPTER 11: MY BEAUTIFUL DARK TWISTED FANTASY

THE BLACK REPUBLICAN NEXT DOOR PLAYLIST (ARTISTS WERE SELECTED BY BLACK
REPUBLICANS INTERVIEWED FOR THE BOOK)

"Sardines," Junkyard Band (Clifford and Belinda, DC)

"Elevators (Me and You)," OutKast (April, Georgia)

"Friends in Low Places," Garth Brooks (Keith, Oklahoma)

"Window Seat," Erykah Badu (Tariq, Texas)

"I Wanna Be Where You Are," Michael Jackson (Charles, Indiana)

"Move B★★ch," Ludacris (Connie, Georgia)

"WTF (Where They From)," Missy Elliott (feat. Pharrell Williams) (Katina, Virginia)

"Homecoming," Kanye West (feat. Chris Martin) (Reign, Illinois)

INTERLUDE: TRADITIONS, TRIGGERS & KEYS

GREATEST MARCH MADNESS MOMENTS IN MEN'S COLLEGE BASKETBALL (BASED ON MY
PERSONAL BIAS)

Illinois beats Syracuse 89–86 (1989)—This was the game that sent my all-time
favorite basketball team, the Flyin' Illini, to the Final Four. It's one of my earliest

sports memories, and I still remember the feeling of watching the team cut down the basketball net. I knew it was especially meaningful for my dad, being one of the greatest boys basketball players out of Syracuse (who was never recruited to play at Syracuse).

University of Illinois–Chicago men's basketball team makes it to the NCAA tournament for the first time in school history (1998)—This happened while I was a student at UIC (right before I flunked out). Being in the room with my dad and his team and seeing the pure joy and elation when they received an at-large bid was one of my proudest daughter moments.

Illinois beats Arizona in overtime 89–90 (2005)—I'd gotten a last-minute ticket to the game and had gone in somewhat neutral, but the game ended up being one of the greatest comebacks I've ever witnessed. Illinois scored twenty points in 3.5 seconds to erase a fifteen-point deficit. In a college basketball game. Unbelievable.

Wisconsin beating Kentucky 71–64 (2015)—My favorite Wisconsin team beat an amazing and previously undefeated Kentucky team in the Final Four. As a Badgers alum, this was just a fun team to watch, if for no other reason than because it was a rare season where they scored over sixty points more often than not.

And finally . . . the entire tournament run of the 2019 University of Virginia (UVA) basketball team—UVA had been good for a while, but this particular UVA team brought my husband a lot of joy as an alum. Putting this team here is my gift to David for granting me permission to write some of our private conversations into the book. Each of UVA's final three games in the tournament were insta-classics, with the title game going into overtime.

CHAPTER 12: THE STORIES WE LIVE WITH

BLACK GOTHIC GIRL READING LIST

Ruby by Cynthia Bond

Fledgling by Octavia Butler

Corregidora by Gayl Jones

Sula by Toni Morrison

We Have Always Lived in the Castle by Shirley Jackson

African American Gothic: Screams from Shadowed Places by Maisha L. Wester

Linden Hills by Gloria Naylor

Incidents in the Life of a Slave Girl by Harriet Ann Jacobs

CONCLUSION: MAGGOT BRAIN

MORE BOOKS TO MESS WITH YOUR HEAD

The Third Wave by Alvin Toffler

Capitalist Realism: Is There No Alternative? by Mark Fisher

Assembling a Black Counter Culture by DeForrest Brown, Jr.

Race after Technology: Abolitionist Tools for the New Jim Code by Ruha Benjamin

Boots Riley: Tell Homeland Security—We Are the Bomb by Boots Riley

Sylvia Wynter: On Being Human as Praxis edited by Katherine McKittrick

Afro-Nostalgia: Feeling Good in Contemporary Black Culture by Badia Ahad-Legardy

The Disordered Cosmos: A Journey into Dark Matter, Spacetime, and Dreams Deferred by Chanda Prescod-Weinstein

Index

About the Author

© Mollye Miller Photography

Brandi Collins-Dexter is the former senior campaign director at Color Of Change, where she oversaw the media, culture, and economic justice departments. She has testified in front of Congress on issues related to race, technology, and corporate accountability, is a regular commentator on racial justice, and was named a "person to watch" by *The Hill* and one of the 100 most influential African Americans by *The Root*. She is a visiting fellow at the Harvard Kennedy School's Shorenstein Center. Brandi comes from a long line of South Side Chicagoans and currently lives in Baltimore with her husband, David, and their cat, Ella.

CELADON
BOOKS

Founded in 2017, Celadon Books, a division of
Macmillan Publishers, publishes a highly curated list
of twenty to twenty-five new titles a year. The list of
both fiction and nonfiction is eclectic and focuses
on publishing commercial and literary books and
discovering and nurturing talent.